Oracle®

PL/SQL™

INTERACTIVE WORKBOOK

ISBN 0-13-015743-0

90000

9 780130 157430

BOOKS IN THIS SERIES

- Baman Motivala
  "Oracle Forms Interactive Workbook"
  0-13-015808-9

- Benjamin Rosenzweig & Elena Silvestrova
  "Oracle PL/SQL Interactive Workbook"
  0-13-015743-0

- Alex Morrison & Alice Rischert
  "Oracle SQL Interactive Workbook"
  0-13-015745-7

Oracle PL/SQL

INTERACTIVE WORKBOOK

Benjamin Rosenzweig
Elena Silvestrova

Prentice Hall PTR
Upper Saddle River, New Jersey 07458
www.phptr.com/Rosenzweig

Library of Congress Cataloging-in-Publication Data

Rosenzweig, Benjamin.
    Oracle PL/SQL interactive workbook / Benjamin Rosenzweig, Elena Silvestrova.
      p. cm.
    ISBN 0-13-015743-0
    1. PL/SQL (Computer program language) 2. Oracle (Computer file) 3. Relational
databases. I. Silvestrova, Elena. II. Title.
    QA76.73.P258 R67 2000
    005.75'65—dc21

                                                    00-021909

Acquisitions editor: *Tim Moore*
Development editor: *Russ Hall*
Marketing manager: *Bryan Gambrel*
Buyer: *Maura Goldstaub*
Editorial Assistant: *Julie Okulicz*
Cover design director: *Jerry Votta*
Cover designer: *Nina Scuderi*
Art director: *Gail Cocker-Bogusz*
Series design: *Meryl Poweski*
Project coordinator: *Anne Trowbridge*
Web site project manager: *Eileen Clark*
Compositor/Production services: *Pine Tree Composition, Inc.*

 © 2000 by Prentice-Hall PTR
Prentice-Hall, Inc.
Upper Saddle River, NJ 07458

Prentice Hall books are widely used by corporations and government agencies
for training, marketing, and resale.

The publisher offers discounts on this book when ordered in bulk quantities.
For more information, contact: Corporate Sales Department, Phone: 800-382-3419;
Fax: 201-236-7141; E-mail: corpsales@prenhall.com; or write: Prentice Hall PTR,
Corp. Sales Dept., One Lake Street, Upper Saddle River, NJ 07458.

All products or services mentioned in this book are the trademarks or service
marks of their respective companies or organizations.

Printed in the United States of America
10 9 8 7 6 5 4 3 2 1

ISBN 0-13-015743-0

Prentice-Hall International (UK) Limited, *London*
Prentice-Hall of Australia Pty. Limited, *Sydney*
Prentice-Hall Canada Inc., *Toronto*
Prentice-Hall Hispanoamericana, S.A., *Mexico*
Prentice-Hall of India Private Limited, *New Delhi*
Prentice-Hall of Japan, Inc., *Tokyo*
Pearson Education Asia Pte. Ltd.
Editora Prentice-Hall do Brasil, Ltda., *Rio de Janeiro*

CONTENTS

ACKNOWLEDGMENTS

ACKNOWLEDGMENTS FROM BEN ROSENZWEIG

I would like to thank my co-author Elena Silvestrova for being a wonderful and knowledgeable colleague to work with. I would also like to thank Douglas Scherer for giving me the opportunity to work on this book as well as providing constant support and assistance through the entire writing process. I am indebted to Carol Brennan for her technical edits, she saved me from errors in every chapter. Finally I would like to thank the many friends and family, especially Edward Clarin and Edward Knopping, for helping me through the long process of putting the whole book together, which included many late nights and weekends.

ACKNOWLEDGMENTS FROM ELENA SILVESTROVA

My contribution to this book reflects the help and advice of many people. I am particularly indebted to the people at Prentice Hall who diligently worked to bring this book to market. Thanks to all of my students at Columbia University, who perennially demonstrated that teaching is learning. Thanks to Carol Brennan for her valuable comments and suggestions. To Ben Rosenzweig and Douglas Scherer, thanks for making this project a rewarding and enjoyable experience. Special thanks to David Dawson, whose insightful ideas and sincere support encourage me to work hard to the very end. Most importantly, thanks to my mom and dad, Natalia and Victor, whose excitement, enthusiasm, inspiration, and support were exceeded only by their love.

FROM THE EDITOR

Prentice Hall's Interactive Workbooks are designed to get you up and running fast, with just the information you need, when you need it.

We are certain that you will find our unique approach to learning simple and straightforward. Every chapter of every Interactive Workbook begins with a list of clearly defined Learning Objectives. A series of labs make up the heart of each chapter. Each lab is designed to teach you specific skills in the form of exercises. You perform these exercises at your computer and answer pointed questions about what you observe. Your answers will lead to further discussion and exploration. Each lab then ends with multiple-choice Self-Review Questions, to reinforce what you've learned. Finally, we have included Test Your Thinking projects at the end of each chapter. These projects challenge you to synthesize all of the skills you've acquired in the chapter.

Our goal is to make learning engaging, and to make you a more productive learner.

And you are not alone. Each book is integrated with its own "Companion Website." The website is a place where you can find more detailed information about the concepts discussed in the Workbook, additional Self-Review Questions to further refine your understanding of the material, and perhaps most importantly, where you can find a community of other Interactive Workbook users working to acquire the same set of skills that you are.

All of the Companion Websites for our Interactive Workbooks can be found at `http://www.phptr.com/Rosenzweig`.

Timothy C. Moore
VP, Executive Editor
Pearson PTR Interactive

INTRODUCTION

The *Oracle Interactive Workbook: PL/SQL* presents the Oracle PL/SQL programming language in a unique and highly effective format. It challenges you to learn Oracle PL/SQL by using it rather than by simply reading about it.

Just as a grammar workbook would teach you about nouns and verbs by first showing you examples and then asking you to write sentences, the Oracle PL/SQL workbook teaches you about cursors, procedures, and triggers by first showing you examples, and then asking you to create these objects yourself.

WHO THIS BOOK IS FOR

This book is intended for anyone who needs a quick but detailed introduction to programming with Oracle's PL/SQL language. The ideal readers are those with some experience with relational databases, with some Oracle experience, specifically with SQL and SQL*Plus, but with little or no experience with PL/SQL, or with most other programming languages.

The content of this book is based on the material that is taught in an Introduction to PL/SQL class at Columbia University's CTA program New York City. The student body is rather diverse, in that there are some students who have years of experience with IT and programming, but no experience with Oracle PL/SQL, and then there are those with absolutely no experience in IT or programming. The content of the book, like the class, is balanced to meet the needs of both extremes.

HOW THIS BOOK IS ORGANIZED

The intent of this workbook is to teach you about Oracle PL/SQL by presenting you with a series of challenges followed by detailed solutions to those challenges. The basic structure of each chapter is as follows:

Chapter

    Lab

        Exercises

        Exercise Answers with Detailed Discussion

        Self-Review Questions

    Lab...

    Test Your Thinking Questions

Each chapter contains interactive Labs that introduce topics about Oracle PL/SQL. The topics are discussed briefly and then explored through exercises, which are the heart of each Lab.

Each Exercise consists of a series of steps that you will follow to perform a specific task, along with questions that are designed to help you discover the important things about PL/SQL programming on your own. The answers to these questions are given at the end of the Exercises, along with more in-depth discussion of the concepts explored.

The Exercises are not meant to be closed book quizzes to test your knowledge. On the contrary, they are intended to act as your guide and walk you through a task. So, you are encouraged to flip back and forth from the Exercise question section to the Exercise answer section so that, if need be, you can read the answers and discussions as you go along.

At the end of each Lab is a series of multiple-choice Self-Review Questions. These are meant to be closed book quizzes to test that you have the Lab material. The answers to these questions appear in Appendix A. There are also additional Self-Review Questions at this book's companion Web site, found at `http://www.phptr.com/Rosenzweig`.

Finally, at the end of each chapter you will find a Test Your Thinking section, which consists of a series of projects designed to solidify all of the skills you have learned in the chapter. If you have successfully completed all of the Labs in the chapter, you should be able to tackle these projects with few problems. You will find guidance and/or solutions to these at the companion Web site.

The chapters should be completed in sequence because PL/SQL builds itself chapter by chapter. Additionally, many of the files you create and save in earlier chapters will be required in later chapters. In the end, all of the skills you have acquired, and files you have created, will come together in Chapter 13 and 14, "Packages" and "Stored Code," where you will create a package.

ABOUT THE COMPANION WEB SITE

The companion Web site is located at

`http://www.phptr.com/Rosenzweig`

Here you will find two very important things:

1) Files you will need **before** you begin reading the workbook.
2) Answers to the Test Your Thinking questions.

All of the Exercises and questions are based on a sample database called STUDENT. The files required to created and install this STUDENT schema are downloadable from the Web site.

The answers to the Test Your Thinking section will also be found at the web site.

In addition to required files and "Test Your Thinking" answers, the Web site will have many other features like additional review questions, a message board, and periodically updated information about the book.

 You should visit the companion Web site and download the required files before starting the Labs and Exercises.

`http://www.phptr.com/Rosenzweig`

WHAT YOU'LL NEED

There are software programs as well as knowledge requirements necessary to complete the exercise sections of the workbook.

SOFTWARE

Oracle8

SQL*Plus

Access to the WWW

Windows 95/98 or NT 4.0

ORACLE8

Oracle8 is Oracle's RDBMS and its flagship product. You can use either Oracle Personal Edition or Oracle Enterprise Edition. If you use Oracle Enterprise Edition, this can be running on a remote server or locally on your own machine. Oracle 8.0.5 Enterprise Edition running locally was used to create the exercises for this book but subsequent versions should be compatible (the web site will also have scripts to create a database that will function for Oracle 7.3 and above).

Additionally, you should have access to and be familiar with SQL*Plus. This book was used running SQL*Plus version 8.0.5.

You have a number of options for how to edit and run scripts from SQL*Plus. There are also many third-party programs to edit and debug PL/SQL. SQL*Plus is used throughout this book, since SQL*Plus comes with the Oracle Personal Edition and Enterprise Edition.

SQL*PLUS

You should be familiar with using SQL*Plus to execute SQL statements (if not then refer to the other book in the Prentice Hall Interactive Oracle Series on this topic Morrison/Rishchert's Oracle Interactive Workbook: SQL). There are a few key differences between executing SQL statement in SQL*Plus and executing PL/SQL statements in SQL*Plus. You will be introduced to these differences so that you can work with the exercises in this book.

You can end an SQL Command in SQL*Plus in one of three ways: 1) with a semicolon (;) 2) with a backslash (/) on a line by itself or 3) with a blank line. The semicolon (;) tells SQL*Plus that you want to run the command that you have just entered. You type the semicolon at the end of the SELECT statement and then press return. SQL*Plus will process what is in the SQL Buffer.

■ FOR EXAMPLE

```
SQL> select sysdate
  2  from dual
  3  ;

SYSDATE

---------
```

```
24-NOV-99

SQL>
```

THE SQL BUFFER

SQL*Plus will store the SQL command or PL/SQL block that you have most recently entered in an area of memory known as the SQL Buffer. The SQL Buffer will remain unchanged until you enter a new command or exit your SQL*Plus session. You can easily edit the contents of the SQL Buffer by typing EDIT at the SQL prompt. The default text editor will open with the contents of the SQL Buffer. You can edit the file and then exit the editor. This will cause the contents of the SQL Buffer to change. SQL*Plus commands such as SET SERVEROUTPUT ON are not captured into the SQL Buffer nor does SQL*Plus store the semicolon or the slash you type to execute a command in the SQL buffer. When you create stored procedures, functions or packages you begin with the CREATE command. When you begin a PL/SQL block, you start by entering the word DECLARE or BEGIN. Typing either BEGIN, DECLARE or CREATE will put the SQL*Plus session into PL/SQL mode.

RUNNING PL/SQL BLOCKS IN SQL*PLUS

Once you are in PL/SQL mode, you will not be able to end the block in the same manner that you ended a SQL block. The semicolon (;) can be used multiple times in a single PL/SQL subprogram, thus when you end a line with a semicolon you will not terminate the PL/SQL subprogram. You can terminate the PL/SQL subprogram by entering a period(.). This will end the block and leave the block in the SQL Buffer, but it will not execute the subprogram. You have a choice, to enter EDIT and edit the program, or execute the subprogram with a backslash (/) or an RUN. A semicolon (;) will not execute these SQL commands as it does other SQL commands.

You might enter and execute a PL/SQL subprogram as follows:

```
SQL> BEGIN

  2     DBMS_OUTPUT.PUT_LINE('This is a PL/SQL Block');

  3   END;

  4   .

SQL> /
```

```
This is a PL/SQL Block

PL/SQL procedure successfully completed.

SQL>
```

If you run a script file that you have saved on your computer, you must remember to complete your program with a period(.). If you simply want to put the code into the SQL Buffer you can end the script with a back-slash (/) which will execute the file.

```
SQL> @scriptFilename.sql
```

The failure to end your PL/SQL block with a period (.) or a backslash (/) will prevent your block from executing.

WINDOWS 95/98 OR NT 4.0

The SQL*Plus development environment is available on a number of different operating system platforms including Microsoft Windows and various flavors of UNIX. The exercises and examples in this workbook were created using Microsoft Windows NT 4.0 with service pack 3. Therefore, they are geared more for those working in a Windows environment.

But, as mentioned before, most of the concepts in this book are rather fundamental and, therefore, apply to all operating systems. So, even if you are developing on a UNIX platform, this book can still be of use to you.

ABOUT THE SAMPLE SCHEMA

The STUDENT schema contains tables and other objects meant to keep information about a registration and enrollment system for a fictitious university. There are ten tables in the system that store data about students, courses, instructors and so on. In addition to storing contact information (address and telephone number) for students and instructors, and descriptive information about courses (COST and PREREQUISITES), the schema also keeps track of the sections for particular courses, and the sections in which students have enrolled.

The SECTION and ENROLLMENT tables are two of the most important tables in the schema. The SECTION table stores data about the individual sections that have been created for each course. Each section record also stores information about where and when the section will meet, and which instructor will teach the section. The section table is related to the course table and the instructor table.

The enrollment table is equally important, because it keeps track of which students have enrolled in which sections. Each enrollment record also stores information about the student's grade and enrollment date. The enrollment table is related to the student table and the section table.

The schema also has a number of other tables that manage grading for each student in each section.

CONVENTIONS USED IN THIS BOOK

There are several conventions that are used in this book to try and make your learning experience easier. These are explained here.

This icon is used to flag notes or advice from the author to you, the reader. For instance, if there is a particular topic or concept that you really need to understand for the exam, or if there's something that you need to keep in mind while working, you will find it set off from the main text like this.

This icon is used to flag tips or especially helpful tricks that will save you time or trouble. For instance, if there is a shortcut for performing a particular task or a method that the author has found useful, you will find it set off from the main text like this.

Computers are delicate creatures and can be easily damaged. Likewise, they can be dangerous to work on if you're not careful. This icon is used to flag information and precautions that will not only save you headaches in the long run, they may even save you or your computer from harm.

This icon is used to flag passages with a reference to the book's companion Web site, which once again is located at:

`http://www.phptr.com/Rosenzweig`

Oracle

PL/SQL

INTERACTIVE WORKBOOK

CHAPTER 1

PROGRAMMING CONCEPTS

Computers play a large role in the modern world. No doubt you realize how crucial they have become to running any business today; they have also become one of the sources of entertainment in our lives. You probably use computers with your everyday tasks as well, such as when sending email, paying bills, shopping, reading the latest news on the Internet, or even when playing games.

A computer is a sophisticated device. However, it is important to remember that it is still only a device and cannot think on its own. In order to be useful, a computer needs instructions to follow. Facilities such as programming languages allow programmers to provide computers with a list of instructions called programs. These programs tell a computer what actions to perform. As a result, programming languages and computer programs play an important role in today's technology.

L A B   1 . 1

THE NATURE OF A COMPUTER PROGRAM AND PROGRAMMING LANGUAGES

LAB OBJECTIVES

After this lab, you will be able to:

✔ Understand the Nature of Computer Programs and Programming Languages

✔ Understand the Differences between Interpreted and Compiled Languages

---

A computer needs instructions to follow because it cannot think on its own. For instance, when playing a game of solitaire you must choose which card to move. Each time a card is moved, a set of instructions has been executed to carry out the move. These instructions compose only a small part of the solitaire program. This program comprises many more instructions that allow a user to perform actions such as beginning or ending a game, selecting a card's color, and so forth. Therefore, a computer program comprises instructions that direct the actions of the computer. In essence, a program plays the role of guide for a computer. It tells the computer what steps in what order should be taken to complete a certain task successfully.

Computer programs are created with the help of programming languages. A programming language is a set of instructions consisting of rules, syntax, numerical and logical operators, and utility functions. Programmers can use programming languages to create a computer program. There are many different programming languages available today. However, all programming languages can be divided into three major groups: machine languages, assembly languages, and high-level languages.

Words such as statement *or* command *are often used when talking about instructions issued by a program to a computer. These terms are interchangeable.*

MACHINE LANGUAGES

Machine language is the native language of a particular computer because it is defined by the hardware of the computer. Each instruction or command is a collection of zeros and ones. As a result, machine language is the hardest language for a person to understand, and it is the only language understood by the computer. All other programming languages must be translated into machine language. Consider the following example of the commands issued in the machine language.

■ FOR EXAMPLE

Consider this mathematical notation $X = X + 1$. In programming, this notation reads *the value of the variable is incremented by one*. So, in the example below, you are incrementing the value of the variable by 1 using machine language specific to an Intel processor.

```
1010 0001 1110 0110 0000 0001
0000 0011 0000 0110 0000 0001 0000 0000
1010 0011 1110 0110 0000 0001
```

ASSEMBLY LANGUAGES

Assembly language uses English-like abbreviations to represent operations performed on the data. A computer cannot understand assembly language directly. The program written in assembly language must be translated into machine language with the help of the special program called an *assembler*. Consider the following example of the commands issued in assembly language.

■ FOR EXAMPLE

In this example, you are increasing the value of the variable by 1 as well. This example is also specific to an Intel processor:

```
MOV AX, [01E6]
ADD AX, 0001
MOV [01E6], AX
```

HIGH-LEVEL LANGUAGES

High-level language uses English-like instructions and common mathematical notations. High-level languages allow programmers to perform complicated calculations with a single instruction. However, it is easier to read and understand than machine and assembly language. As a result, it is not as time-consuming to create a program in high-level language as it is in machine or assembly language.

■ FOR EXAMPLE

```
variable := variable + 1;
```

This example shows a simple mathematical operation of addition. This instruction can be easily understood by anyone without programming experience and with basic mathematical knowledge.

DIFFERENCES BETWEEN INTERPRETED AND COMPILED LANGUAGES

High-level languages can be divided into two groups: interpreted and compiled. Interpreted languages are translated into machine language with the help of another program called an *interpreter*. The interpreter translates each statement in the program into machine language and executes it immediately before the next statement is examined.

Compiled languages are translated into machine language with the help of the program called a *compiler*. Compilers translate English-like statements into machine language. However, all of the statements must be translated before a program can be executed. The compiled version of the program is sometimes referred to as an *executable*.

An interpreted program must be translated into machine language every time it is run. A compiled program is translated into machine language only once when it is compiled. The compiled version of the program can then be executed as many times as needed.

LAB 1.1 EXERCISES

1.1.1 UNDERSTANDING THE NATURE OF COMPUTER PROGRAMS AND PROGRAMMING LANGUAGES

Answer the following questions:

a) What is a program?

_____

_____

Consider this scenario: You have been hired to work for the ABC Company. One of your responsibilities is to produce a daily report that contains complicated calculations.

b) Without using a computer program to fulfill this responsibility, what potential problems do you foresee in generating this report every day?

_____

_____

c) Based on your observations in question b, how do you think a computer program would make that task easier?

_____

_____

d) What is a programming language?

_____

_____

For the next question, consider the following code:

```
0010 0000 1110 0110 0000 0001
0000 0011 0000 0110 1000 0000
1010 0001 1111 0110 0000 0001
```

e) What type of programming language is this code written in?

_____

_____

For the next question, consider the following code:

```
MOV AX, [01E9]
ADD AX, 0010
MOV [01E6], AX
```

f) What type of programming language is this code written in?

_____

_____

For the next question, consider the following code:

```
variable := 2 * variable - 10;
```

g) What type of programming language is this code written in?

_____

_____

1.1.2 UNDERSTANDING THE DIFFERENCES BETWEEN COMPILED AND INTERPRETED LANGUAGES

Answer the following questions:

a) What is an interpreted language?

_____

_____

b) What is a compiled language?

_____

_____

c) Which do you think will run quicker, an interpreted or a compiled program?

_____

_____

LAB 1.1 EXERCISE ANSWERS

1.1.1 ANSWERS

a) What is a program?

Answer: A computer program comprises instructions that direct the actions of the computer.

b) Without using a computer program to fulfill this responsibility, what potential problems do you foresee in generating this report every day?

Answer: Programs help us with repetitive, time-consuming, and error-prone tasks. If you do not have a program that helps you create this report, it might take you a whole day to collect the needed information for the report and perform the needed calculations. As a result, you will not be able to concentrate on your other responsibilities. In addition, sooner or later you will probably make mistakes while creating the report.

c) Based on your observations in question b, how do you think a computer program would make that task easier?

Answer: Using a program guarantees fast retrieval of needed information and accurate results, assuming that the program does not contain any errors. Furthermore, once a program is created, the same set of steps is repeated on a daily basis. Consequently, a well-written program is not susceptible to human frailties such as typographical errors or the accidental exclusion of a formula.

d) What is a programming language?

Answer: A programming language is a set of instructions consisting of rules, syntax, numerical and logical operators, and utility functions.

e) What type of programming language is this code an example of?

Answer: This is an example of a machine language.

Machine languages can be understood directly by the computer. Each statement in the machine language is represented by the string of zeros and ones.

This example illustrates the nonintuitive nature of machine languages. However, a computer can read these instructions directly and execute them instantly. You can see that creating a program in a machine language can be a slow and tedious process. To facilitate program creation, programmers use higher-level languages that are closer to human language.

f) What type of programming language is this code an example of?

Answer: This is an example of an assembly language.

Assembly language uses mnemonic symbols to represent the binary code of machine language. Each assembly instruction is directly translated into a machine language instruction. You may notice that assembly language is slightly easier to understand than machine language.

g) What type of programming language is this code an example of?

Answer: This is an example of a high-level language.

Programs created in high-level languages are portable. They can be moved from one computer to another because a high-level programming language is not machine-specific. High-level languages must be translated into machine language with the help of interpreter or compiler.

1.1.2 ANSWERS

a) What is an interpreted language?

Answer: Interpreted languages are translated into machine language with the help of another program called an interpreter. The interpreter translates statement in the program into machine language and executes it immediately before the next statement is examined.

b) What is a compiled language?

Answer: Compiled languages are translated into machine language with the help of the program called a compiler. Compilers translate English-like statements into machine language.

c)   Which do you think will run quicker, an interpreted or a compiled program?

Answer: Generally, interpreted programs run slower than compiled programs.

As you observed earlier, an interpreted program must be translated into machine language every time it is run. A compiled program is translated into machine language only once when it is compiled, and then it can be executed as many times as needed. As a result, an interpreted program runs slower than a compiled program.

LAB 1.1 SELF-REVIEW QUESTIONS

In order to test your progress, you should be able to answer the following questions.

1)   What group of programming languages is easiest for the computer to understand?
   a) _____The machine languages
   b) _____The high-level languages
   c) _____The assembly languages

2)   Programs created in the machine languages are which of the following?
   a) _____Portable
   b) _____Machine-specific

3)   Which of the following is true of interpreted programs?
   a) _____All statements are translated and only then executed.
   b) _____Each statement is translated and executed before the next statement.

4)   Before a program written in a high-level language can be executed, which of the following must take place?
   a) _____A program must be interpreted.
   b) _____A program must be compiled.
   c) _____A program can be executed immediately.

5)   Which of the following is true of the interpreter?
   a) _____It translates instructions written in assembler language into machine language.
   b) _____It translates machine language into a high-level language.
   c) _____It translates a high-level language into machine language.

   Quiz answers appear in Appendix A, Section 1.1.

LAB 1.2

GOOD PROGRAMMING PRACTICES

LAB OBJECTIVES

After this lab, you will be able to:

✔ Understand the Nature of Good Programming Practices

✔ Understand Formatting Guidelines

In the previous section of this chapter you encountered the terms *computer program* and *programming language*. You will recall that a program is a set of instructions, and a programming language is a tool that allows programmers to provide computers with these instructions. However, the process of creating a computer program is not as simple as just writing down instructions. Sometimes it can become a tedious and complicated task. Before a computer can be provided with these instructions, the programmer needs to know what instructions must be specified. In essence, the process of creating a program is akin to the process of applied problem solving.

Consider this mathematical word problem:

> The 1980's speed record for human-powered vehicles was set on a measured 200 meter run by a sleek machine called Vector. Pedaling back-to-back, its two drivers averaged 69.92 miles per hour.

> This awkward mix of units is the way data appeared in an article reporting the event. Determine the speed of the vehicle in meters per second.

This word problem involves conversion from miles per hour to meters per second. However, it contains information that has nothing to do with its solution such as the name of the vehicle and the number of people needed to operate it. In order to achieve correct results, you must be able to filter out needed information and discard the rest. Next, you need to know what formulas must be used for actual conversion.

This is a relatively straightforward example of a problem-solving process that can be used for academic purposes. However, in the business world, problem descriptions are often incomplete or ambiguous. They are also harder to solve. These problems require the ability to ask questions that help clarify the problem and an ability to organize the problem into logical parts. By breaking down the problem, you will be able to focus better on possible solutions and more easily manage each part. Once each part is fully understood, the solution to the overall problem will readily develop.

This technique of breaking the problem into parts and solving each part is called a *top-down approach* to problem solving. When writing a program, you can also approach your task in a top-down manner. However, to solve the problem efficiently, you need to approach it in a structured manner.

STRUCTURED PROGRAMMING

Structured programming embodies a disciplined approach to writing clear code that is easy to understand, test, maintain, and modify. A program can be organized into modules called *subroutines*. These subroutines focus on a particular part of the overall problem that the program addresses. Subroutines are easier to understand and manage because they are only components of the overall program. Together, all of the subroutines compose the overall program.

Structured programming also embodies the following three attributes: sequence, selection, and iteration. These attributes or structures describe how statements in the program are executed. Furthermore, a program can contain any of these structures or a combination of them.

SEQUENCE

Sequence refers to the linear execution of code. In other words, the control is passed from one statement to the next statement in consecutive order. Consider Figure 1.1.

**LAB
1.2**

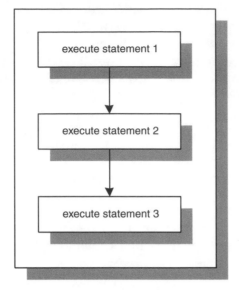

Figure 1.1 ■ Sequence structure.

Figure 1.1 contains rectangular symbols. The rectangular symbol in the diagram can represent not only a single statement, but a subroutine as well. The arrows represent the flow of the control between statements. The control is passed from statement 1 to statement 2 and then to statement 3. Thus, these statements are executed in the sequential order.

SELECTION

Selection refers to the decision-making process. For example: When I am trying to choose between different activities for this weekend, I start with the knowledge that on Friday night I want to go to the movies, Saturday night I want to go dancing, and Sunday I want to spend a quiet evening at home. In order for me to choose one of the activities, I need to know what day of the week it is. The logic for my decision on the weekend activities can be illustrated below:

```
IF TODAY IS 'FRIDAY'
    I AM GOING TO SEE A MOVIE
IF TODAY IS 'SATURDAY'
    I AM GOING DANCING
IF TODAY IS 'SUNDAY'
    I AM SPENDING A QUIET EVENING AT HOME
```

The test conditions "TODAY IS . . ." can evaluate either to TRUE or FALSE based on the day of the week. If today happens to be Friday, the first test

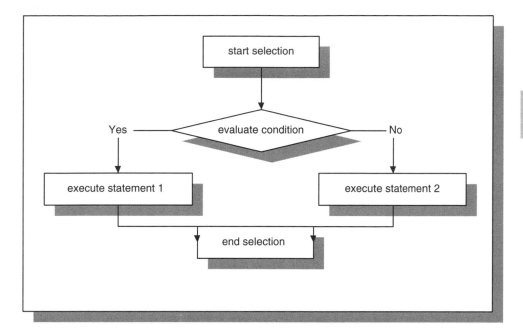

Figure 1.2 ■ Selection structure.

condition "TODAY is 'FRIDAY'" becomes TRUE, and other test conditions become FALSE. In this case, I am going to see a movie, and the other activities can be discarded.

Figure 1.2 illustrates general flow of the control of the selection structure.

Figure 1.2 contains a new diamond shape called the decision symbol. This indicates that a decision must be made or a certain test condition must be evaluated. This test condition evaluates to TRUE (Yes) or FALSE (No). If the test condition yields TRUE, statement 1 is executed. If the test condition yields FALSE, statement 2 is executed. It is important for you to remember that a rectangle can represent a set of statements or a subroutine.

ITERATION

Iteration refers to an action that needs to be repeated a finite number of times. The number of times this action is repeated is based on some terminating factor. Consider the following example. You are reading a chapter from this book. Each chapter has a finite number of pages. In order to finish the chapter, you need to read through all the pages. This is indicated below:

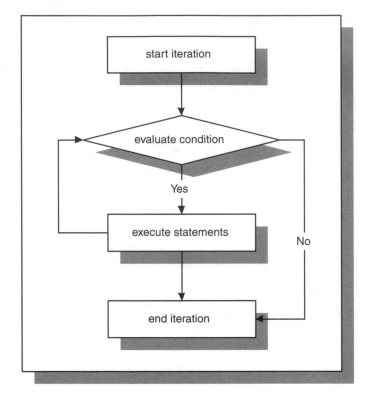

Figure 1.3 ■ Iteration structure.

```
WHILE THERE ARE MORE PAGES IN THE CHAPTER TO READ
    READ THE CURRENT PAGE
    GO TO THE NEXT PAGE
```

The terminating factor in this example is the number of pages in the chapter. As soon as the last page in the chapter is read, the iteration is complete.

Figure 1.3 illustrates general flow of the control of the iteration structure.

As long as the condition evaluates to TRUE, the statements inside iteration structure are repeated. As soon as the condition evaluates to FALSE, the flow of the control is passed to the exit point of the iteration structure.

DIFFERENCES BETWEEN STRUCTURED AND NON-STRUCTURED PROGRAMMING

Before structured programming became widely used, programs were simply sequential lines of code. This code was not organized into modules and did not employ many of the structures you encountered earlier in this chapter. The result was a meandering set of statements that was difficult to maintain and understand. In addition, these programs used multiple GOTO statements that allow program control to jump all over the code. Almost all programs that use GOTO statements can be rewritten using structures such as selection and iteration.

FORMATTING GUIDELINES

It was mentioned earlier that structured programming allows us to write clear code that is easy to understand, test, maintain, and modify. However, structured programming alone is not enough to create readable and manageable code. Formatting is a very important aspect of writing a program. Moreover, your formatting style should stay consistent throughout your programs.

Consider this example of the SELECT statement that has not been formatted.

■ FOR EXAMPLE

```
SELECT s.first_name, s.last_name, e.final_grade FROM
student s, enrollment e WHERE s.student_id =
e.student_id AND e.final_grade IS NOT NULL;
```

Even though this example contains only a very simple SELECT statement, you can see that the logic is hard to follow.

Consider the same SELECT statement with few formatting changes.

■ FOR EXAMPLE

```
SELECT s.first_name, s.last_name, e.final_grade
  FROM student s, enrollment e
 WHERE s.student_id = e.student_id
   AND e.final_grade IS NOT NULL;
```

You have probably noticed that the second version of the SELECT statement is much easier to read and understand. It is important to realize that both SELECT statements are syntactically correct. They produce the same output when run.

Usually, the logic depicted in the program is more complex than that of the SELECT statement. Therefore, proper formatting of the code is extremely important for two major reasons. First, a well-formatted program will facilitate any changes made later by the program's author. In other words, even the author will understand the logic of the program easier if he or she needs to modify the program later. Second, any person who has to maintain the program can more easily follow the logical structure of the program.

In order for the program to be readable and understandable, there are two main guidelines to follow. First, *the format of the program must illustrate the logical structure of the program*. You can reveal the logical structure of the program by using indentation in your code. Consider the example of the selection structure used earlier in this chapter.

■ *FOR EXAMPLE*

```
IF TODAY IS 'FRIDAY'
    I AM GOING TO SEE A MOVIE
IF TODAY IS 'SATURDAY'
    I AM GOING DANCING
IF TODAY IS 'SUNDAY'
    I AM SPENDING A QUIET EVENING AT HOME
```

You have probably noticed that each statement following IF clause is indented. As a result, it is easier to understand what activity is taken based on the day of the week. You could take this example and format it differently.

■ *FOR EXAMPLE*

```
IF TODAY IS 'FRIDAY' I AM GOING TO SEE A MOVIE
IF TODAY IS 'SATURDAY' I AM GOING DANCING
IF TODAY IS 'SUNDAY' I AM SPENDING A QUIET EVENING AT
HOME
```

This example also shows a formatted version of the selection structure. However, this formatting style does not reveal the logical structure of the selection as well as the previous example. As a matter of fact, this example looks like extremely short story rather than program.

Second, *your program should contain comments*. Comments will help you to explain what you are trying to accomplish. However, you should be careful because too many comments can make your code confusing.

You can use the code format seen in this book's examples as you write your programs. It is not the only good format available, but hopefully it will be a good example of formatting technique, which will help you to develop your own style. However, regardless of your style, you should follow these guidelines when creating a program.

LAB 1.2 EXERCISES

1.2.1 UNDERSTANDING THE NATURE OF GOOD PROGRAMMING PRACTICES

Answer the following questions:

a) What is a top-down approach?

_____

_____

b) What is structured programming?

_____

_____

c) Create the following selection structure. Determine which season each month of the year belongs to.

_____

_____

d) Create the following iteration structure. For every day of the week display its name.

_____

_____

e) Create the following structure. For every day that falls within business week display its name. For every day that falls within weekend display 'The weekend is here, and it is here to stay!!!'

Hint: you will need to use iteration and selection structures. The selection structure must be placed inside the iteration structure.

_____

_____

1.2.2 UNDERSTANDING FORMATTING GUIDELINES

Answer the following questions:

a) What is the reason for formatting your code?

_____

_____

b) What are two main guidelines of good formatting?

_____

_____

LAB 1.2 EXERCISE ANSWERS

1.2.1 ANSWERS

a) What is a top-down approach?

Answer: The technique of breaking the problem into parts and solving each part is called a top-down approach to problem solving. By breaking down the problem, it is easier to focus on possible solutions and manage each part. Once each part is fully understood, the solution to the overall problem can be readily developed.

b) What is structured programming?

Answer: Structured programming embodies a disciplined approach to writing clear code that is easy to understand, test, maintain, and modify. A program can be organized into modules called subroutines. These subroutines focus on a particular part of the overall problem that the program addresses. Subroutines are easier to understand and manage because they are only components of the overall program. Together, all of the subroutines compose the overall program.

c) Create the following selection structure. Determine which season each month of the year belongs to.

Answer: Your selection structure should look similar to the following:

```
IF MONTH IN ('DECEMBER', 'JANUARY', 'FEBRUARY')
   IT IS WINTER
IF MONTH IN ('MARCH', 'APRIL', 'MAY')
   IT IS SPRING
```

```
IF MONTH IN ('JUNE', 'JULY', 'AUGUST')
    IT IS SUMMER
IF MONTH IN ('SEPTEMBER', 'OCTOBER', 'NOVEMBER')
    IT IS FALL
```

The test conditions of this selection structure use operator IN. This operator allows us to construct the list of valid months for every season. It is important to realize the use of the parenthesis. In this case, it is not done for the sake of a syntax rule. This use of the parenthesis allows us to define clearly the list of values for a specific month, hence helping us to outline the logic of the structure.

Now, consider the fragment of the selection structure below:

```
IF MONTH IS 'DECEMBER'
    IT IS WINTER
IF MONTH IS 'JANUARY'
    IT IS WINTER
IF MONTH IS 'FEBRUARY'
    IT IS WINTER
    ...
```

This selection structure causes the same outcome, yet it is much longer. As a result it does not look well structured, even though it has been formatted properly.

d) Create the following iteration structure. For every day that falls within the business week display its name.

Answer: Your selection structure should look similar to the following:

```
WHILE THERE ARE MORE DAYS IN THE WEEK
    DISPLAY THE NAME OF THE CURRENT DAY
    GO TO THE NEXT DAY
```

Assume that you are starting your week on Monday—there are six days left. Next, you will display the name of the current day of the week, which is Monday for the first iteration. Then, you move to the next day. Next day is Tuesday, and there are five more days in the week. So, you will display the name of the current day—Tuesday—and move to the next day, and so forth. Once, the name of the seventh day (Sunday) has been displayed, the iteration structure has completed.

e) Create the following structure. For every day that falls within the business week display its name. For every day that falls within weekend display 'The weekend is here, and it is here to stay!!!'

Answer: *Your structure should look similar to the following:*

```
WHILE THERE ARE MORE DAYS IN THE WEEK
    IF DAY BETWEEN 'MONDAY' AND 'FRIDAY'
        DISPLAY THE NAME OF THE CURRENT DAY
    IF DAY IN ('SATURDAY', 'SUNDAY')
        DISPLAY 'THE WEEKEND IS HERE AND IT IS HERE TO
                STAY!!!'
    GO TO THE NEXT DAY
```

LAB 1.2

This structure is a combination of two structures: iteration and selection. The iteration structure will repeat its steps for each day of the week. The selection structure will display the name of the current day or the message "The weekend is. . . ."

Assume that you are starting your week on Monday again. There are six days left. Next, the control of the flow is passed to the selection structure. Because the current day happens to be Monday, and it falls within business week, its name is displayed. Then, the control of the flow passed back to the iteration structure, and you are ready to move to the next day.

The next day is Tuesday, and there are five more days in the week. So, the control is passed to the iteration structure again. Tuesday also falls within business week, so its name is displayed as well. Next, the control is passed back to the iteration structure, and you go to the next day, and so forth. Once, the day falls within weekend, the message "The weekend is . . ." is displayed.

1.2.2 ANSWERS

a) What is the reason for formatting your code?

Answer: *A well-formatted program is easier to understand and maintain because format can reveal the logical structure of the program.*

b) What are two main guidelines of good formatting?

Answer: *First, the code of the program should be indented so that the logical structure of the program is clear. Second, the program should contain comments describing what is being accomplished.*

LAB 1.2 SELF-REVIEW QUESTIONS

In order to test your progress, you should be able to answer the following questions.

1) Which one is not a feature of the structured programming?
   a) _____Iteration
   b) _____Sequence
   c) _____GOTO
   d) _____Modularity

2) Structured programming allows the control of the program to jump all over the code.
   a) _____True
   b) _____False

3) Which of the following is true about sequence structure?
   a) _____It refers to the decision-making process.
   b) _____It refers to the linear execution of code.
   c) _____It refers to the repetition of code.

4) A test condition must evaluate to which of the following in order for the selection to execute?
   a) _____TRUE
   b) _____FALSE
   c) _____None of the above

5) A poorly formatted SELECT statement produces output different from a well-formatted SELECT statement.
   a) _____True
   b) _____False
   c) _____None of the above

Quiz answers appear in Appendix A, Section 1.2.

C H A P T E R   1

TEST YOUR THINKING

In this chapter you have learned what a program is. You also defined the concepts of structured programming. Here are some projects that will help you test the depth of your understanding.

1) Create the following structure: Based on the value of a number, determine if it is even or odd. *Hint: Before you decide how to define even and odd numbers, you should decide what structure must be used to achieve the desired results.*

2) Create the following structure: The structure you created in the previous exercise is designed to work with a single number. Modify it so that it can work with a list of numbers.

C H A P T E R   2

PL/SQL CONCEPTS

In the previous chapter, you were introduced to some elements of computer programming languages. In this chapter, you will be introduced to the elements of a specific programming language, PL/SQL, and how it fits in the client-server architecture.

PL/SQL stands for "Procedural Language Extensions to SQL." PL/SQL extends SQL by adding programming structures and subroutines available in any high-level language. In this chapter, you will see examples that will illustrate the syntax and the rules of the language.

PL/SQL is used for both server-side and client-side development. For example, database triggers (code that is attached to tables, discussed in a later chapter) on the server-side and logic behind an Oracle Developer tool on the client-side can be written using PL/SQL. In addition, PL/SQL can be used to develop applications for browsers such as Netscape when used in conjunction with the Oracle Application Server and the PL/SQL Web Development Toolkit.

L A B   2 . 1

PL/SQL IN CLIENT-SERVER ARCHITECTURE

> ## LAB OBJECTIVES
>
> After this lab, you will be able to:
>
> ✔ Use PL/SQL Anonymous Blocks
> ✔ Understand How PL/SQL Gets Executed

Many Oracle applications are built using client-server architecture. The Oracle database resides on the server. The program that makes requests against this database resides on the client machine. This program can be written in C, Java, or PL/SQL.

While PL/SQL is just like any other programming language, it has syntax and rules that determine how programming statements work together. It is important for you to realize that PL/SQL is not a stand-alone programming language. PL/SQL is a part of the Oracle RDBMS, and it can reside in two environments, the client and the server. As a result, it is very easy to move PL/SQL modules between server-side and client-side applications.

In both environments, any PL/SQL block or subroutine is processed by the PL/SQL engine, which is a special component of many Oracle products. Some of these products are Oracle server, Oracle Forms, and Oracle Reports. The PL/SQL engine processes and executes any PL/SQL statements and sends any SQL statements to the SQL statement processor. The SQL statement processor is always located on the Oracle server. Figure 2.1 illustrates the PL/SQL engine residing in Oracle server.

When the PL/SQL engine is located on the server, the whole PL/SQL block is passed to the PL/SQL engine on the Oracle server. The PL/SQL engine processes the block according to the Figure 2.1.

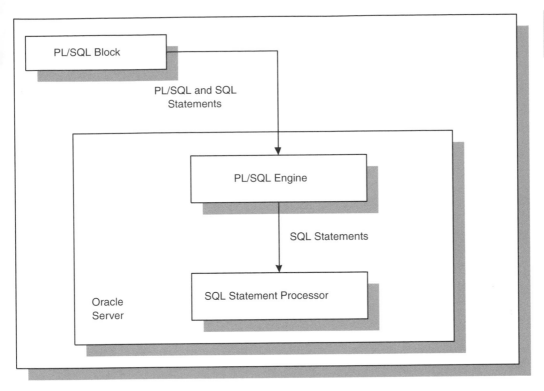

Figure 2.1 ■ The PL/SQL engine and Oracle server.

When the PL/SQL engine is located on the client, as it is in the Oracle Developer Tools, the PL/SQL processing is done on the client side. All SQL statements that are embedded within the PL/SQL block are sent to the Oracle server for further processing. When PL/SQL block contains no SQL statement, the entire block is executed on the client side.

Using PL/SQL has several advantages. For example, when you issue a SELECT statement in SQL*Plus against the STUDENT table, it retrieves a list of students. The SELECT statement you issued at the client computer is sent to the database server to be executed. The results of this execution are then sent back to the client. As a result, you will see rows displayed on your client machine.

Now, assume that you need to issue multiple SELECT statements. Each SELECT statement is a request against the database and is sent to the Oracle server. The results of each SELECT statement are sent back to the client. Each time a SELECT statement is executed, network traffic is generated. Hence, multiple SELECT statements will result in multiple round trip transmissions, adding significantly to the network traffic.

When these SELECT statements are combined into a PL/SQL program, they are sent to the server as a single unit. The SELECT statements in this PL/SQL program are executed at the server. The server sends the results of these SELECT statements back to the client, also as a single unit. Therefore, a PL/SQL program encompassing multiple SELECT statements can be executed at the server and have the results returned to the client in one round trip. This obviously is a more efficient process than having each SELECT statement executed independently. This model is illustrated in the Figure 2.2.

Figure 2.2 compares two applications. The first application uses four independent SQL statements that generate eight trips on the network. The second application combines SQL statements into a single PL/SQL block. This PL/SQL block is then sent to the PL/SQL engine. The engine sends SQL statements to the SQL Statement Processor and checks the syntax of PL/SQL statements. As you can see, only two trips are generated on the network.

In addition, applications written in PL/SQL are portable. They can run in any environment Oracle can run. Since PL/SQL does not change from one environment to the next, different tools can use a PL/SQL script.

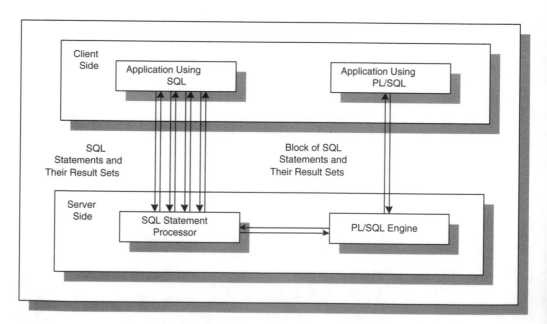

Figure 2.2 ■ PL/SQL in client-server architecture.

PL/SQL BLOCK STRUCTURE

A block is the most basic unit in PL/SQL. All PL/SQL programs are combined into blocks. These blocks can also be nested one within the other. Usually, PL/SQL blocks combine statements that represent a single logical task. Therefore, different tasks within a single program can be separated into blocks. As a result, it is easier to understand and maintain the logic of the program.

PL/SQL blocks can be divided into two groups: named and anonymous. Named blocks are used when creating subroutines. These subroutines are procedures, functions, and packages. The subroutines then can be stored in the database and referenced by their names later on. In addition, subroutines such as procedures and functions can be defined within the anonymous PL/SQL block. These subroutines exist as long as this block is executing and cannot be referenced outside the block. In other words, subroutines defined in one PL/SQL block cannot be called by another PL/SQL block or referenced by their names later on. Subroutines are discussed in Chapters 11 through 14. Anonymous PL/SQL blocks, you have probably guessed, do not have names. As a result, they cannot be stored in the database and referenced later.

PL/SQL blocks contain three sections: declaration section, executable section, and exception-handling section. The executable section is the only mandatory section of the block. Both the declaration and exception-handling sections are optional. As a result, a PL/SQL block has the following structure:

```
DECLARE
    Declaration statements
BEGIN
    Executable statements
EXCEPTION
    Exception-handling statements
END;
```

DECLARATION SECTION

The *declaration section* is the first section of the PL/SQL block. It contains definitions of PL/SQL identifiers such as variables, constants, cursors, and so on. PL/SQL identifiers are covered in detail throughout the book.

■ *FOR EXAMPLE*

```
DECLARE
    v_first_name VARCHAR2(35);
```

```
v_last_name VARCHAR2(35);
v_counter NUMBER := 0;
```

The example given above shows a declaration section of an anonymous PL/SQL block. It begins with the keyword DECLARE and contains two variable declarations and one constant declaration. The names of the variables, `v_first_name` and `v_last_name`, are followed by their datatypes and sizes. The name of the constant, `v_counter`, is followed by its datatype and a value assigned to it. Notice that a semicolon terminates each declaration.

EXECUTABLE SECTION

The *executable section* is the next section of the PL/SQL block. This section contains executable statements that allow you to manipulate the variables that have been declared in the declaration section.

■ *FOR EXAMPLE*

```
BEGIN
    SELECT first_name, last_name
      INTO v_first_name, v_last_name
      FROM student
     WHERE student_id = 123;
    DBMS_OUTPUT.PUT_LINE
        ('Student name: '||v_first_name||' '||
          v_last_name);
END;
```

The example given above shows the executable section of the PL/SQL block. It begins with the keyword BEGIN and contains a SELECT statement from the STUDENT table. First and last names for student ID 123 are selected into two variables: `v_first_name` and `v_last_name`. Then the values of the variables, `v_first_name` and `v_last_name`, are displayed on the screen with the help of DBMS_OUTPUT.PUT_LINE statement. This statement will be covered later in this chapter in greater detail. The end of the executable section of this block is marked by the keyword END. *The executable section of any PL/SQL block always begins with the keyword BEGIN and ends with the keyword END.*

EXCEPTION-HANDLING SECTION

The *exception-handling section* is the last section of the PL/SQL block. This section contains statements that are executed when a runtime error occurs within the block. Runtime errors occur while the program is running and cannot be detected by the PL/SQL compiler. Once a runtime error occurs, the control is passed to the exception-handling section of the block. The error is then evaluated, and a specific exception is raised or executed. This is best illustrated by the example below.

■ FOR EXAMPLE

```
BEGIN
    SELECT first_name, last_name
      INTO v_first_name, v_last_name
      FROM student
     WHERE student_id = 123;
    DBMS_OUTPUT.PUT_LINE
        ('Student name: '||v_first_name||' '||
          v_last_name);
EXCEPTION
    WHEN NO_DATA_FOUND THEN
        DBMS_OUTPUT.PUT_LINE
            ('There is no student with student id 123');
END;
```

This shows the exception-handling section of the PL/SQL block. It begins with the keyword EXCEPTION. The WHEN clause evaluates which exception must be raised. In this example, there is only one exception called NO_DATA_FOUND, and it is raised when SELECT statement does not return any rows. If there is no record for student ID 123 in the STUDENT table, the control is passed to the exception-handling section and DBMS_OUTPUT.PUT_LINE statement is executed. Chapters 6, 9, and 10 contain more detailed explanation of exception-handling section.

You have seen examples of declaration section, executable section, and exception-handling section. Consider combining these examples into a single PL/SQL block.

■ FOR EXAMPLE

```
DECLARE
    v_first_name VARCHAR2(35);
    v_last_name VARCHAR2(35);
BEGIN
    SELECT first_name, last_name
      INTO v_first_name, v_last_name
      FROM student
     WHERE student_id = 123;
    DBMS_OUTPUT.PUT_LINE
        ('Student name: '||v_first_name||' '||
```

```
                v_last_name);
      EXCEPTION
         WHEN NO_DATA_FOUND THEN
            DBMS_OUTPUT.PUT_LINE
               ('There is no student with student id 123');
      END;
```

How PL/SQL Gets Executed

Every time an anonymous PL/SQL block is executed, the code is sent to the PL/SQL engine on the server where it is compiled. The named PL/SQL block is compiled only at the time of its creation, or if it has been changed. The compilation process includes syntax checking, binding, and p-code generation.

Syntax checking involves checking PL/SQL code for syntax or compilation errors. Syntax error occurs when a statement does not exactly correspond to the syntax of the programming language. Errors such as misspelled keyword, missing semicolon at the end of the statement, or undeclared variable are examples of syntax errors.

Once the programmer corrects syntax errors, the compiler can assign a storage address to program variables that are used to hold data for Oracle. This process is called *binding*. It allows Oracle to reference storage addresses when the program is run. At the same time, the compiler checks references to the stored objects such as table name or column name in the SELECT statement, or a call to a named PL/SQL block.

Next, p-code is generated for the PL/SQL block. *P-code* is a list of instructions to the PL/SQL engine. For named blocks, p-code is stored in the database, and it is used the next time the program is executed. Once the process of compilation has completed successfully, the status for a named PL/SQL block is set to VALID, and also stored in the database. If the compilation process was not successful, the status of a named PL/SQL block is set to INVALID.

 It is important to remember that successful compilation of the named PL/SQL block does not guarantee successful execution of this block in the future. If, at the time of the execution, any one of the stored objects referenced by the block is not present in the database or not accessible to the block, the execution will fail. The status of the named PL/SQL block will be changed to INVALID.

LAB 2.1 EXERCISES

2.1.1 USING PL/SQL ANONYMOUS BLOCKS

Answer the following questions:

a) Why it is more efficient to combine SQL statements into PL/SQL blocks?

_____

_____

b) What are the differences between named and anonymous PL/SQL blocks?

_____

_____

For the next two questions, consider the following code:

```
DECLARE
   v_name VARCHAR2(50);
   v_total NUMBER;
BEGIN
   SELECT i.first_name||' '||i.last_name, COUNT(*)
     INTO v_name, v_total
     FROM instructor i, section s
    WHERE i.instructor_id = s.instructor_id
      AND i.instructor_id = 102
    GROUP BY i.first_name||' '||i.last_name;
   DBMS_OUTPUT.PUT_LINE
      ('Instructor '||v_name||' teaches '||v_total||
       ' courses');
EXCEPTION
   WHEN NO_DATA_FOUND THEN
      DBMS_OUTPUT.PUT_LINE
         ('There is no such instructor');
END;
```

c) Based on the example provided above, describe the structure of PL/SQL block.

_____

_____

d) What happens when runtime error NO_DATA_FOUND occurs in the PL/SQL block shown above?

_____

_____

2.1.2 UNDERSTANDING HOW PL/SQL GETS EXECUTED

Answer the following questions:

a) What happens when an anonymous PL/SQL block is executed?

_____

_____

b) What steps are included in the compilation process of a PL/SQL block?

_____

_____

c) What is a syntax error?

_____

_____

d) How does a syntax error differ from a run-time error?

_____

_____

LAB 2.1 EXERCISE ANSWERS

2.1.1 ANSWERS

a) Why it is more efficient to combine SQL statements into PL/SQL blocks?

Answer: It is more efficient to use SQL statements within PL/SQL blocks because network traffic can be decreased significantly, and an application becomes more efficient as well.

When a SQL statement is issued on the client computer, the request is made to the database on the server, and the result set is sent back to the client. As a result, a single SQL statement causes two trips on the network. If multiple SELECT statements are issued, the network traffic can increase significantly very fast. For example, four SELECT statements cause eight network trips. If these statements are part of the PL/SQL block, there are still only two network trips made as in case of a single SELECT statement.

b) What are the differences between named and anonymous PL/SQL blocks?

Answer: Named PL/SQL blocks can be stored in the database and referenced by their names later. Since anonymous PL/SQL blocks do not have names, they cannot be stored in the database and referenced later.

c) Based on the example provided above, describe the structure of PL/SQL block.

Answer: PL/SQL blocks contain three sections: declaration section, executable section, and exception-handling section. The executable section is the only mandatory section of the PL/SQL block.

The declaration section holds definitions of PL/SQL identifiers such as variables, constants, and cursors. The declaration section starts with the keyword DECLARE. The declaration section

```
DECLARE
    v_name VARCHAR2(50);
    v_total NUMBER;
```

contains definitions of two variables, `v_name` and `v_total`.

The executable section holds executable statements. It starts with keyword BEGIN and ends with keyword END. The executable section shown in bold letters

```
BEGIN
   SELECT i.first_name||' '||i.last_name, COUNT(*)
     INTO v_name, v_total
     FROM instructor i, section s
    WHERE i.instructor_id = s.instructor_id
      AND i.instructor_id = 102
    GROUP BY i.first_name||' '||i.last_name;
   DBMS_OUTPUT.PUT_LINE
        ('Instructor '||v_name||' teaches '||v_total||
         ' courses');
EXCEPTION
   WHEN NO_DATA_FOUND THEN
      DBMS_OUTPUT.PUT_LINE
         ('There is no such instructor');
END;
```

contains a SELECT INTO statement that assigns values to the variables v_name and v_total, and a DBMS_OUTPUT.PUT_LINE statement that displays their values on the screen.

The exception-handling section of the PL/SQL block contains statements that are executed only if runtime errors occur in the PL/SQL block. The following exception-handling section

```
EXCEPTION
   WHEN NO_DATA_FOUND THEN
      DBMS_OUTPUT.PUT_LINE
         ('There is no such instructor');
```

contains the DBMS_OUTPUT.PUT_LINE statement that is executed when run-time error NO_DATA_FOUND occurs.

d) What happens when run-time error NO_DATA_FOUND occurs in the PL/SQL block shown above?

Answer: When a runtime error occurs in the PL/SQL block, the control is passed to the exception-handling section of the block. The exception NO_DATA_FOUND is evaluated then with the help of the WHEN clause.

When the SELECT INTO statement

```
SELECT i.first_name||' '||i.last_name, COUNT(*)
  INTO v_name, v_total
  FROM instructor i, section s
 WHERE i.instructor_id = s.instructor_id
   AND i.instructor_id = 102
GROUP BY i.first_name||' '||i.last_name;
```

does not return any rows, the control of the execution is passed to the exception-handling section of the block. Next, the DBMS_OUTPUT.PUT_ LINE statement associated with the exception NO_DATA_FOUND is executed. As a result, the message "There is no such instructor" is displayed on the screen.

2.1.2 ANSWERS

a) What happens when an anonymous PL/SQL block is executed?

Answer: When an anonymous PL/SQL block is executed, the code is sent to the PL/SQL engine on the server where it is compiled.

b) What steps are included in the compilation process of a PL/SQL block?

Answer: The compilation process includes syntax checking, binding, and p-code generation.

Syntax checking involves checking PL/SQL code for compilation errors. Once syntax errors have been corrected, a storage address is assigned to the variables that are used to hold data for Oracle. This process is called binding. Next, p-code is generated for PL/SQL block. P-code is a list of instructions to the PL/SQL engine. For named blocks, p-code is stored in the database, and it is used the next time the program is executed.

c) What is a syntax error?

Answer: A syntax error occurs when a statement does not correspond to the syntax rules of the programming language. Undefined variable or a misplaced keyword are examples of syntax error.

d) How does a syntax error differ from a runtime error?

Answer: A syntax error can be detected by the PL/SQL compiler. A runtime errors occur while the program is running and cannot be detected by the PL/SQL compiler.

A misspelled keyword is an example of the syntax error. For example, the script

```
BEIN
   DBMS_OUTPUT.PUT_LINE('This is a test');
END;
```

contains a syntax error. You should try to find this error.

A SELECT INTO statement returning no rows is an example of the runtime error. This error can be handled with the help of the exception-handling section of the PL/SQL block.

LAB 2.1 SELF-REVIEW QUESTIONS

In order to test your progress, you should be able to answer the following questions.

1) SQL statements combined into PL/SQL blocks cause an increase in the network traffic
   a) _____True
   b) _____False

2) Which one of the following sections is mandatory for a PL/SQL block?
   a) _____Exception-handling section
   b) _____Executable section
   c) _____Declaration section

3) The exception section in a PL/SQL block is used to
   a) _____handle compilation errors.
   b) _____handle runtime errors.
   c) _____handle both compilation and runtime errors.

4) A PL/SQL compiler can detect
   a) _____syntax errors.
   b) _____runtime errors.
   c) _____both compilation and runtime errors.

5) P-code is stored in the database for
   a) _____anonymous PL/SQL blocks.
   b) _____named PL/SQL blocks.

Quiz answers appear in Appendix A, Section 2.1.

L A B   2 . 2

PL/SQL IN SQL*PLUS

LAB OBJECTIVES

After this lab, you will be able to:

✔ Use Substitution Variables
✔ Use DBMS_OUTPUT.PUT_LINE statement

SQL*Plus is an interactive tool that allows you to type SQL or PL/SQL statements at the command prompt. These statements are then sent to the database. Once they are processed, the results are sent back from the database and displayed on the screen. However, there are some differences between entering SQL and PL/SQL statements.

Consider the following example of SQL statement.

■ *FOR EXAMPLE*

```
SELECT first_name, last_name
  FROM student;
```

The semicolon terminates this SELECT statement. Therefore, as soon as you type semicolon and hit the ENTER key, the result set is displayed to you.

Now, consider example of PL/SQL block used in the previous lab.

■ *FOR EXAMPLE*

```
DECLARE
   v_first_name VARCHAR2(35);
   v_last_name VARCHAR2(35);
BEGIN
   SELECT first_name, last_name
     INTO v_first_name, v_last_name
     FROM student
```

```
              WHERE student_id = 123;
          DBMS_OUTPUT.PUT_LINE
             ('Student name: '||v_first_name||' '||
                v_last_name);
      EXCEPTION
         WHEN NO_DATA_FOUND THEN
            DBMS_OUTPUT.PUT_LINE
                ('There is no student with student id 123');
      END;
      .
      /
```

There are two additional lines at the end of the block containing "." and "/". The "." marks the end of the PL/SQL block and is optional. The "/" executes the PL/SQL block and is required.

When SQL*Plus reads SQL statement, it knows that the semicolon marks the end of the statement. Therefore, the statement is complete and can be sent to the database. When SQL*Plus reads a PL/SQL block, a semicolon marks the end of the individual statement within the block. In other words, it is not a block terminator. Therefore, SQL*Plus needs to know when the block has ended. As you have seen in the example above, it can be done with period and forward slash.

SUBSTITUTION VARIABLES

You noted earlier that PL/SQL is not a stand-alone programming language. It only exists as a tool within Oracle programming environment. As a result, it does not really have capabilities to accept input from a user. However, SQL*Plus allows a PL/SQL block to receive input information with the help of substitution variables. Substitution variables cannot be used to output the values because no memory is allocated for them. SQL*Plus will substitute a variable before the PL/SQL block is sent to the database. Substitution variables are usually prefixed by the ampersand (&) character or double ampersand (&&) character. Consider following example.

■ FOR EXAMPLE

```
DECLARE
   v_student_id NUMBER := &sv_student_id;
   v_first_name VARCHAR2(35);
   v_last_name VARCHAR2(35);
BEGIN
   SELECT first_name, last_name
```

```
        INTO v_first_name, v_last_name
        FROM student
       WHERE student_id = v_student_id;
     DBMS_OUTPUT.PUT_LINE
         ('Student name: '||v_first_name||' '||
           v_last_name);
  EXCEPTION
     WHEN NO_DATA_FOUND THEN
         DBMS_OUTPUT.PUT_LINE('There is no such student');
  END;
```

**LAB
2.2**

When this example is executed, the user is asked to provide a value for the student ID. The student's name is then retrieved from the STUDENT table if there is a record with the given student ID. If there is no record with the given student ID, the message from the exception section is displayed on the screen.

The example shown above uses a single ampersand for the substitution variable. When a single ampersand is used throughout the PL/SQL block, the user is asked to provide a value for each occurrence of the substitution variable. Consider the following example.

■ FOR EXAMPLE

```
BEGIN
   DBMS_OUTPUT.PUT_LINE('Today is '||'&sv_day');
   DBMS_OUTPUT.PUT_LINE('Tomorrow will be
      '||'&sv_day');
END;
```

This example produces the following output:

```
Enter value for sv_day: Monday
old    2:    DBMS_OUTPUT.PUT_LINE('Today is
'||'&sv_day');
new    2:    DBMS_OUTPUT.PUT_LINE('Today is
'||'Monday');
Enter value for sv_day: Tuesday
old    3:    DBMS_OUTPUT.PUT_LINE('Tomorrow will be
'||'&sv_day');
new    3:    DBMS_OUTPUT.PUT_LINE('Tomorrow will be
'||'Tuesday');
Today is Monday
Tomorrow will be Tuesday
PL/SQL procedure successfully completed.
```

When a substitution variable is used in the script, the output produced by the program contains the statements that show how the substitution was done. For example, consider the following lines of the output produced by the example above:

```
old    2:   DBMS_OUTPUT.PUT_LINE('Today is
                 '||'&sv_day');

new    2:   DBMS_OUTPUT.PUT_LINE('Today is
                 '||'Monday');
```

If you do not want to see these lines displayed in the output produced by the script, use the SET command option before you run the script as shown below:

```
SET VERIFY OFF;
```

Then, the output changes as shown below:

```
Enter value for sv_day: Monday

Enter value for sv_day: Tuesday

Today is Monday

Tomorrow will be Tuesday

PL/SQL procedure successfully completed.
```

You have probably noticed that substitution variable `sv_day` appears twice in this PL/SQL block. As a result, when this example is run, the user is asked twice to provide the value for the same variable. Now, consider an altered version of example as follows (changes are shown in bold).

■ FOR EXAMPLE

```
BEGIN
    DBMS_OUTPUT.PUT_LINE('Today is '||'&&sv_day');
    DBMS_OUTPUT.PUT_LINE('Tomorrow will be
        '||'&sv_day');
END;
```

In this example, substitution variable `sv_day` is prefixed by double ampersand in the first DBMS_OUTPUT.PUT_LINE statement. As a result, this version of the example produces different output.

```
Enter value for sv_day: Monday
old    2:   DBMS_OUTPUT.PUT_LINE('Today is
                 '||'&&sv_day');
```

```
new     2:      DBMS_OUTPUT.PUT_LINE('Today is
                '||'Monday');
old     3:      DBMS_OUTPUT.PUT_LINE('Tomorrow will be
                '||'&sv_day');
new     3:      DBMS_OUTPUT.PUT_LINE('Tomorrow will be
                '||'Monday');
Today is Monday
Tomorrow will be Monday
PL/SQL procedure successfully completed.
```

From the output shown above, it is clear that the user is asked only once to provide the value for the substitution variable sv_day. As a result, both DBMS_OUTPUT.PUT_LINE statements use the value of Monday entered previously by the user.

When a substitution variable is assigned to the string (text) datatype, it is a good practice to enclose it by single quotes. You cannot always guarantee that a user will provide text information in single quotes. This practice will make your program less error prone. Consider the following example.

■ FOR EXAMPLE

```
v_course_no VARCHAR2(5)  := '&sv_course_no';
```

As mentioned earlier, substitution variables are usually prefixed by the ampersand (&) character or double ampersand (&&) characters. These are default characters that denote substitution variables. There is a special SET command option available in SQL*Plus that allows to change the default character (&) to any other character or disable the substitution variable feature. This SET command has the following syntax:

SET DEFINE *character*

or

SET DEFINE ON

or

SET DEFINE OFF

The first set command option changes the prefix of the substitution variable from an ampersand to another character. However, it is important for you to note that this character cannot be alphanumeric or white space. The second (ON option) and third (OFF option) control whether

SQL*Plus will look for substitution variables or not. In addition, ON option changes the value of the *character* back to the ampersand.

DBMS_OUTPUT.PUT_LINE

You already have seen some examples of how the DBMS_OUTPUT.PUT_LINE statement can be used. This statement is used to display information on the screen. It is very helpful when you want to see how your PL/SQL block is executed. For example, you might want to see how variables change their values throughout the program or debug it.

The DBMS_OUTPUT.PUT_LINE is a call to the procedure PUT_LINE. This procedure is a part of the DBMS_OUTPUT package that is owned by the Oracle user SYS.

DBMS_OUTPUT.PUT_LINE writes information to the buffer for storage. Once a program has been completed, the information from the buffer is displayed on the screen. The size of the buffer can be set between 2000 and 1,000,000 bytes. Before you can see the output printed on the screen, one of the following statements must be entered before the PL/SQL block.

```
SET SERVEROUTPUT ON;
```

or

```
SET SERVEROUTPUT ON SIZE 5000;
```

The first SET statement enables the DBMS_OUTPUT.PUT_LINE statement, and the default value for the buffer size is used. The second SET statement not only enables the DBMS_OUTPUT.PUT_LINE statement. The buffer size is changed from its default value to 5000 bytes.

Similarly, if you do not want information to be displayed on the screen by the DBMS_OUTPUT.PUT_LINE statement, following SET command can be issued prior to the PL/SQL block.

```
SET SERVEROUTPUT OFF;
```

LAB 2.2 EXERCISES

2.2.1 USING SUBSTITUTION VARIABLES

In this exercise, you will calculate the square of a number. The value of the number will be provided with the help of a substitution variable. Then, the result will be displayed on the screen.

Create the following PL/SQL script:

```
-- ch02_1a.sql, version 1.0
SET SERVEROUTPUT ON
DECLARE
    v_num NUMBER := &sv_num;
    v_result NUMBER;
BEGIN
    v_result := POWER(v_num, 2);
    DBMS_OUTPUT.PUT_LINE
        ('The value of v_result is: '||v_result);
END;
```

Execute the script, then answer the following questions:

a) If the value of v_num is equal to 10, what output is printed on the screen?

_____

_____

b) What is the purpose of using a substitution variable?

_____

_____

c) Why it is considered a good practice to enclose substitution variable with single quotes for string datatypes?

_____

_____

2.2.2 USING DBMS_OUTPUT.PUT_LINE STATEMENT

In this exercise, you will determine the day of the week based on today's date. You will then display the results on the screen.

Create the following PL/SQL script

```
-- ch02_2a.sql, version 1.0
SET SERVEROUTPUT ON
```

```
DECLARE
    v_day VARCHAR2(20);
BEGIN
    v_day := TO_CHAR(SYSDATE, 'Day');
    DBMS_OUTPUT.PUT_LINE ('Today is '||v_day);
END;
```

**LAB
2.2**

Execute the script, then answer the following questions:

a) What was printed on the screen?

_____

_____

b) What will be printed on the screen if the statement SET SERVER-OUTPUT OFF is issued? Why?

_____

_____

c) How would you change the script to display the time of the day as well?

_____

_____

LAB 2.2 EXERCISE ANSWERS

2.2.1 ANSWERS

a) If the value of v_num is equal to 10, what output is printed on the screen?

Answer: Your output should look like the following:

```
Enter value for v_num: 10
old    2:    v_num    NUMBER := &sv_num;
new    2:    v_num    NUMBER := 10;
The value of v_result is: 100
PL/SQL procedure successfully completed.
```

The first line of the output asks you to provide a value for sv_num. Then, the actual substitution is shown to you in the lines 2 and 3. In the second line, you can see the original statement from the PL/SQL block. In the third line, you can see the same statement with substitution value. The next line shows the output produced by the DBMS_OUTPUT.PUT_LINE statement. Finally, the last line informs you that your PL/SQL block was executed successfully.

b) What is the purpose of using a substitution variable?

Answer: A substitution variable allows the PL/SQL block to accept information provided by the user at the time of the execution. Substitution variables are used for input purposes only. They cannot be used to output values for a user.

c) Why it is considered a good practice to enclose substitution variable with single quotes for string datatypes?

Answer: A program cannot depend wholly on a user to provide text information is single quotes. Enclosing a substitution variable with single quotes allows a program to be less error prone.

2.2.2 ANSWERS

a) What was printed on the screen?

Answer: Your output should look like the following:

```
Today is Friday
PL/SQL procedure successfully completed.
```

In this example, SQL*Plus does not ask you to enter the value of the v_day variable because there is no substitution variable used. The value of v_day is computed with the help of TO_CHAR and SYSDATE functions. Then, it is displayed on the screen with the help of DBMS_OUTPUT.PUT_LINE statement.

b) What will be printed on the screen if the statement SET SERVEROUT-PUT OFF is issued? Why?

Answer: If the statement SET SERVEROUTPUT OFF is issued prior to the execution of the PL/SQL block, no output will be printed on the screen. The output will look like following:

```
PL/SQL procedure successfully completed.
```

It is important to note that when substitution variables are used, the user is prompted to enter the value for the variable regardless of the SERVER-

OUTPUT setting. The prompt for the user is provided by SQL*Plus and does not depend on the option chosen for the SERVEROUTPUT.

c) How would you change the script to display time of the day as well?

Answer: Your script should look similar to this script.

```
-- ch02_2b.sql, version 2.0
SET SERVEROUTPUT ON
DECLARE
    v_day VARCHAR2(20);
BEGIN
    v_day := TO_CHAR(SYSDATE, 'Day, HH24:MI');
    DBMS_OUTPUT.PUT_LINE ('Today is '|| v_day);
END;
```

The statement shown in bold has been changed in order to display time of the day as well. The output produced by this PL/SQL block is shown below:

```
Today is Friday   , 23:09
PL/SQL procedure successfully completed.
```

LAB 2.2 SELF-REVIEW QUESTIONS

In order to test your progress, you should be able to answer the following questions.

1) SQL*Plus understands a semicolon as a terminating symbol of a PL/SQL block.
    a) _____True
    b) _____False

2) Substitution variables are used to
    a) _____read input information provided by a user.
    b) _____provide a user with output information.
    c) _____Both a and b.

3) PUT_LINE is one of the procedures from DBMS_OUTPUT package.
    a) _____True
    b) _____False

4) DBMS_OUTPUT.PUT_LINE writes information to the buffer for storage before it is displayed on the screen.
    a) _____True
    b) _____False

5)   The SET command SET SERVEROUTPUT ON SIZE 8000, is used to
   a)   _____enable the DBMS_OUTPUT.PUT_LINE statement only.
   b)   _____change the buffer size only.
   c)   _____enable the DBMS_OUTPUT.PUT_LINE statement and change the buffer size.

Quiz answers appear in Appendix A, Section 2.2.

C H A P T E R   2

TEST YOUR THINKING

In this chapter you have learned about PL/SQL concepts. You explored PL/SQL block structure, substitution variables, and the DBMS_OUTPUT.PUT_LINE statement. Here are some exercises that will help you test the depth of your understanding.

1) In order to calculate the area of a circle, the circle's radius must be squared and then multiplied by *pi*. Write a program that calculates the area of a circle. The value for the radius should by provided with the help of the substitution variable. Use 3.14 for the value of *pi*. Once the area of the circle is calculated, display it on the screen.

2) Rewrite the script ch02_2b.sql, version 2.0. In the output produced by the script, extra spaces appear after the day of the week. The new script must remove the extra spaces after the day of the week.

The current output:

```
Today is Friday   , 23:09
```

The new output should have the format as shown below:

```
Today is Friday, 23:09
```

CHAPTER 3

GENERAL PROGRAMMING LANGUAGE FUNDAMENTALS

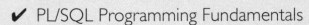

CHAPTER OBJECTIVES

In this chapter, you will learn about:

✔ PL/SQL Programming Fundamentals   Page 50

In the first two chapters you have learned about the difference between machine language and a programming language. You have also learned how PL/SQL is different from SQL and about PL/SQL basic block structure. This is similar to learning the history behind a foreign language and in what context it is used. In order to use the PL/SQL language, you will have to learn the key words, what they mean, and when and how to use them. First, you will encounter the different types of key words and then their full syntax. Finally, in this chapter, you will expand upon simple block structure with an exploration of scope and nesting blocks.

L A B   3 . 1

PL/SQL PROGRAMMING FUNDAMENTALS

LAB OBJECTIVES

After this lab, you will be able to:

✔ Make Use of PL/SQL Language Components
✔ Make Use of PL/SQL Variables
✔ Make Use of Anchored Datatypes
✔ Declare and Initialize Variables
✔ Understand the Scope of a Block, Nested Blocks, and Labels

In most languages, you only have two sets of characters: numbers and letters. Some languages, such as Hebrew or Tibetan, have specific characters for vowels that are not placed in line with consonants. Additionally, other languages, such as Japanese, have three character sets: one for words originally taken from the Chinese language, another set for native Japanese words, and then a third for other foreign words. In order to speak any foreign language, you have to begin by learning these character sets. Then you progress to learn how to make words from these character sets; finally, you learn the parts of speech and you can begin talking. You can think of PL/SQL as being a more complex language because it has many character types and, additionally, many types of words or lexical units that are made from these character sets. Once you learn these, you progress to learn the structure of the PL/SQL language.

CHARACTER TYPES

The PL/SQL engine accepts four types of characters: letters, digits, symbols (*, +, -, = ..etc), and white space. When elements from one of these character types are joined together, they will create a lexical unit (these lexical units can be a combination of character types). The lexical units are the words of the PL/SQL language. First you need to learn the PL/SQL vocabulary, and then you will move on to the syntax or grammar. Soon you can start talking in PL/SQL.

Although PL/SQL can be considered a language, don't try talking to your fellow programmers in PL/SQL. For example, at a dinner table of programmers, if you say "BEGIN, LOOP FOR PEAS IN PLATE EXECUTE EAT PEAS, END LOOP, EXCEPTION WHEN BROCCOLI FOUND EXECUTE SEND TO PRESIDENT BUSH, END EAT PEAS." You may not be considered human. This type of language is reserved for Terminators and the like.

LEXICAL UNITS

A language like English contains different parts of speech. Each part of speech, such as a verb or noun, behaves in a different way and must be used accordingly. Likewise, a programming language has *lexical units* that are the building blocks of the language. PL/SQL lexical units fall within one of the following five groups:

1. *Identifiers*. Identifiers must begin with a letter and may be up to 30 characters long. See a PL/SQL manual for a more detailed list of restrictions; generally, if you stay with characters, numbers, and ' ' and avoid reserved words, you will not run into problems.
2. *Reserved Words*. Reserved words are words that PL/SQL saves for its own use (e.g., BEGIN, END, SELECT).
3. *Delimiters*. These are characters that have special meaning to PL/SQL, such as arithmetic operators and quotation marks.
4. *Literals*. A literal is any value (character, numeric, or Boolean [true/false]) that is not an identifier. 123, "Declaration of Independence" and FALSE are examples of literals.
5. *Comments*. These can be either single-line comments (i.e., --) or multi-line comments (i.e., /* */).

See Appendix B, "PL/SQL Formatting Guide," for details on formatting.

In the following exercises, you will practice putting these units together.

LAB 3.1 EXERCISES

3.1.1 MAKING USE OF PL/SQL LANGUAGE COMPONENTS

Now that you have the character types and the lexical units, it is equivalent to knowing the alphabet and how to spell out words.

a) Why does PL/SQL have so many different types of characters? What are they used for?

_____

_____

b) What would be the equivalent of a verb and a noun in English in PL/SQL? Do you speak PL/SQL?

_____

_____

3.1.2 MAKING USE OF PL/SQL VARIABLES

Variables may be used to hold a temporary value.

```
Syntax : <variable-name> <datatype> [optional default
assignment]
```

■ FOR EXAMPLE

```
-- ch03_1a.pls
DECLARE
   v_name VARCHAR2(30);
   v_dob DATE;
   v_us_citizen BOOLEAN;
BEGIN
   DBMS_OUTPUT.PUT_LINE(v_name||'born on'||v_dob);
END;
```

a) If you ran the previous example in a SQL*Plus, what would be the result?

_____

_____

b) Run the example and see what happens. Explain what is happening as focus moves from one line to the next.

_____

_____

3.1.3 MAKING USE OF ANCHORED DATATYPES

The datatype that you assign to a variable can be based on a database object. This is called an *anchored declaration* since the variable's datatype is dependent on that of the underlying object. It is wise to make use of this when possible so that you do not have to update your PL/SQL when the datatypes of base objects change.

```
Syntax:   <variable_name> <type attribute>%TYPE
```

The type is a direct reference to a database column.

■ FOR EXAMPLE

```
-- ch03_2a.pls
DECLARE
    v_name student.first_name%TYPE;
    v_grade grade.grade_numeric%TYPE;
BEGIN
    DMBS_OUTPUT.PUT_LINE(NVL(v_name, 'No Name ')||
        ' has grade of '||NVL(v_grade, 'no grade'));
END;
```

a) In the previous example, what has been declared? State the datatype and value.

_____

_____

3.1.4 DECLARING AND INITIALIZING VARIABLES

In PL/SQL, variables must be declared in order to be referenced. This is done in the initial declarative section of a PL/SQL block. Remember that each declaration must be terminated with a semicolon. Variables can be assigned using

LAB
3.1

the assignment operator ":=" . If you declare a numeric variable to be a constant, it will retain the same value throughout the block; in order to do this, you must give it a value at declaration.

Type the following into a text file and run the script from a SQL*Plus session.

```
-- ch03_3a.pls
SET SERVEROUTPUT ON
DECLARE
    v_cookies_amt NUMBER := 2;
    v_calories_per_cookie CONSTANT NUMBER := 300;
BEGIN
    DBMS_OUTPUT.PUT_LINE('I ate ' || v_cookies_amt ||
        ' cookies with ' || v_cookies_amt *
        v_calories_per_cookie || ' calories.');
    v_cookies_amt := 3;
    DBMS_OUTPUT.PUT_LINE('I really ate ' ||
        v_cookies_amt
        || ' cookies with ' || v_cookies_amt *
        v_calories_per_cookie || ' calories.');
    v_cookies_amt := v_cookies_amt + 5;
    DBMS_OUTPUT.PUT_LINE('The truth is, I actually ate '
        || v_cookies_amt || ' cookies with ' ||
    v_cookies_amt * v_calories_per_cookie
        || ' calories.');
END;
```

a) What will the output be for the above script? Explain what is being declared and what the value of the variable is throughout the scope of the block.

_____

_____

■ FOR EXAMPLE

```
-- ch03_3a.pls
DECLARE
    v_lname VARCHAR2(30);
    v_regdate DATE;
    v_pctincr CONSTANT NUMBER(4,2) := 1.15;
    v_counter NUMBER := 0;
    v_new_cost course.crsecost%TYPE;
    v_YorN BOOLEAN := TRUE;
```

```
BEGIN
    NULL; — ...
END;
```

b) In the previous example, replace the null with the following, then explain the value of the variables at the beginning and at the end of the script.

```
v_counter := NVL(v_counter, 0) + 1;
v_new_cost := 800 * v_pctincr;
```

PL/SQL variables are held together with expressions and operators. An expression is a sequence of variables and literals, separated by operators, and is used to manipulate data, perform calculations, and compare data.

Expressions are composed of a combination of operand and operators. An *operand* is an argument to the operator; it can be a variable, a constant, a function call. The *operator* is what specifies the action (+,**,/, OR, etc).

You can use parentheses to control the order in which Oracle evaluates an expression. Continue to add to your SQL script the following:

```
v_counter := ((v_counter + 5)*2) / 2;
v_new_cost := (v_new_cost * v_counter)/4;
```

c) What will be the values of the variables at the end of the script?

3.1.5 UNDERSTANDING THE SCOPE OF A BLOCK, NESTED BLOCKS, AND LABELS

SCOPE OF A BLOCK

The scope or existence of structures defined in the declaration section are local to that block. The block also provides the scope for exceptions that are declared and raised. Exceptions will be covered in more detail in Chapters 6, 9, and 10, "Exceptions."

LABELS AND NESTED BLOCKS

Labels can be added to a block in order to improve readability and to qualify the names of elements that exist under the same name in nested blocks. The name of the block must proceed the first line of executable code (either the BEGIN or DECLARE) as follows:

■ *FOR EXAMPLE*

```
-- ch03_4a.pls
-- set serveroutput on
   <<find_stu_num>>
   BEGIN
      DBMS_OUTPUT.PUT_LINE('The procedure
                   find_stu_num has been executed.');
   END find_stu_num;
```

The label optionally appears after END. In SQL*Plus, the first line of a PL/SQL block cannot be a label. For commenting purposes, you may alternatively use "- -" or /*, ending with */

Blocks can be nested in the main section or in an exception handler. A *nested block* is a block that is placed fully within another block. This has an impact on the scope and visibility of variables. The scope of a variable is the period when memory is being allocated for the variable and extends from the moment of declaration until the END of the block from which it was declared. The visibility of a variable is the part of the program where the variable can be accessed.

a) If the following example were run in SQL*Plus, what will be displayed?

_____

_____

```
-- ch03_5a.pls
DECLARE
   e_show_exception_scope EXCEPTION;
   v_student_id            NUMBER := 123;
BEGIN
  DBMS_OUTPUT.PUT_LINE('outer student id is '
     ||v_student_id);
   DECLARE
     v_student_id     VARCHAR2(8) := 125;
```

```
      BEGIN
         DBMS_OUTPUT.PUT_LINE('inner student id is '
            ||v_student_id);
         RAISE e_show_exception_scope;
      END;
EXCEPTION
   WHEN e_show_exception_scope
   THEN
      DBMS_OUTPUT.PUT_LINE('When am I displayed?');
      DBMS_OUTPUT.PUT_LINE('outer student id is '
         ||v_student_id);
END;
```

b) Now run the example and see if it produced what you expected. Explain how the focus moves from one block to another in this example.

_____

_____

LAB 3.1 EXERCISE ANSWERS

3.1.1 ANSWERS

a) Why does PL/SQL have so many different types of characters? What are they used for?

Answer: The PL/SQL engine recognizes different characters as having different meaning and therefore processes them differently. PL/SQL is neither a pure mathematical language nor a spoken language, yet it contains elements of both. Letters will form various lexical units such as identifiers or key words, mathematic symbols will form lexical units known as delimiters that will perform an operation, and other symbols such as /* indicate comments that should not be processed.

b) What would be the equivalent of a verb and a noun in English in PL/SQL? Do you speak PL/SQL?

Answer: A noun would be similar to the lexical unit known as an identifier. A verb would be similar to the lexical unit known as a delimiter. Delimiters can simply be a quote but others perform a function such as multiply "*".

3.1.2 ANSWERS

a) If you ran the previous example in a SQL*Plus, what would be the result?

Answer: Assuming SET SERVEROUTPUT ON *had been issued, you would only get* **born on***. The reason is that the variables* v_name *and* v_dob *have no values.*

b) Run the example and see what happens. Explain what is happening as focus moves from one line to the next.

Answer: Three variables are declared. When each one is declared, its initial value is null. v_name *is set as a varchar2 with a length of 30,* v_dob *is set as a character type date, and* v_us_citizen *is set to BOOLEAN. Once the executable section begins, the variables have no value and therefore when the DBMS_OUTPUT is told to print their values, it prints nothing.*

This can be seen if the variables were replaced as follows: Instead of v_name, put NVL(v_name, 'No Name') and instead of v_dob put NVL (v_dob, '01-Jan-1999'), then run the same block and you will get:

```
No Name born on 01-Jan-1999
```

In order to make use of a variable, you must declare it in the declaration section of the PL/SQL block. You will have to give it a name and state its data type. You also have the option to give your variable an initial value. Note that if you do not assign a variable an initial value, it will be null. It is also possible to constrain the declaration to "not null," in this case you must assign an initial value. Variables must first be declared and then they can be referenced. PL/SQL does not allow forward references. You can set the variable to be a constant, which means it cannot change.

3.1.3 ANSWERS

a) In the previous example, what has been declared? State the datatype and value.

Answer: The variable v_name *was declared with the identical datatype as the column* first_name *from the database table STUDENT—varchar2(25). Additionally, the variable* v_grade *was declared the identical datatype as the column* grade_ numeric *on the GRADE database table—number(3). Each has a value of null.*

Most Common Datatypes

VARCHAR2(maximum_length)

- Stores variable-length character data.
- Takes a required parameter that specifies a maximum length up to 32767 bytes.
- Does not use a constant or variable to specify the maximum length; an integer literal must be used.
- Although the maximum length of a VARCHAR2(n) variable is 32,767 bytes, the maximum width of a VARCHAR2 database column is 2000 bytes; therefore, values longer than 2000 bytes cannot be inserted into a VARCHAR2 column.

CHAR[(maximum_length)]

- Stores fixed-length (blank-padded if necessary) character data.
- Takes an optional parameter that specifies a maximum length up to 32,767 bytes.
- Does not use a constant or variable to specify the maximum length; an integer literal must be used. If maximum length is not specified, it defaults to 1.
- Although the maximum length of a CHAR(n) variable is 32,767 bytes, the maximum width of a CHAR database column is 255 bytes; therefore, you cannot insert values longer than 255 bytes into a CHAR column.

NUMBER[(precision, scale)]

- Stores fixed or floating-point numbers of virtually any size.
- Precision is the total number of digits.
- Scale determines where rounding occurs.
- It is possible to specify precision and omit scale, in which case scale is 0 and only integers are allowed.
- Constants or variables cannot be used to specify precision and scale; integer literals must be used.
- Maximum precision of a NUMBER value is 38 decimal digits.
- Scale can range from −84 to 127.
- For instance, a scale of 2 rounds to the nearest hundredth (3.456 becomes 3.46).
- Scale can be negative, which causes rounding to the left of the decimal point. For example, a scale of −3 rounds to the nearest thousand (3456 becomes 3000). A scale of zero rounds to the nearest whole number. If you do not specify the scale, it defaults to zero.

BINARY_INTEGER

- Stores signed integer variables.
- Compares to the NUMBER datatype. BINARY_INTEGER variables are stored in the binary format, which takes less space.
- Calculations are faster.
- Can store any integer value in the range –2,147,483,747 through 2,147,483,747.

DATE

- Stores fixed-length date values.
- Valid dates for DATE variables include January 1, 4712 BC to December 31, 4712 AD.
- When stored in a database column, date values include the time of day in seconds since midnight. The date portion defaults to the first day of the current month; the time portion defaults to midnight.
- Dates are actually stored in binary format and will be displayed according to the default format.

BOOLEAN

- Stores the values TRUE and FALSE and the non-value NULL. Recall that NULL stands for a missing, unknown, or inapplicable value.
- Only the values TRUE and FALSE and the non-value NULL can be assigned to a BOOLEAN variable.
- The values TRUE and FALSE cannot be inserted into a database column.

LONG

- Stores variable-length character strings.
- The LONG datatype is like the VARCHAR2 datatype, except that the maximum length of a LONG value is 32,760 bytes.
- Any LONG value can be inserted into a LONG database column because the maximum width of a LONG column is 2,147,483,647 bytes. However, you cannot select a value longer than 32,760 bytes from a LONG column into a LONG variable.
- LONG columns can store text, arrays of characters, or even short documents. You can reference LONG columns in UPDATE, INSERT, and (most) SELECT statements, but not in expressions, SQL function calls, or certain SQL clauses such as WHERE, GROUP BY, and CONNECT BY.

ROWID
- Internally, every Oracle database table has a ROWID pseudocolumn, which stores binary values called rowids.
- Rowids uniquely identify rows and provide the fastest way to access particular rows.
- Use the ROWID datatype to store rowids in a readable format.
- When you select or fetch a rowid into a ROWID variable, you can use the function ROWIDTOCHAR, which converts the binary value to an 18-byte character string and returns it in the format.
- Row ID in Oracle 8i is as follows: OOOOOOFFFBBBBBBRRR OOOOOO: This number signifies the database segment. FFF: This number indicates the tablespace-relative datafile number of the datafile that contains the row. BBBBBB: This number is the data block that contains the row. RRR: This number is the row in the block (keep in mind that this may change in future versions of Oracle).

3.1.4 ANSWERS

a) What will the output be for the above script? Explain what is being declared and what the value of the variable is throughout the scope of the block.

Answer. The server output will be:

```
I ate 2 cookies with 600 calories.
I really ate 3 cookies with 900 calories.
The truth is, I actually ate 8 cookies with 2400
calories.
PL/SQL procedure successfully completed.
```

Initially the variable v_cookies_amt *is declared to be a number with the value of two and the variable* v_calories_per_cookie *is declared to be a constant with a value of 300 (since it is declared to be a constant, it will not change its value). In the course of the procedure the value of* v_cookies_amt *is later set to be 3, and then finally it is set to be its current value (3) plus 5 thus becoming 8.*

b) In the previous example, replace the null with the following, then explain what that value of the variables at the end of the script. When in doubt, add DBMS_OUTPUT to view the values of the variables.

Answer: Initially the variable v_lname *is declared as a datatype varchar2 length of 30 and a value of null. The variable* v_regdate *is declared as datatype date with a* value of null. The variable v_pctincr *is declared as constant number with length of 4 and precision of 2 and a value of 1.15. The variable* v_counter *is declared as number with a value of 0. The variable* v_YorN *is declared as variable of boolean datatype and a value of TRUE.*

Once the executable section is complete, the variable v_counter *will be changed from null to 1. And the value of* v_new_cost *will change from null to 1200 (800 times 1.15).*

Note that a common way to find out the value of a variable at different points in block is to add a DBMS_OUTPUT.PUT_LINE(v_variable_name); throughout the block.

c) What will be the values of the variables at the end of the script?

Answer: The value of v_counter *will then change from 1 to 6 ((1 + 5) *2))/2 and the value of* new_cost *will go from 1200 to 1800 (800 * 6)/4.*

Operators(Delimiters)—the Separators in an Expression

Arithmetic (** , * , / , + , -)
Comparison(=, <> , != , < , > , <= , >= , LIKE , IN , BETWEEN , IS NULL)
Logical (AND, OR, NOT)
String (||, LIKE)

Expressions

Operator Precedence

   ** , NOT

   +, - (arithmetic identity and negation) *, / + , - , || =, <>, != , <= ,
   >= , < , > , LIKE, BETWEEN, IN, IS NULL

 AND—logical conjunction
 OR—logical inclusion

3.1.5 ANSWERS

a) If the following example were run in SQL*Plus, what will be displayed?

Answer: The following would result:

```
outer student id is 123
inner student id is 125
```

```
When am I displayed?
outer student id is 123
PL/SQL procedure successfully completed.
```

b) Now run the example and see if it produced what you expected. Explain how the focus moves from one block to another in this example.

Answer: The variable `e_Show_Exception_Scope` *will be declared as an exception type in the declaration section of the block. There is also be a declaration of the variable called* `v_student_id` *of datatype NUMBER that will be initialized to the number 123. This variable will have a scope of the entire block but it will only be visible outside of the inner block. Once the inner block begins, another variable named* `v_student_id` *is declared. This time it is of datatype varchar2(8) and is initialized to 125. This variable will have a scope and visibility only within the inner block. The use of DBMS_OUTPUT helps to show which variable is visible. The inner block raises the exception* `e_Show_Exception_Scope`, *this means focus will move out of the execution section and into the exception section.. Focus will look for an exception named* `e_Show_Exception_Scope`. *Since the inner block has no exception with this name, focus will move to the outer block's exception section and it will find the exception. The inner variable* `v_student_id` *is now out of scope and visibility. The outer variable* `v_student_id` *(which has always been in scope) now regains visibility. Because the exception has an IF/THEN construct, it will execute the DBMS_OUTPUT call. This is a simple use of nested blocks. Later in the book you will see more complex examples. Once you have covered exception handling in depth in Chapter 6 and 9, you will see there is greater opportunity to make use of nested blocks.*

LAB 3.1 SELF-REVIEW QUESTIONS

In order to test your progress, you should be able to answer the following questions.

1) If a variable is declared as follows, what are the results?

```
v_fixed_amount CONSTANT NUMBER;
```

a) _____ A number variable called `v_fixed_amount` has been declared (it will remain as a constant once initialized).

b) _____ A number variable called `v_fixed_amount` has been declared (it will remain as null).

c) _____ An error message will result because constant initialization must be done in the executable section of the block.

d) _____ An error message will result because the declaration for the constant is missing an assignment to a number.

2) Which of the following are valid character types for PL/SQL?
    a) _____ Numbers
    b) _____ English letters
    c) _____ Paragraph returns
    d) _____ Arithmetic symbols
    e) _____ Japanese Kanji

3) A variable may be used for which of the following?
    a) _____ To hold a constant, such as the value of π.
    b) _____ To hold the value of a counter that keeps changing.
    c) _____ To place a value that will be inserted into the database.
    d) _____ To hold onto the function of an operand.
    e) _____ To hold any value as long as you declare it.

4) Which of the following will declare a variable that is of the identical datatype as the `student_id` in the database table student in the CTA database?
    a) _____ `v_id student_id := 123;`
    b) _____ `v_id binary integer;`
    c) _____ `v_id number := 24;`
    d) _____ `v_id student_id%type;`

5) The value of a variable is set to null after the 'end;' of the block is issued.
    a) _____ True
    b) _____ False

Quiz answers appear in Appendix A, Section 3.1.

Go to the companion website for this book, located at `http://www.phptr.com/Rosenzweig` *for more review questions on datatypes.*

C H A P T E R   3

TEST YOUR THINKING

Before starting these projects, take a look at the formatting guidelines in Appendix B. Make your variable names conform to the standard. At the top of the Declare section, put a comment stating which naming standard you are using.

1. Write a PL/SQL block:

    a) Include declarations for the following variables:

    A VARCHAR2 datatype that can contain the string "Introduction to Oracle PL/SQL"

    A NUMBER that can be assigned 987654.55, but not 987654.567 or 9876543.55

    A CONSTANT (you choose the correct datatype) that is auto-initialized to the value "603D"

    A BOOLEAN

    A DATE datatype autoinitialized to one week from today

    b) In the body of the PL/SQL block, put a DBMS_OUTPUT.PUT_LINE message for each of the variables that received an auto initialization value.

    c) In a comment at the bottom of the PL/SQL block, state the value of your number datatype.

2. Alter the PL/SQL block you created in (1) above to conform to the following specs.

    a) Remove the DBMS_OUTPUT.PUT_LINE messages.

    b) In the body of the PL/SQL block, write a selection test (IF) that does the following—use a nested if statement where appropriate.

    i) Check if the VARCHAR2 you created contains the course named "Introduction to Underwater Basketweaving."

ii) If it does, then put a DBMS_OUTPUT.PUT_LINE message on the screen that says so.

iii) If it does not, then test to see if the CONSTANT you created contains the room number 603D.

iv) If it does, then put a DBMS_OUTPUT.PUT_LINE message on the screen that states the course name and the room name that you've reached in this logic.

v) If it does not, then put a DBMS_OUTPUT.PUT_LINE message on the screen that states that the course and location could not be determined.

c) Add a WHEN OTHERS EXCEPTION that puts a DBMS_OUTPUT.PUT_ LINE message on the screen that says that an error occurred.

C H A P T E R   4

SQL IN PL/SQL

This chapter is a collection of some fundamental elements of using SQL statements in PL/SQL blocks. In the previous chapter, you initialized variables with the ":=" syntax; in this chapter, we will introduce the method of using an SQL select statement to update the value of a variable. These variables can then be used in DML statements (INSERT, DELETE, or UPDATE). Additionally, we will demonstrate how you can use a sequence in your DML statements within a PL/SQL block much as you would in a stand-alone SQL statement.

A *transaction* in Oracle is a series of SQL statements that have been grouped together into a logical unit by the programmer. A programmer chooses to do this in order to maintain data integrity. Each application (SQL*Plus, Procedure Builder, and so forth) maintains a single database session for each instance of a user login. The changes to the database that have been executed by a single application session are not actually "saved" into the database until a COMMIT occurs. Work within a transaction up to and just prior to the commit can be rolled back; work done prior to the commit cannot be rolled back.

In order to exert *transaction control*, a SAVEPOINT can be used to break down large SQL statements into individual units that are easier to manage. In this chapter, we will cover the basic elements of *transaction control* so you will know how to manage your PL/SQL code by use of COMMIT, ROLLBACK, and principally SAVEPOINT.

LAB 4.1

MAKING USE OF DML IN PL/SQL

LAB OBJECTIVES

After this lab, you will be able to:

✔ Use the SELECT INTO Syntax for Variable Initialization
✔ Use DML in a PL/SQL Block
✔ Make Use of a Sequence in a PL/SQL Block

VARIABLE INITIALIZATION WITH SELECT INTO

In PL/SQL, there are two main methods of giving value to variables in a PL/SQL block. The first one, which you learned in Chapter 2, "PL/SQL Concepts," is initialization with the ":=" syntax. In this lab we will learn how to initialize a variable with a select statement by making use of SELECT INTO syntax.

A variable that has been declared in the declaration section of the PL/SQL block can later be given a value with a SELECT statement. The correct syntax is as follows:

```
SELECT item_name
    INTO variable_name
    FROM table_name;
```

It is important to note that any single row function can be performed on the item to give the variable a calculated value.

■ *FOR EXAMPLE*

```
--   ch04_1a.sql
SET SERVEROUTPUT ON
DECLARE
   v_average_cost VARCHAR2(10);
BEGIN
   SELECT TO_CHAR(AVG(cost), '$9,999.99')
     INTO v_average_cost
     FROM course;
   DBMS_OUTPUT.PUT_LINE('The average cost of a '||
     'course in the CTA program is '||
     v_average_cost');
END;
```

In this example, a variable is given the value of the average cost of a course in the course table. First, the variable must be declared in the declaration section of the PL/SQL block. In this example, the variable is given the datatype of VARCHAR2(10) because of the functions used on the data. The same select statement that would produce this outcome in SQL*Plus would be:

```
SELECT TO_CHAR(AVG(cost), '$9,999.99')
  FROM course;
```

The TO_CHAR function is used to format the cost; in doing this, the number datatype is converted to a character datatype. Once the variable has a value, it can be displayed to the screen in SQL*Plus using the PUT_LINE procedure of the DBMS_OUTPUT package.

LAB 4.1 EXERCISES

4.1.1 USING THE *SELECT INTO* SYNTAX FOR *VARIABLE INITIALIZATION*

Run the PL/SQL block from the pre-exercise example

a) What is displayed on the SQL*Plus screen? Explain the results.

_____

_____

b) Take the same PL/SQL block and place the line with the DBMS_OUTPUT before the SELECT INTO statement. What is displayed on the SQL*Plus screen? Explain what the value of the variable is at each point in the PL/SQL block.

Data definition language (DDL) is not valid in a simple PL/SQL block (more advanced techniques such as procedures in the DBMS_SQL package will enable you to make use of DDL), yet data manipulation (DML) is easily achieved either by use of variables or by simply putting a DML statement into a PL/SQL block. Here is an example of a PL/SQL block that UPDATES an exiting entry in the zipcode table.

■ *FOR EXAMPLE*

```
--   ch04_2a.sql
DECLARE
    v_city zipcode.city%TYPE;
BEGIN
    SELECT 'COLUMBUS'
      INTO v_city
      FROM dual;
    UPDATE zipcode
       SET city = v_city
     WHERE ZIP = 43224;
END;
```

It is also possible to insert data into a database table in a PL/SQL block as shown in the following example.

■ *FOR EXAMPLE*

```
--   ch04_3a.sql
DECLARE
    v_zip zipcode.zip%TYPE;
    v_user zipcode.created_by%TYPE;
    v_date zipcode.created_date%TYPE;
BEGIN
    SELECT 43438, USER, SYSDATE
      INTO v_zip, v_user, v_date
      FROM dual;
    INSERT INTO zipcode
```

```
      (ZIP, CREATED_BY ,CREATED_DATE, MODIFIED_BY,
       MODIFIED_DATE
      )
      VALUES(v_zip, v_user, v_date, v_user, v_date);
END;
```

SELECT statements that return no rows or too many rows will cause an error to occur that can be trapped by using an exception. You will learn more about handling exceptions in Chapters 6, 9, and 10, "Exceptions."

4.1.2 USING DML IN A PL/SQL BLOCK

a) Write a PL/SQL block that will insert a new student in the student table. Use your own information for the data.

_____

_____

USING AN ORACLE SEQUENCE

An Oracle *sequence* is an Oracle database object that can be used to generate unique numbers. You can use sequences to automatically generate primary key values.

ACCESSING AND INCREMENTING SEQUENCE VALUES Once a sequence is created, you can access its values in SQL statements with these pseudo-columns:

CURRVAL   Returns the current value of the sequence.

NEXTVAL   Increments the sequence and returns the new value.

■ FOR EXAMPLE

This statement creates the sequence ESEQ:

```
CREATE SEQUENCE eseq
   INCREMENT BY 10
```

The first reference to ESEQ.NEXTVAL returns 1. The second returns 11. Each subsequent reference will return a value 10 greater than the one previous.

(Even though you will be guaranteed unique numbers, you are not guaranteed contiguous numbers. In some systems this may be a problem, for example, when generating invoice numbers.)

DRAWING NUMBERS FROM A SEQUENCE Beginning with Oracle v7.3, a sequence value can be inserted directly into a table without first selecting it. Previously it was necessary to use the SELECT INTO syntax and put the new sequence number into a variable and then insert the variable.

■ FOR EXAMPLE

For this example, a table called test01 will be used: First the table test01 is created, then the sequence test_seq, then the sequence is used to populate the table.

```
--  ch04_3a.sql
CREATE TABLE test01 (col1 number);
CREATE SEQUENCE test_seq
    INCREMENT BY 5;
BEGIN
    INSERT INTO test01
        VALUES (test_seq.NEXTVAL);
END;
```

4.1.3 MAKING USE OF A SEQUENCE IN A PL/SQL BLOCK

In this last exercise for this lab, you will make use of all the material covered so far in this chapter.

> **a)** Write a PL/SQL block that will insert a new student in the STUDENT table. Use your own information for the data. Create two variables that are used in the select statement. Get the USER and SYSDATE for the variables. Finally, use the existing `student_id_seq` sequence to generate a unique id for the new student.

LAB 4.1 EXERCISE ANSWERS

4.1.1 ANSWERS

Run the PL/SQL block from the pre-exercise example.

a) What is displayed on the SQL*Plus screen? Explain the results.

Answer: You will see the following result:

```
The average cost of a course in the CTA program is
$1,198.33.
PL/SQL procedure successfully completed.
```

In the declaration section of the PL/SQL block, the variable v_average_ cost is declared as a varchar2. In the executable section of the block, this variable is given the value of the average cost from the course table by means of the SELECT INTO syntax. The SQL function TO_CHAR is issued to format the number. The DBMS_OUTPUT is then used to show the result to the screen.

b) Take the same PL/SQL block and place the line with the DBMS_OUT-PUT before the SELECT INTO statement. What is displayed on the SQL*Plus screen? Explain what the value of the variable is at each point in the PL/SQL block.

Answer: You will see the following result:

```
The average cost of a course in the CTA program is
PL/SQL procedure successfully completed.
```

The variable v_average_ cost will be set to NULL when it is first declared. Because the DBMS_OUTPUT is placed before the variable is given a value, the output for the variable will be NULL. After the SELECT INTO, the variable will be given the same value as in the original block described in question A, but it will not be displayed because there is not another DBMS_OUTPUT line in the PL/SQL block.

4.1.2 ANSWERS

a) Write a PL/SQL block that will insert a new student in the STUDENT table. Use your own information for the data.

Answer: The following is one example of how this could be handled:

```
--   ch04_4a.sql
DECLARE
   v_max_id number;
BEGIN
   SELECT MAX(student_id)
     INTO v_max_id
     FROM student;
   INSERT into student
      (student_id, last_name, zip,
       created_by, created_date,
       modified_by, modified_date,
       registration_date
      )
     VALUES (v_max_id + 1, 'Rosenzweig',
             11238, 'BROSENZ ', '01-JAN-99',
             'BOSENZ', '01-JAN-99', '01-JAN-99'
             );
END;
```

In order to generate a unique ID, the maximum `student_id` is selected into a variable and then it is incremented by one. It is important to remember in this example that there is foreign key on the zip item in the student table, which means that the zipcode you choose to enter must be in the ZIPCODE table.

4.1.3 ANSWERS

a) Write a PL/SQL block that will insert a new student in the STUDENT table. Use your own information for the data. Create two variables that are used in the select statement. Get the USER and SYSDATE for the variables. Finally, use the existing `student_id_seq` sequence to generate a unique id for the new student.

Answer: The following is one example of how this could be handled:

```
--   ch04_5a.sql
DECLARE
   v_user student.created_by%TYPE;
   v_date student.created_date%TYPE;
BEGIN
   SELECT USER, sysdate
     INTO  v_user, v_date
     FROM dual;
   INSERT INTO student
```

```
      (student_id, last_name, zip,
       created_by, created_date, modified_by,
       modified_date, registration_date
       )
      VALUES (student_id_seq.nextval, 'Smith',
              11238, v_user, v_date, v_user, v_date,
              v_date
              );
END;
```

In the declaration section of the PL/SQL block, two variables are declared. They are both set to be datatypes within the student table using the %TYPE method of declaration. This ensures the datatypes match the columns of the tables into which they will be inserted. The two variables v_user and v_date are given values from the system by means of SELECT INTO. The value of the student_id is generated by using the next value of the student_id_seq sequence.

LAB 4.1 SELF-REVIEW QUESTIONS

In order to test your progress, you should be able to answer the following questions.

1) Which of the following are valid methods to initialize value for a variable?
   a) _____ Declare a sequence
   b) _____ The ":=" syntax
   c) _____ SET SERVEROUPUT ON
   d) _____ SELECT INTO statement

2) Which of the following are valid DML or DDL statements in a PL/SQL Block?
   a) _____ INSERT
   b) _____ CREATE TABLE
   c) _____ CREATE SEQUENCE
   d) _____ UPDATE

3) Complete the following statement with the correct syntax for inserting a sequence in a PL/SQL BLOCK.

```
   INSERT INTO STUDENT (student_id, last_name)
```
   a) _____ VALUES (student_id_seq.currval, 'Smith');
   b) _____ VALUES ('Smith', student_id_seq.currval);
   a) _____ VALUES (student_id_seq.nextval, 'Smith');
   a) _____ VALUES (nextval, 'Smith');

4) Which of the following are true statements about an Oracle Sequence?

a) _____ It can be use a DML statement only in stand-alone SQL, not in a PL/SQL block.

b) _____ It is a database object.

d) _____ It is useful for generating contiguous numbers for invoicing.

d) _____ It can be used to generate unique primary keys.

Quiz answers appear in Appendix A, Section 4.1.

L A B   4 . 2

MAKING USE
OF SAVEPOINT

LAB OBJECTIVES

After this lab, you will be able to:

✔ Make Use of COMMIT, ROLLBACK, and SAVEPOINT in a PL/SQL Block

Transactions are a means to break programming code into manageable units. Grouping transactions into smaller elements is a standard practice that ensures an application will save only correct data. Initially, any application will have to connect to the database in order to access the data. It is important to point out that when a user is issuing DML statements in an application, the changes are not visible to other users until a COMMIT or ROLLBACK has been issued. Oracle guarantees a read-consistent view of the data. Until that point, all data that has been inserted or updated will be held in memory and only be available to the current user. The rows that have been changed will be locked by the current user and will not be available for updating to other users until the locks have been released. A COMMIT or a ROLLBACK statement will release these locks. Transactions can be more readily controlled by marking points of the transaction with the SAVEPOINT command.

For more details on transaction control (such as row locking issues), see the companion volume, Oracle DBA Interactive Workbook, *by Douglas Scherer and Melanie Caffrey (Prentice Hall, 2000).*

The definition of a *transaction* is simply a logical unit of work. The set of SQL statements comprising a transaction either succeed or fail as a unit. The PL/SQL block for one transaction ends with COMMIT or ROLLBACK.

- **COMMIT** Makes events within a transaction permanent.
- **ROLLBACK** Erases events within a transaction.

Additionally, one can use a SAVEPOINT to control transactions. Transactions are defined in the PL/SQL block from one SAVEPOINT to another. The use of the SAVEPOINT command allows you to break your SQL statements into units so that in a given PL/SQL block, some units can be *committed* (saved to the database), some can be *rolled back* (undone), and so forth.

Note that there is a distinction between transaction and a PL/SQL block. The start and end of a PL/SQL block do not necessarily mean the start and end of a transaction.

In order to demonstrate the need for transaction control, we will examine a two-step data-manipulation process. For example, suppose that the fees for all courses in the CTA database that had a prerequisite course needed to be increased by 10 percent and at the same time all courses that did not have a prerequisite needed to be decreased by 10 percent. This is a two-step process. If one step had been successful but the second step was not, then the data concerning course cost would be inconsistent in the database. Because this adjustment is based on a change in percentage, there would be no way to track what part of this course adjustment had been successful and what had not been.

■ FOR EXAMPLE

In this example, you see one PL/SQL block that performs two updates on the cost item in the course table. In the first step (this code is commented for the purpose of emphasizing each update), the cost is updated with a cost that is 10 percent less whenever the course does not have a prerequisite. In the second step, the cost is increased by 10 percent when the course has a prerequisite.

```
--  ch04_6a.sql
BEGIN
-- STEP 1
   UPDATE course
      SET cost = cost  - (cost * 0.10)
    WHERE prerequisite IS NULL;
-- STEP 2
   UPDATE course
      SET cost = cost  + (cost * 0.10)
```

```
        WHERE prerequisite IS NOT NULL;
END;
```

Let's assume that the first update statement succeeds, but the second update statement fails because the network went down. The data in the course table is now inconsistent because courses with no prerequisite have had their cost reduced but courses with prerequisites have not been adjusted. To prevent this sort of situation, statements must be combined into a transaction. So, either both statements will succeed, or both statements will fail.

A transaction usually combines SQL statements that represent a logical unit of work. The transaction begins with the first SQL statement issued after the previous transaction, or the first SQL statement issued after connecting to the database. The transaction ends with the COMMIT or ROLLBACK statement.

COMMIT

When a COMMIT statement is issued to the database, the transaction has ended, and the following statements are true:

- All work done by the transaction becomes permanent.
- Other users can see changes in data made by the transaction.
- Any locks acquired by the transaction are released.

A COMMIT statement has the following syntax:

```
COMMIT [WORK];
```

The word *WORK* is optional and is used to improve readability. Until a transaction is committed, only the user executing that transaction can see changes in the data made by his session.

■ FOR EXAMPLE

Suppose User A issues the following command on a student table that exists in another schema but has a public synonym of student:

```
--  ch04_6a.sql
INSERT INTO student
    (student_id, last_name, zip, registration_date,
     created_by, created_date, modified_by,
     modified_date
    )
```

```
VALUES (student_id_seq.nextval, 'Tashi', 10015,
        '01-JAN-99', 'STUDENTA', '01-JAN-99',
        'STUDENTA', '01-JAN-99'
       );
```

Then User B enters the following command to query table known by its public synonym student, while logged on to his session.

```
SELECT *
    FROM student
    WHERE first_name = 'Tashi';
```

Then User A issues the following command:

```
COMMIT;
```

Now if User B enters the same query again, he will not see the same results.

In this next example, there are two sessions: User A and User B. User A inserts a record into the student table. User B queries the student table, but does not get the record was inserted by User A. User B cannot see the information because User A has not committed the work. When User A commits the transaction, User B, upon resubmitting the query, sees the records inserted by User A.

 Note that this is covered in more depth in the companion volume, Oracle DBA Interactive Workbook, *by Douglas Scherer and Melanie Caffrey (Prentice Hall, 2000).*

ROLLBACK

When a ROLLBACK statement is issued to the database, the transaction has ended and the following statements are true:

- All work done by the user is undone, as if it hadn't been issued.
- Any locks acquired by the transaction are released.

A ROLLBACK statement has following syntax:

```
ROLLBACK [WORK];
```

The *WORK* keyword is optional and is available for increased readability.

SAVEPOINT

The ROLLBACK statement undoes all work done by the user in a specific transaction. With the SAVEPOINT command, however, only part of the transaction can be undone. A SAVEPOINT command has following syntax:

```
SAVEPOINT name;
```

The word *name* is the SAVEPOINT's name. Once a SAVEPOINT is defined, the program can roll back to the SAVEPOINT. A ROLLBACK statement, then, has the following syntax:

```
ROLLBACK [WORK] to SAVEPOINT name;
```

When a ROLLBACK to SAVEPOINT statement is issued to the database, the following statements are true:

- Any work done since the SAVEPOINT is undone. The SAVE-POINT remains active, however, until a full COMMIT or ROLL-BACK is issued. It can be rolled back to again, if desired.
- Any locks and resources acquired by the SQL statements since the SAVEPOINT will be released.
- The transaction is not finished, because SQL statements are still pending.

LAB 4.2 EXERCISES

4.2.1 MAKING USE OF *COMMIT, ROLLBACK,* AND *SAVEPOINT* IN A *PL/SQL* BLOCK

Log into the CTA schema and enter the following series of commands. (Optionally, you can write the PL/SQL block in a text file and then run the script from the SQL*Plus prompt.)

```
--   ch04_7a.sql
BEGIN
   INSERT INTO student
       ( student_id, Last_name, zip,
registration_date,
       created_by, created_date, modified_by,
       modified_date
     )
```

```
        VALUES ( student_id_seq.nextval, 'Tashi',
10015,
               '01-JAN-99', 'STUDENTA', '01-JAN-99',
               'STUDENTA','01-JAN-99'
          );
    SAVEPOINT A;
    INSERT INTO student
        ( student_id, Last_name, zip,
registration_date,
          created_by, created_date, modified_by,
          modified_date
        )
        VALUES (student_id_seq.nextval, 'Sonam', 10015,
               '01-JAN-99', 'STUDENTB','01-JAN-99',
               'STUDENTB', '01-JAN-99'
               );
    SAVEPOINT B;
    INSERT INTO student
        ( student_id, Last_name, zip, registration_date,
          created_by, created_date, modified_by,
          modified_date
        )
        VALUES (student_id_seq.nextval, 'Norbu', 10015,
               '01-JAN-99', 'STUDENTB', '01-JAN-99',
               'STUDENTB', '01-JAN-99'
               );
    SAVEPOINT C;
    ROLLBACK TO B;
END;
```

a) If you issue the following command, what would you expect to see? Why?

```
    SELECT *
      FROM student
     WHERE last_name = 'Norbu';
```

_____

_____

b) Try it. What happened? Why?

_____

_____

Now issue:

```
ROLLBACK to SAVEPOINT A;
```

c) What happened?

_____

_____

d) If you issue the following, what do you expect to see?

```
SELECT last_name
  FROM student
 WHERE last_name = 'Tashi';
```

_____

_____

e) Issue the command and explain your findings.

_____

_____

SAVEPOINT is often used before a complicated section of the transaction. If this part of the transaction fails, it can be rolled back, allowing the earlier part to continue.

It is important to note the distinction between transactions and PL/SQL blocks. When a block starts, it does not mean that the transaction starts. Likewise, the start of the transaction need not coincide with the start of a block.

LAB 4.2 EXERCISE ANSWERS

4.2.1 ANSWERS

a) If you issue the following command, what would you expect to see? Why?

```
SELECT *
  FROM student
 WHERE last_name = 'Norbu';
```

Answer: You will not be able to see any data because the ROLLBACK to (SAVEPOINT) B has undone the last insert statement where the student 'Norbu' was inserted.

b) Try it. What happened? Why?

Answer: When you issue this command, you will get the message "no rows selected."

Three students were inserted in this PL/SQL block. First, Sonam in SAVE-POINT A, then Tashi in SAVEPOINT B, and finally Norbu was inserted in SAVEPOINT C. Then when the command ROLLBACK to B was issued, the insert of Norbu was undone.

Now issue:

```
ROLLBACK to SAVEPOINT A;
```

c) What happened?

Answer: The insert in SAVEPOINT B was just undone. This deleted the insert of Tashi who was inserted in SAVEPOINT B.

d) If you issue the following, what do you expect to see?

```
SELECT *
  FROM student
 WHERE last_name = 'Tashi';
```

Answer: You will see the data for Tashi.

e) Issue the command and explain your findings.

Answer: You will see one entry for Tashi, as follows:

```
LAST_NAME
-------------------------
Tashi
```

Tashi was the only student that was successfully entered into the database. The ROLLBACK to SAVEPOINT A undid the insert statement for Norbu and Sonam.

> ### A Single PL/SQL Block Can Contain Multiple Transactions
>
> For Example:
> ```
> Declare
>    v_Counter NUMBER;
> BEGIN
>    v_counter := 0;
>    FOR i IN 1..100
>    LOOP
>       v_counter := v_counter + 1;
>       IF v_counter = 10
>       THEN
>          COMMIT;
>          v_counter := 0;
>       END IF;
>    END LOOP;
> END;
> ```
> In this example, as soon as value of v_counter becomes equal to 10, the work is committed. So, there will be a total of 10 transactions contained in this one PL/SQL block.

LAB 4.2 SELF-REVIEW QUESTIONS

In order to test your progress, you should be able to answer the following questions.

1) User A can ROLLBACK User B's insert statement.
   a) _____ True
   b) _____ False

2) When a COMMIT has been issued, which of the following are true? Choose all that apply.
   a) _____ All memory holds on the data have been released.
   b) _____ All data inserts are available to other users.
   c) _____ You have to get married.
   c) _____ The transaction is not finished because SQL statements are still pending.

**LAB
4.2**

3)   What defines a logical unit of work?
    a) _____ From one SAVEPOINT to the next.
    b) _____ From one ROLLBACK to the next.
    c) _____ From one COMMIT to the next.
    d) _____ All of the above.

4)   The advantage of using SAVEPOINTS in a PL/SQL block are:
    a) _____ It prevents inconsistent data.
    b) _____ It allows one to group code into manageable units.
    c) _____ It prevents one from duplicating a primary key.
    d) _____ It locks rows and prevents other users from updating the same row.

Quiz answers appear in Appendix A, Section 4.2.

CHAPTER 4

TEST YOUR THINKING

In the chapter discussion, you learned how to use numerous SQL techniques in a PL/SQL block. First, you learned how to use SELECT INTO to generate values for a variable. Then you learned the various DML methods, including the use of a sequence. Finally, you learned how to manage transactions by using SAVEPOINTS. Complete the following projects by writing the code for each step, running it, and then going on to the next step.

1) Create a table called CHAP4 with two columns, one is ID (a number) and the second is NAME, which is a varchar2(20).

2) Create a sequence called CHAP4_SEQ that increments by units of 5.

3) Write a PL/SQL block that performs the following in this order:

   a) Declares 2 variables, one for the `v_name` and one for `v_id`. The `v_name` variable can be used throughout the block for holding the name that will be inserted, realize that the value will change in the course the block.

   b) The block then inserts into the table the name of the student that is enrolled in the most classes and uses a sequence for the id; afterwards, there is SAVEPOINT A.

   c) Then the student with the least enrollments is inserted; afterwards, there is SAVEPOINT B.

   d) Then the instructor who is teaching the maximum number of courses is inserted in the same way. Afterwards, there is SAVEPOINT C.

   e) Using a SELECT INTO statement, hold the value of the instructor in the variable `v_id`.

   f) Undo the instructor insert by use of ROLLBACK.

   g) Insert the instructor teaching the least number of courses but do not use the sequence to generate the ID; instead use the value from the first instructor whom you have since undone.

    h)   Now insert the instructor teaching the most number of courses and use the sequence to populate his ID.

4) Add DBMS_OUTPUT throughout the block to display the values of the variables as they change. (This is good practice for debugging.)

C H A P T E R 5

CONDITIONAL CONTROL

CHAPTER OBJECTIVES

In this chapter, you will learn about:

In almost every program that you write, you need to make decisions. For example, if it is the end of the fiscal year, bonuses must be distributed to the employees based on their salaries. In order to compute employee bonuses, a program needs to have a conditional control. In other words, it needs to employ a selection structure (you learned about selection structure in Chapter 1).

Conditional control allows you to control the flow of the execution of the program based on a condition. In programming terms, it means that the statements in the program are not executed sequentially. Rather, one group of statements, or another will be executed depending on how the condition is evaluated.

In PL/SQL, there are two types of conditional control: IF statement and ELSIF statement. In this chapter, you will explore both types of conditional control and how these types can be nested one inside of another.

L A B   5 . 1

IF STATEMENTS

> ## LAB OBJECTIVES
>
> After this lab, you will be able to:
>
> ✔ Use IF-THEN Statements
> ✔ Use IF-THEN-ELSE Statements

An IF statement has two forms: IF-THEN and IF-THEN-ELSE. An IF-THEN statement allows you to specify only one group of actions to take. In other words, this group of actions is taken only when a condition evaluates to TRUE. An IF-THEN-ELSE statement allows you to specify two groups of actions, and the second group of actions is taken when a condition evaluates to FALSE.

IF-THEN STATEMENTS

An IF-THEN statement is the most basic kind of a conditional control and has the following structure:

```
IF CONDITION
THEN
    STATEMENT 1;
    ...
    STATEMENT N;
END IF;
```

The reserved word IF marks the beginning of the IF statement. Statements 1 through N are a sequence of executable statements that consist of one or more of the standard programming structures. The word *CONDITION* between keywords IF and THEN determines whether these statements are executed. END IF is a reserved phrase that indicates the end of the IF-THEN construct.

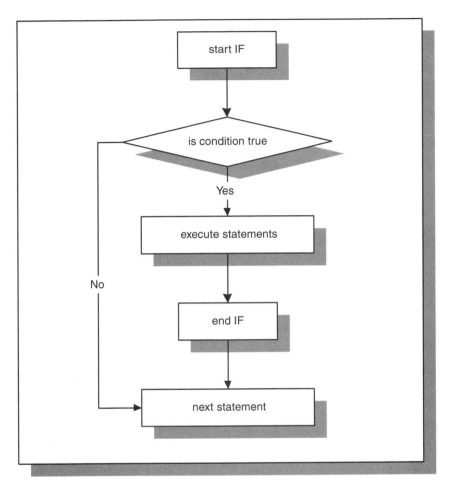

Figure 5.1 ■ IF-THEN statement.

This flow of the logic from the preceding structure on the IF-THEN statement is illustrated in the Figure 5.1.

When an IF-THEN statement is executed, a condition is evaluated to either TRUE or FALSE. If the condition evaluates to TRUE, control is passed to the first executable statement of the IF-THEN construct. If the condition evaluates to FALSE, the control is passed to the first executable statement after the END IF statement.

Consider the following example. You have two numeric values stored in the variables, v_num1 and v_num2. You need to arrange your values so that the smaller value is always stored in v_num1, and the larger value is always stored in the v_num2.

■ *FOR EXAMPLE*

```
DECLARE
    v_num1 NUMBER := 5;
    v_num2 NUMBER := 3;
    v_temp NUMBER;
BEGIN
    -- if v_num1 is greater than v_num2 rearrange their
    -- values
    IF v_num1 > v_num2
    THEN
        v_temp := v_num1;
        v_num1 := v_num2;
        v_num2 := v_temp;
    END IF;
    -- display the values of v_num1 and v_num2
    DBMS_OUTPUT.PUT_LINE('v_num1 = '||v_num1);
    DBMS_OUTPUT.PUT_LINE('v_num2 = '||v_num2);
END;
```

In this example, condition 'v_num1 > v_num2' evaluates to TRUE because 5 is greater that 3. Next, the values are rearranged so that 3 is assigned to v_num1, and 5 is assigned to v_num2. It is done with the help of the third variable, v_temp, that is used as a temporary storage.

This example produces the following output:

```
v_num1 = 3
v_num2 = 5
PL/SQL procedure successfully completed.
```

IF-THEN-ELSE STATEMENT

An IF-THEN statement specifies the sequence of statements to execute only if the condition evaluates to TRUE. When this condition evaluates to FALSE, there is no special action to take except to proceed with execution of the program.

An IF-THEN-ELSE statement enables you to specify two groups of statements. One group of statements is executed when the condition evaluates to TRUE. Another group of statements is executed when the condition evaluates to FALSE. This is indicated as follows:

```
IF CONDITION
THEN
```

```
     STATEMENT 1;
ELSE
     STATEMENT 2;
END IF;
STATEMENT 3;
```

When *CONDITION* evaluates to TRUE, control is passed to STATEMENT 1; when *CONDITION* evaluates to FALSE, control is passed to STATE-MENT 2. After the IF-THEN-ELSE construct has completed, STATEMENT 3 is executed. This flow of the logic is illustrated in the Figure 5.2.

The IF-THEN-ELSE construct should be used when trying to choose be-tween two mutually exclusive actions. Consider the following example.

```
DECLARE
     v_num NUMBER := &sv_user_num;
BEGIN
```

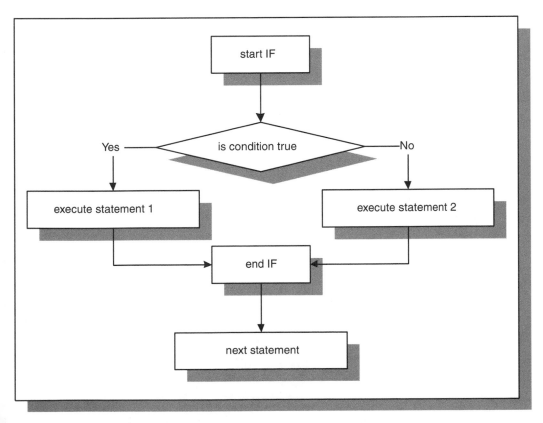

Figure 5.2 ■ IF-THEN-ELSE statement.

```
                    -- test if the number provided by the user is even
                    IF  MOD(v_num,2) = 0
                    THEN
                        DBMS_OUTPUT.PUT_LINE(v_num||' is even number');
                    ELSE
                        DBMS_OUTPUT.PUT_LINE(v_num||' is odd number');
                    END IF;
                    DBMS_OUTPUT.PUT_LINE('Done...');
                 END;
```

It is important to realize that for any given number only one of the DBMS_OUTPUT.PUT_LINE statements is executed. Hence, the IF-THEN-ELSE construct enables you to specify two and only two mutually exclusive actions.

When run, this example produces the following output:

```
Enter value for v_user_num: 24
old   2:     v_num  NUMBER := &v_user_num;
new   2:     v_num  NUMBER := 24;
24 is even number
Done...
PL/SQL procedure successfully completed.
```

NULL CONDITION

In some cases, a condition used in an IF statement can be evaluated to NULL instead of TRUE or FALSE. For the IF-THEN construct, the statements will not be executed if an associated condition evaluates to NULL. Next, control will be passed to the first executable statement after END IF. For the IF-THEN-ELSE construct, the statements specified after the keyword ELSE will be executed if an associated condition evaluates to NULL.

■ *FOR EXAMPLE*

```
DECLARE
    v_num1 NUMBER := 0;
    v_num2 NUMBER;
BEGIN
    IF v_num1 = v_num2
    THEN
        DBMS_OUTPUT.PUT_LINE('v_num1 = v_num2');
    ELSE
        DBMS_OUTPUT.PUT_LINE('v_num1 != v_num2');
    END IF;
END;
```

This example produces the following output:

```
v_num1 != v_num2
PL/SQL procedure successfully completed.
```

The condition

```
v_num1 = v_num2
```

is evaluated to NULL because a value is not assigned to the variable
v_num2. Therefore, variable v_num2 is NULL. Notice that IF-THEN-ELSE
construct is behaving as if the condition evaluated to FALSE, and second
DBMS_OUTPUT.PUT_LINE statement is executed.

LAB 5.1 EXERCISES

5.1.1 USING THE IF-THEN STATEMENT

In this exercise, you will use the IF-THEN statement to test if the date provided by the user falls on weekend. In other words, if the day happens to be
Saturday or Sunday.

Create the following PL/SQL script:

```
-- ch05_1a.sql, version 1.0
SET SERVEROUTPUT ON
DECLARE
    v_date DATE :=
        TO_DATE('&sv_user_date', 'DD-MON-YYYY');
    v_day VARCHAR2(15);
BEGIN
    v_day := RTRIM(TO_CHAR(v_date, 'DAY'));
    IF v_day IN ('SATURDAY', 'SUNDAY')
    THEN
        DBMS_OUTPUT.PUT_LINE(v_date||' falls on week-
end');
    END IF;
    — control resumes here
    DBMS_OUTPUT.PUT_LINE('Done...');
END;
```

In order to test this script fully, execute it twice. For the first run enter
'07-JUL-1999', and for the second run enter '11-JUL-1999'. Execute the script,
then answer the following questions:

a) What output was printed on the screen (for both dates)?

_____

_____

b) Explain why the output produced for two dates is different?

_____

_____

Remove the RTRIM function from the assignment statement for `v_day` as follows:

```
v_day := TO_CHAR(v_date, 'DAY');
```

Run the script again entering '11-JUL-1999' for `v_date`.

c) What output was printed on the screen? Why?

_____

_____

d) Rewrite this script using the LIKE operator instead of the IN operator, so that it produces the same results for dates specified earlier.

_____

_____

e) Rewrite this script using the IF-THEN-ELSE construct. If the date specified does not fall on the weekend, display a message to the user saying so.

_____

_____

5.1.2 USING THE *IF-THEN-ELSE* STATEMENT

In this exercise, you will use the IF-THEN-ELSE statement to check how many students are enrolled for course number 25, section 1. If there are 15 or more students enrolled, section 1 of course number 25 is full. Otherwise, section 1 of course number 25 is not full and more students can register for it. In both cases, a message should be displayed to a user indicating whether section 1 is full. Try to answer the questions *before* you run the script. Once you have answered the questions, run the script and check your answers.

Create the following PL/SQL script:

```
-- ch05_2a.sql, version 1.0
SET SERVEROUTPUT ON
DECLARE
   v_total NUMBER;
BEGIN
   SELECT COUNT(*)
   INTO v_total
   FROM enrollment e, section s
   WHERE e.section_id = s.section_id
     AND s.course_no = 25
     AND s.section_no = 1;
   -- check if section 1 of course 25 is full
   IF v_total >= 15
   THEN
      DBMS_OUTPUT.PUT_LINE
         ('Section 1 of course 25 is full');
   ELSE
      DBMS_OUTPUT.PUT_LINE
         ('Section 1 of course 25 is not full');
   END IF;
   -- control resumes here
END;
```

Try to answer the following questions first and then execute the script:

a) What DBMS_OUTPUT.PUT_LINE statement will be displayed if there are 15 students enrolled in section 1 of course number 25?

_____

_____

b) What DBMS_OUTPUT.PUT_LINE statement will be displayed if there are 3 students enrolled in section 1 of course number 25?

_____

_____

c) What DBMS_OUTPUT.PUT_LINE statement will be displayed if there is no section 1 for course number 25?

_____

_____

d) How would you change this script so that both course and section numbers are provided by a user?

_____

_____

e) How would you change this script so that if there are less than 15 students enrolled in section 1 of course number 25, a message indicating how many students can still be enrolled is displayed?

_____

_____

LAB 5.1 EXERCISE ANSWERS

5.1.1 ANSWERS

a) What output was printed on the screen (for both dates)?

Answer: The first output produced for the date is 07-JUL-1999. The second output is produced for the date 11-JUL-1999.

```
Enter value for sv_user_date: 07-JUL-1999
old    2:    v_date   DATE := TO_DATE('&sv_user_date',
'DD-MON-YYYY');
new    2:    v_date   DATE := TO_DATE('07-JUL-1999',
'DD-MON-YYYY');
```

Done...
PL/SQL procedure successfully completed.

When the value of 07-JUL-1999 is entered for `v_date`, the day of the week is determined for the variable `v_day` with the help of the function TO_CHAR and RTRIM. Next, the following condition is evaluated:

```
v_day IN ('SATURDAY', 'SUNDAY')
```

Because the value of `v_day` is 'WEDNESDAY,' the condition evaluates to FALSE. Then, control is passed to the first executable statement after END IF. As a result, 'Done...' is displayed on the screen.

```
Enter value for sv_user_date: 11-JUL-1999
old    2:    v_date  DATE := TO_DATE('&sv_user_date',
'DD-MON-YYYY');
new    2:    v_date  DATE := TO_DATE('11-JUL-1999',
'DD-MON-YYYY');
11-JUL-1999 falls on weekend
Done...
PL/SQL procedure successfully completed.
```

The value of `v_day` is derived from the value of `v_date`. Next, the condition of the IF-THEN statement is evaluated. Because it evaluates to TRUE, the statement after the keyword THEN is executed. So, '11-JUL-1999 falls on weekend' is displayed on the screen. Next, control is to the last DBMS_OUTPUT.PUT_LINE statement, and 'Done...' is displayed on the screen.

   b) Explain why the output produced for two dates is different.

   Answer: The first date, 07-JUL-1999, is Wednesday. As a result, the condition, `v_day` *IN ('SATURDAY,' 'SUNDAY'), does not evaluate to TRUE. So, control is transferred to the statement after END IF, and 'Done...' is displayed on the screen.*

   The second date, 11-JUL-1999, is Sunday. Because Sunday falls on weekend, the condition evaluates to TRUE, and the message '11-JUL-1999 falls on weekend' is displayed on the screen. Next, the last DBMS_OUTPUT.PUT_LINE statement is executed, and 'Done...' is displayed on the screen.

Remove the RTRIM function from the assignment statement for `v_day` as follows:

```
v_day := TO_CHAR(v_date, 'DAY');
```

Run the script again entering '11-JUL-1999' for `v_date`.

c) What output was printed on the screen? Why?

Answer: This answer contains only the portion of the code that helps to illustrate the changes.

```
-- ch05_1b.sql, version 2.0
SET SERVEROUTPUT ON
DECLARE
   ...
BEGIN
   v_day := TO_CHAR(v_date, 'DAY');
   ...
END;
/
```

This script produces the following output:

```
Enter value for sv_user_date: 11-JUL-1999
old    2:    v_date  DATE := TO_DATE('&sv_user_date',
'DD-MON-YYYY');
new    2:    v_date  DATE := TO_DATE('11-JUL-1999',
'DD-MON-YYYY');
Done...
PL/SQL procedure successfully completed.
```

In the original example, the variable v_day is calculated with the help of the statement, RTRIM(TO_CHAR(v_date, 'DAY')). First, the function TO_CHAR returns the day of the week padded with blanks. The size of the value retrieved by the function TO_CHAR is always 9 bytes. Next, the RTRIM function removes trailing spaces.

In the statement

```
v_day := TO_CHAR(v_date, 'DAY')
```

the TO_CHAR function is used without the RTRIM function. Therefore, trailing blanks are not removed after the day of the week has been derived. As a result, the condition of the IF-THEN statement evaluates to FALSE even though given date falls on the weekend, and control is passed to the last DBMS_OUTPUT.PUT_LINE statement.

d) Rewrite this script using LIKE operator instead of IN operator, so that it produces the same results for dates specified earlier.

Answer: This answer contains only the portion of the code that helps to illustrate the changes.

```
-- ch05_1c.sql, version 3.0
SET SERVEROUTPUT ON
DECLARE
    ...
BEGIN
    v_day := RTRIM(TO_CHAR(v_date, 'DAY'));
    IF v_day LIKE 'S%'
    THEN
        DBMS_OUTPUT.PUT_LINE(v_date||' falls on weekend');
    END IF;
    ...
END;
```

Both days, Saturday and Sunday, are the only days of the week that start with the letter 'S'. As a result, there is no need to spell out the names of the days or specify any additional letters for the LIKE operator.

e) Rewrite this script using the IF-THEN-ELSE construct. If the date specified does not fall on the weekend, display a message to the user saying so.

Answer: Your script should look similar to the following:

```
-- ch05_1d.sql, version 4.0
SET SERVEROUTPUT ON
DECLARE
    v_date DATE := TO_DATE('&sv_user_date', 'DD-MON-
YYYY');
    v_day VARCHAR2(15);
BEGIN
    v_day := RTRIM(TO_CHAR(v_date, 'DAY'));
    IF v_day IN ('SATURDAY', 'SUNDAY')
    THEN
        DBMS_OUTPUT.PUT_LINE(v_date||' falls on week-
end');
    ELSE
        DBMS_OUTPUT.PUT_LINE
            (v_date||' does not fall on the weekend');
    END IF;
    -- control resumes here
    DBMS_OUTPUT.PUT_LINE('Done...');
END;
```

In order to modify the script, the ELSE part was added to the IF statement. The rest of the script has not been changed.

5.1.2 ANSWERS

a) What DBMS_OUTPUT.PUT_LINE statement will be displayed if there are 15 students enrolled in section 1 of course number 25?

Answer: If there are 15 or more students enrolled in section 1 of course number 25, the first DBMS_OUTPUT.PUT_LINE statement is displayed on the screen.

The condition

```
v_total >= 15
```

evaluates to TRUE, and as a result, the statement

```
DBMS_OUTPUT.PUT_LINE
    ('Section 1 of course 25 is full');
```

is executed.

b) What DBMS_OUTPUT.PUT_LINE statement will be displayed if there are 3 students enrolled in section 1 of course number 25?

Answer: If there are 3 students enrolled in section 1 of course number 25, second DBMS_OUTPUT.PUT_LINE statement is displayed on the screen.

The condition

```
v_total >= 15
```

evaluates to FALSE, and the ELSE part on the IF-THEN-ELSE statement is executed. As a result, the statement

```
DBMS_OUTPUT.PUT_LINE
    ('Section 1 of course 25 is not full');
```

is executed.

c) What DBMS_OUTPUT.PUT_LINE statement will be displayed if there is no section 1 for course number 25?

Answer: If there is no section 1 for course number 25, the ELSE part of the IF-THEN-ELSE statement will be executed. So, the second DBMS_OUTPUT.PUT_LINE statement will be displayed on the screen.

The COUNT function used in the SELECT statement

```
SELECT COUNT(*)
  INTO v_total
  FROM enrollment e, section s
 WHERE e.section_id = s.section_id
   AND s.course_no = 25
   AND s.section_no = 1;
```

returns 0. Then, the condition of the IF-THEN-ELSE statement evaluates to FALSE. Therefore, the ELSE part of the IF-THEN-ELSE statement is executed, and second DBMS_OUTPUT.PUT_LINE statement is displayed on the screen.

d) How would you change this script so that both course and section numbers are provided by a user?

Answer: This answer contains only the portion of the code that helps to illustrate the changes.

Two addition variables must be declared and initialized with the help of the substitution variables as follows:

```
-- ch05_2b.sql, version 2.0
SET SERVEROUTPUT ON
DECLARE
   v_total NUMBER;
   v_course_no CHAR(6) := '&sv_course_no';
   v_section_no NUMBER := &sv_section_no;
BEGIN
   SELECT COUNT(*)
    INTO v_total
    FROM enrollment e, section s
   WHERE e.section_id = s.section_id
     AND s.course_no = v_course_no
     AND s.section_no = v_section_no;
   -- check if a specific section of a course is full
   IF v_total >= 15
   THEN
      ...
```

e) How would you change this script so that if there are less than 15 students enrolled in section 1 of course number 25, a message indicating how many students can still be enrolled is displayed?

Answer: Your script should look similar to the following:

```
-- ch05_2c.sql, version 3.0
SET SERVEROUTPUT ON
```

```
DECLARE
   v_total NUMBER;
   v_students NUMBER;
BEGIN
   SELECT COUNT(*)
     INTO v_total
     FROM enrollment e, section s
    WHERE e.section_id = s.section_id
      AND s.course_no = 25
      AND s.section_no = 1;
   -- check if section 1 of course 25 is full
   IF v_total >= 15
   THEN
      DBMS_OUTPUT.PUT_LINE
          ('Section 1 of course 25 is full');
   ELSE
      v_students := 15 - v_total;
      DBMS_OUTPUT.PUT_LINE
          (v_students||' students can still enroll '||
           'into section 1 of course 25');
   END IF;
   -- control resumes here
END;
```

Notice, if the IF-THEN-ELSE statement evaluates to FALSE, the statements associated with the ELSE part are executed. In this case, the value of the variable of `v_total` is subtracted from 15. The result of this operation indicates how many more students can enroll into the section 1 of course number 25.

LAB 5.1 SELF-REVIEW QUESTIONS

In order to test your progress, you should be able to answer the following questions.

1) An IF construct is a control statement for which of the following?
   a) _____ Sequence structure
   b) _____ Iteration structure
   c) _____ Selection structure

2) In order for the statements of an IF-THEN construct to be executed, the condition must evaluate to which of the following?
   a) _____ TRUE
   b) _____ FALSE
   c) _____ NULL

3) When a condition of the IF-THEN-ELSE construct is evaluated to NULL, control is passed to the first executable statement after END IF.
   a) _____ True
   b) _____ False

4) How many actions can you specify in an IF-THEN-ELSE statement?
   a) _____Only one
   b) _____Only two
   c) _____Only four
   d) _____As many as you require

5) The IF-THEN-ELSE construct should be used to achieve which of the following?
   a) _____ Three mutually exclusive actions
   b) _____ Two mutually exclusive actions
   c) _____ Two actions that are not mutually exclusive

Quiz answers appear in Appendix A, Section 5.1.

LAB 5.2

ELSIF STATEMENTS

> ## LAB OBJECTIVES
>
> After this lab, you will be able to:
>
> ✔ Use the ELSIF Statement

An ELSIF statement has the following structure:

```
IF CONDITION 1
THEN
    STATEMENT 1;
ELSIF CONDITION 2
THEN
    STATEMENT 2;
ELSIF CONDITION 3
THEN
    STATEMENT 3;
...
ELSE
    STATEMENT N;
END IF;
```

The reserved word IF marks the beginning of an ELSIF construct. The words *CONDITION 1* through *CONDITION N* are a sequence of the conditions that evaluate to TRUE or FALSE. These conditions are mutually exclusive. In other words, if *CONDITION 1* evaluates to TRUE, STATEMENT 1 is executed, and control is passed to the first executable statement after the reserved phrase END IF. The rest of the ELSIF construct is ignored. When *CONDITION 1* evaluates to FALSE, the control is passed to the ELSIF part and *CONDITION 2* is evaluated, and so forth. If none of the specified conditions yield TRUE, the control is passed to the ELSE part of the ELSIF construct. An ELSIF statement can contain any number of ELSIF clauses.

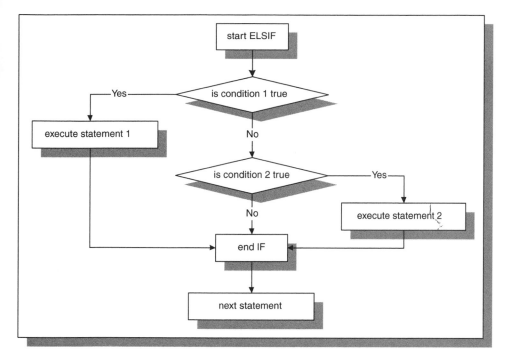

Figure 5.3 ■ ELSIF statement.

This flow of the logic is illustrated in the Figure 5.3.

Figure 5.3 shows that if condition 1 is evaluated to TRUE, statement 1 is executed, and the control is passed to the first statement after END IF. If condition 1 evaluates to FALSE, the control is passed to condition 2. If condition 2 yields TRUE, statement 2 is executed. Otherwise, the control is passed to the statement following END IF, and so forth. Consider the following example.

■ *FOR EXAMPLE*

```
DECLARE
    v_num NUMBER := &sv_num;
BEGIN
    IF v_num < 0
    THEN
        DBMS_OUTPUT.PUT_LINE
            (v_num||' is a negative number');
    ELSIF v_num = 0
    THEN
        DBMS_OUTPUT.PUT_LINE(v_num||' is equal to zero');
    ELSE
```

```
        DBMS_OUTPUT.PUT_LINE
            (v_num||' is a positive number');
    END IF;
END;
```

The value of v_num is provided at runtime and evaluated with the help of the ELSIF statement. If the value of v_num is less that zero, the first DBMS_OUTPUT.PUT_LINE statement executes, and the ELSIF construct terminates. If the value of v_num is greater that zero, both conditions

v_num < 0 and **v_num = 0**

evaluate to FALSE, and the ELSE part of the ELSIF construct executes.

Assume the value of v_num equals five at runtime. This example produces the output shown below:

```
Enter value for sv_num: 5
old    2:    v_num  NUMBER := &sv_num;
new    2:    v_num  NUMBER := 5;
5 is a positive number
PL/SQL procedure successfully completed.
```

Remember the following information about an ELSIF statement:

♦ *Always match IF with an END IF*

♦ *There must be a space between END and IF. When the space is omitted, the compiler produces the following error:*

```
ERROR at line 22:
ORA-06550: line 22, column 4:
PLS-00103: Encountered the symbol ";" when expecting
one of the following:
if
```

As you can see, this error message is not very clear, and it can take you sometime to correct this error especially if you have not encountered it before.

♦ *There is no second "E" in the "ELSIF"*

♦ *Conditions of an ELSIF statement must be mutually exclusive. These conditions are evaluated in sequential order, from the first to the last. Once a condition evaluates to TRUE, the remaining conditions of the*

ELSIF statement are not evaluated at all. Consider this example of an ELSIF construct:

```
   IF v_num >= 0
THEN
   DBMS_OUTPUT.PUT_LINE ('v_num is greater than 0');
ELSIF v_num =< 10
THEN
   DBMS_OUTPUT.PUT_LINE ('v_num is less than 10');
ELSE
    DBMS_OUTPUT.PUT_LINE
        ('v_num is less than ? or greater than ?');
END IF;
```

Assume that the value of v_num *is equal to 5. Both conditions of the ELSIF statement potentially can evaluate to TRUE because 5 is greater than 0, and 5 is less than 10. However, once the first condition,* v_num >= 0 *evaluates to TRUE, the rest of the ELSIF construct is ignored.*

For any value of v_num *that is greater or equal to 0 and less or equal to 10, these conditions are not mutually exclusive. Therefore, DBMS_OUTPUT.PUT_LINE statement associated with ELSIF clause will not execute for any such value of* v_num. *In order for the second condition,* v_num <= 10, *to yield TRUE, the value of* v_num *must be less than 0.*

How would you rewrite this ELSIF construct to capture any value v_num *between 0 and 10 and display it on the screen with a single condition?*

When using an ELSIF construct, it is not necessary to specify what action should be taken if none of the conditions evaluate to TRUE. In other words, an ELSE clause is not required in the ELSIF construct. Consider the example shown below:

■ *FOR EXAMPLE*

```
DECLARE
   v_num NUMBER := &sv_num;
BEGIN
   IF v_num < 0
   THEN
      DBMS_OUTPUT.PUT_LINE
         (v_num||' is a negative number');
   ELSIF v_num > 0
```

```
THEN
    DBMS_OUTPUT.PUT_LINE
        (v_num||' is a positive number');
END IF;
DBMS_OUTPUT.PUT_LINE('Done...');
END;
```

As you can see, there is no action specified when v_num is equal to zero. If the value of v_num is equal to zero, both conditions will evaluate to FALSE, and the ELSIF statement will not execute at all. When value of zero is specified for v_num, this example produces the following output.

```
Enter value for sv_num: 0
old    2:    v_num   NUMBER := &sv_num;
new    2:    v_num   NUMBER := 0;
Done...
PL/SQL procedure successfully completed.
```

You probably noticed that for all IF statement examples, the reserved words THEN, ELSIF, and ELSE are entered on a separate line and aligned with the word IF. In addition, all executable statements in the IF construct are indented. The format of the IF construct makes no difference to the compiler. However, the meaning of the IF construct becomes obvious to us.

The IF-THEN-ELSE statement

```
IF x = y THEN v_text := 'YES'; ELSE v_text := 'NO';
END IF;
```

is equivalent to

```
IF x = y
THEN
    v_text := 'YES';
ELSE
    v_text := 'NO';
END IF;
```

The formatted version of the IF construct is easier to read and understand.

LAB 5.2 EXERCISES

5.2.1 USING THE ELSIF STATEMENT

In this exercise, you will use an ELSIF statement to display a letter grade for a student registered for a specific section of the course number 25.
Create the following PL/SQL script:

```
-- ch05_3a.sql, version 1.0
SET SERVEROUTPUT ON
DECLARE
   v_student_id NUMBER := 102;
   v_section_id NUMBER := 89;
   v_final_grade NUMBER;
   v_letter_grade CHAR(1);
BEGIN
   SELECT final_grade
     INTO v_final_grade
     FROM enrollment
    WHERE student_id = v_student_id
      AND section_id = v_section_id;

   IF v_final_grade BETWEEN 90 AND 100
   THEN
      v_letter_grade := 'A';
   ELSIF v_final_grade BETWEEN 80 AND 89
   THEN
      v_letter_grade := 'B';
   ELSIF v_final_grade BETWEEN 70 AND 79
   THEN
      v_letter_grade := 'C';
   ELSIF v_final_grade BETWEEN 60 AND 69
   THEN
      v_letter_grade := 'D';
   ELSE
      v_letter_grade := 'F';
   END IF;
   -- control resumes here
   DBMS_OUTPUT.PUT_LINE
      ('Letter grade is: '||v_letter_grade);
END;
```

Try to answer the following questions first, and then execute the script:

LAB 5.2

a) What letter grade will displayed on the screen:

i) if the value of `v_final_grade` is equal to 85?

ii) if the value of `v_final_grade` is NULL?

iii) if the value of `v_final_grade` is greater than 100?

_____

_____

b) How would you change this script so that a message `'v_final_grade is null'` is displayed if `v_final_grade` is null?

_____

_____

c) How would you change this script so that student ID and section ID are provided by a user?

_____

_____

d) How would you change the script to define a letter grade without specifying upper limit of the final grade? In the statement, `v_final_grade` BETWEEN 90 and 100, number 100 is the upper limit.

_____

_____

LAB 5.2 EXERCISE ANSWERS

5.2.1 ANSWERS

a) What letter grade will displayed on the screen:

i) if the value of v_final_grade is equal to 85?
ii) if the value of v_final_grade is NULL?
iii) if the value of v_final_grade is greater than 100?

> *Answer: If the value of* v_final_grade *is equal to 85, value "B" of the letter grade will be displayed of the screen.*

The conditions of the ELSIF statement are evaluated in the sequential order. So, the first condition

v_final_grade BETWEEN 90 AND 100

evaluates to FALSE, and control is passed to the first ELSIF part of the ELSIF statement. Then, the second condition

v_final_grade BETWEEN 80 AND 89

evaluates to TRUE, and the letter "B" is assigned to the variable v_letter_grade. The control is then passed to first executable statement after END IF, and message

Letter grade is : B

is displayed on the screen.

> *If the value of* v_final_grade *is NULL, value "F" of the letter grade will be displayed of the screen.*

If the value of the v_final_grade is undefined or NULL, then all conditions of the ESLIF statement evaluate to NULL (notice, they do not evaluate to FALSE). As a result, the ELSE part of the ELSIF statement is executed, and letter "F" is assigned to the v_letter_grade.

> *If the value of* v_final_grade *is greater than 100, value "F" of the letter grade will be displayed of the screen.*

The conditions specified for the ELSIF statement cannot handle the value of v_final_grade greater than 100. So, for any student whose letter grade should be A+, will result in a letter grade of "F." After the ELSIF statement has terminated, "The letter grade is: F" is displayed on the screen.

b) How would you change this script so that a message "v_final_grade is null" is displayed if v_final_grade is null?

> *Answer: This answer contains only a portion of the code that helps to illustrate the changes.*

```
-- ch03_3b.sql, version 2.0
SET SERVEROUTPUT ON
...
BEGIN
```

```
...
IF v_final_grade IS NULL
THEN
    DBMS_OUTPUT.PUT_LINE('v_final_grade is null');
ELSIF v_final_grade BETWEEN 90 AND 100
THEN
    ...
END;
```

One more condition has been added to the ELSIF statement. The condition

v_final_grade BETWEEN 90 AND 100

becomes first ELSIF condition. Now, if the value v_final_grade is NULL, the message "v_final_grade is null" is displayed on the screen. However, there is no value assigned to the variable v_letter_grade. The message "The letter grade is:" is displayed on the screen as well.

c) How would you change this script so that both the student ID and the section ID are provided by a user?

Answer: This answer contains only a portion of the code that helps to illustrate the changes.

```
-- ch05_3c.sql, version 3.0
SET SERVEROUTPUT ON
DECLARE
    v_student_id NUMBER := &sv_student_id;
    v_section_id NUMBER := &sv_section_id;
    v_final_grade NUMBER;
    v_letter_grade NUMBER;
BEGIN
    ...
END;
```

d) How would you change the script to define a letter grade without specifying the upper limit of the final grade? In the statement, v_final_grade BETWEEN 90 and 100, number 100 is the upper limit.

Answer:

```
-- ch05_3d.sql, version 4.0
SET SERVEROUTPUT ON
DECLARE
```

```
      v_student_id NUMBER := 102;
      v_section_id NUMBER := 89;
      v_final_grade NUMBER;
      v_letter_grade CHAR(1);
   BEGIN
      SELECT final_grade
        INTO v_final_grade
        FROM enrollment
       WHERE student_id = v_student_id
         AND section_id = v_section_id;

      IF v_final_grade >= 90
      THEN
         v_letter_grade := 'A';
      ELSIF v_final_grade >= 80
      THEN
         v_letter_grade := 'B';
      ELSIF v_final_grade >= 70
      THEN
         v_letter_grade := 'C';
      ELSIF v_final_grade >= 60
      THEN
         v_letter_grade := 'D';
      ELSE
         v_letter_grade := 'F';
      END IF;
      — control resumes here
      DBMS_OUTPUT.PUT_LINE
         ('Letter grade is: '||v_letter_grade);
   END;
```

LAB
5.2

In this example, there is no upper limit specified for the variable `v_final_grade` because BETWEEN operator has been replaced with ">=" operator. Thus, this script is able to handle the value of `v_final_grade` that is greater than 100. Instead of assigning letter "F" to the `v_letter_grade` (in the version 1.0 of the script), the letter "A" is assigned to the variable `v_letter_grade`. As a result, this script produces more accurate results.

LAB 5.2 SELF-REVIEW QUESTIONS

In order to test your progress, you should be able to answer the following questions.

1)   An ELSIF construct can have only one ELSIF clause present.
   a) _____ True
   b) _____ False

**LAB
5.2**

2) There multiple ELSE clauses present in an ELSIF construct.
  a) _____ True
  b) _____ False

3) What part of the ELSIF statement is executed when all of the conditions speci-fied evaluate to NULL?
  a) _____ IF part
  b) _____ One of the ELSIF parts
  c) _____ ELSE part
  d) _____ ELSIF statement is not executed at all

4) When the conditions of the ELSIF statement are not mutually exclusive, which of the following occur?
  a) _____ ELSIF statement causes an error.
  b) _____ ELSIF statement is not executed at all.
  c) _____ Statements associated with the first condition that evaluates to TRUE are executed.
  d) _____ Statements associated with the last condition that evaluates to TRUE are executed.

5) An ELSIF statement without ELSE part causes a syntax error.
  a) _____ True
  b) _____ False

Quiz answers appear in Appendix A, Section 5.2.

LAB 5.3

NESTED IF STATEMENTS

> ## LAB OBJECTIVES
>
> After this lab, you will be able to:
>
> ✔ Use Nested IF Statements

You have encountered different types of conditional controls: IF-THEN statement, IF-THEN-ELSE statement, and ELSIF statement. These types of conditional controls can be nested inside of another—for example, an IF statement can be nested inside an ELSIF and vice versa. Consider the following:

■ FOR EXAMPLE

```
DECLARE
    v_num1 NUMBER := &sv_num1;
    v_num2 NUMBER := &sv_num2;
    v_total NUMBER;
BEGIN
    IF v_num1 > v_num2
    THEN
        DBMS_OUTPUT.PUT_LINE('IF part of the outer IF');
        v_total := v_num1 - v_num2;
    ELSE
        DBMS_OUTPUT.PUT_LINE('ELSE part of the outer IF');
        v_total := v_num1 + v_num2;
        IF v_total < 0
        THEN
            DBMS_OUTPUT.PUT_LINE('Inner IF');
            v_total := v_total * (-1);
```

```
        END IF;
    END IF;
    DBMS_OUTPUT.PUT_LINE('v_total = '||v_total);
END;
```

The IF-THEN-ELSE statement is called an *outer IF statement* because it encompasses the IF-THEN statement. The IF-THEN statement is called an *inner IF statement* because it is enclosed by the body of the IF-THEN-ELSE statement.

Assume that the value for v_num1 and v_num2 are –4 and 3 respectively. First, the condition

```
v_num1 > v_num2
```

of the outer IF statement is evaluated. Since –4 is not greater than 3, the ELSE part of the outer IF statement is executed. As a result, the message

```
ELSE part of the outer IF
```

is displayed, and the value of v_total is calculated. Next, the condition

```
v_total < 0
```

of the inner IF statement is evaluated. Since that value of v_total is equal –l, the condition yields TRUE, and message

```
Inner IF
```

is displayed. Next, the value of v_total is calculated again. This logic is demonstrated by the output produced by the example:

```
Enter value for sv_num1: -4
old   2:     v_num1   NUMBER := &sv_num1;
new   2:     v_num1   NUMBER := -4;
Enter value for sv_num2: 3
old   3:     v_num2   NUMBER := &sv_num2;
new   3:     v_num2   NUMBER := 3;
ELSE part of the outer IF
Inner IF
v_total = 1
PL/SQL procedure successfully completed.
```

LOGICAL OPERATORS

So far in this chapter, you have seen examples of different IF statements. All these examples used test operators such as >, <, and =, to test a condition. Logical operators can be used to evaluate a condition as well. In addition, they allow a programmer to combine multiple conditions into a single condition if there is such a need.

■ *FOR EXAMPLE*

```
DECLARE
    v_letter CHAR(1) := '&sv_letter';
BEGIN
    IF (v_letter >= 'A' AND v_letter <= 'Z')
        OR (v_letter >= 'a' AND v_letter <= 'z')
    THEN
        DBMS_OUTPUT.PUT_LINE('This is a letter');
    ELSE
        DBMS_OUTPUT.PUT_LINE('This is not a letter');
        IF v_letter BETWEEN '0' and '9'
        THEN
            DBMS_OUTPUT.PUT_LINE('This is a number');
        ELSE
            DBMS_OUTPUT.PUT_LINE('This is not a number');
        END IF;
    END IF;
END;
```

In the example above, the condition

```
(v_letter >= 'A' AND v_letter <= 'Z')
 OR (v_letter >= 'a' AND v_letter <= 'z')
```

uses logical operators AND and OR. There are two conditions

```
(v_letter >= 'A' AND v_letter <= 'Z')
```

and

```
(v_letter >= 'a' AND v_letter <= 'z')
```

combined into one with the help of the OR operator. It is also important for you to realize the purpose of the parentheses. In this example, they are used to improve the readability only because the operator AND takes precedence over the operator OR.

When the symbol "?" is entered at runtime, this example produces the following output

```
Enter value for sv_letter: ?
old   2:     v_letter CHAR(1) := '&sv_letter';
new   2:     v_letter CHAR(1) := '?';
This is not a letter
This is not a number
PL/SQL procedure successfully completed.
```

LAB 5.3 EXERCISES

5.3.1 USING NESTED IF STATEMENTS

In this exercise, you will use nested IF statements. This script will convert the value of a temperature from one system to another. If the temperature is supplied in Fahrenheit, it will be converted to Celsius, and vice versa.

Create the following PL/SQL script:

```
-- ch05_4a.sql, version 1.0
SET SERVEROUTPUT ON
DECLARE
   v_temp_in NUMBER := &sv_temp_in;
   v_scale_in CHAR := '&sv_scale_in';
   v_temp_out NUMBER;
   v_scale_out CHAR;
BEGIN
   IF v_scale_in != 'C' OR v_scale_in != 'F'
   THEN
      DBMS_OUTPUT.PUT_LINE('This is not a valid scale');
   ELSE
      IF v_scale_in = 'C'
      THEN
         v_temp_out := ( (9*v_temp_in) / 5 ) + 32;
         v_scale_out := 'F';
      ELSE
         v_temp_out := ( (v_temp_in - 32)*5 ) / 9;
         v_scale_out := 'C';
      END IF;
      DBMS_OUTPUT.PUT_LINE
         ('New scale is: '||v_scale_out);
      DBMS_OUTPUT.PUT_LINE
```

```
                ('New temperature is: '||v_temp_out);
        END IF;
    END;
```

Execute the script, then answer the following questions:

a) What output is printed on the screen if the value of 100 is entered for the temperature, and the letter "C" is entered for the scale?

LAB
5.3

_____

_____

b) Try to run this script without providing value for the temperature. What message will be displayed on the screen? Why?

_____

_____

c) Try to run this script providing invalid letter for the temperature scale, for example letter "V." What message will be displayed on the screen? Why?

_____

_____

d) Rewrite this script so that if an invalid letter is entered for the scale, v_temp_out is initialized to zero and v_scale_out is initialized to C.

_____

_____

LAB 5.3 EXERCISE ANSWERS

5.3.1 ANSWERS

a) What output is printed on the screen if the value of 100 is entered for the temperature, and the letter "C" is entered for the scale?

Answer: Your output should look like the following:

```
Enter value for sv_temp_in: 100
old   2:     v_temp_in     NUMBER := &sv_temp_in;
new   2:     v_temp_in     NUMBER := 100;
Enter value for sv_scale_in: C
old   3:     v_scale_in    CHAR := '&sv_scale_in';
new   3:     v_scale_in    CHAR := 'C';
New scale is: F
New temperature is: 212
PL/SQL procedure successfully completed.
```

Once the values for v_temp_in and v_scale_in have been entered, the condition

```
v_scale_in != 'C' OR v_scale_in != 'F'
```

of the outer IF statement evaluates to FALSE, and control is passed to the ELSE part of the outer IF statement. Next, the condition

```
v_scale_in = 'C'
```

of the inner IF statement evaluates to TRUE, and the values of the variables v_temp_out and v_scale_out are calculated. The control is then passed back to the outer IF statement, and the new value for the temperature and the scale are displayed on the screen.

b) Try to run this script without providing value for the temperature. What message will be displayed on the screen? Why?

Answer: If the value for the temperature is not entered, the script will not compile at all.

The compiler will try to assign a value to v_temp_in with the help of the substitution variable. Because the value for v_temp_in has not been entered, the assignment statement will fail, and the following error message will be displayed.

```
Enter value for sv_temp_in:
old    2:     v_temp_in    NUMBER := &sv_temp_in;
new    2:     v_temp_in    NUMBER := ;
Enter value for sv_scale_in: C
old    3:     v_scale_in    CHAR := '&sv_scale_in';
new    3:     v_scale_in    CHAR := 'C';
   v_temp_in     NUMBER := ;
                        *
ERROR at line 2:
ORA-06550: line 2, column 27:
PLS-00103: Encountered the symbol ";" when expecting
one of the following:
( - + mod not null <an identifier>
<a double-quoted delimited-identifier> <a bind
variable> avg
count current exists max min prior sql stddev sum
variance
cast <a string literal with character set
specification>
<a number> <a single-quoted SQL string>
The symbol "null" was substituted for ";" to
continue.
```

You have probably noticed that even though the mistake seems small and insignificant, the error message is fairly long and confusing.

c) Try to run this script providing invalid letter for the temperature scale, for example letter "V." What message will be displayed on the screen? Why?

Answer: If invalid letter is entered on for the scale, message "This is not a valid scale" will be displayed on the screen. Messages, "New scale is:" and "New temperature is:," will be displayed as well.

None of the conditions specified in the inner IF statement will evaluate to TRUE. As a result, the ELSE part of this statement will be executed. Then the control will be passed back to the outer IF statement, and messages for new scale and new temperature will be displayed. However, there will not be new values specified for them.

Assume that letter "V" was typed by mistake. This example will produce the following output:

```
Enter value for sv_temp_in: 45
old    2:     v_temp_in    NUMBER := &sv_temp_in;
new    2:     v_temp_in    NUMBER := 45;
```

```
Enter value for sv_scale_in: V
old    3:     v_scale_in    CHAR := '&sv_scale_in';
new    3:     v_scale_in    CHAR := 'V';
This is not a valid scale
New scale is:
New temperature is:
PL/SQL procedure successfully completed.
```

d) Rewrite this script so that if invalid letter is entered for the scale `v_temp_out` is initialized to zero, and `v_scale_out` is initialized to C.

Answer: This answer contains only a portion of the code that helps to illustrate the changes. Notice, two last DBMS_OUTPUT.PUT_LINE statements have been moved from the body of the outer IF statement.

```
-- ch05_4b.sql, version 2.0
...
BEGIN
   IF v_scale_in != 'C' OR v_scale_in != 'F'
   THEN
       DBMS_OUTPUT.PUT_LINE('This is not a valid
scale.');
       v_temp_out := 0;
       v_scale_out := 'C';
   ELSE
     IF v_scale_in = 'C'
       ...
       END IF;
   END IF;
   DBMS_OUTPUT.PUT_LINE
      ('New scale is: '||v_scale_out);
   DBMS_OUTPUT.PUT_LINE
      ('New temperature is: '||v_temp_out);
END;
```

The script above produces the following output:

```
Enter value for sv_temp_in: 100
old    2:     v_temp_in     NUMBER := &sv_temp_in;
new    2:     v_temp_in     NUMBER := 100;
Enter value for sv_scale_in: V
old    3:     v_scale_in    CHAR := '&sv_scale_in';
new    3:     v_scale_in    CHAR := 'V';
This is not a valid scale.
New scale is: C
```

```
New temperature is: 0
PL/SQL procedure successfully completed.
```

LAB 5.3 SELF-REVIEW QUESTIONS

In order to test your progress, you should be able to answer the following questions.

1) What types of IF statements can be nested one inside another?
   a) _____ IF-THEN statement can only be nested inside ELSIF statement.
   b) _____ IF-THEN-ELSE statement cannot be nested at all.
   c) _____ Any IF statement can be nested inside another IF statement.

2) How many IF statements can be nested inside another?
   a) _____ One
   b) _____ Two
   c) _____ Any number

3) Only a single logical operator can be used with a condition of an IF statement.
   a) _____ True
   b) _____ False

4) When using nested IF statements, their conditions do not need to be mutually exclusive.
   a) _____ True
   b) _____ False

5) When the condition of the outer IF statement evaluates to FALSE, which of the following happens?
   a) _____ The control is transferred to the inner IF statement.
   b) _____ The error message is generated.
   c) _____ The control is transferred to the first executable statement after the outer END IF statement.

Quiz answers appear in Appendix A, Section 5.3.

LAB
5.3

CHAPTER 5

TEST YOUR THINKING

In this chapter you have learned about different types of IF statements. You also learned that all these different IF statements can be nested one inside another. Here are some exercises that will help you test the depth of your understanding.

1) Rewrite the `ch05_1a.sql`. Instead of getting information from the user for the variable `v_date`, define its value with the help of the function SYSDATE. After it has been determined if a certain day falls on the weekend, check to see if the time is before or after the noon. Display the time of the day together with the day.

2) Create a new script. For a given instructor, determine how many sections he or she is teaching. If the number is greater or equal to 3, display a message saying the instructor needs a vacation. Otherwise, display a message saying how many sections this instructor is teaching.

3) Execute two PL/SQL blocks below and explain why they produce different output for the same value of the variable `v_num`. Remember to issue the SET SERVER-OUTPUT ON command before running this script.

```
-- Block 1
DECLARE
   v_num NUMBER := NULL;
BEGIN
   IF v_num > 0
   THEN
      DBMS_OUTPUT.PUT_LINE
         ('v_num is greater than 0');
   ELSE
      DBMS_OUTPUT.PUT_LINE
         ('v_num is not greater than 0');
   END IF;
END;

-- Block 2
DECLARE
   v_num NUMBER := NULL;
BEGIN
```

```
    IF v_num > 0
    THEN
        DBMS_OUTPUT.PUT_LINE
            ('v_num is greater than 0');
    END IF;
    IF NOT (v_num > 0)
    THEN
        DBMS_OUTPUT.PUT_LINE
            ('v_num is not greater than 0');
    END IF;
END;
```

CHAPTER 6

EXCEPTION HANDLING AND BUILT-IN EXCEPTIONS

In Chapter 2, you encountered two types of errors that can be found in a program: compilation errors and runtime errors. You will recall that there is a special section in a PL/SQL block that handles the runtime errors. This section is called the *exception-handling section*, and in it, runtime errors are referred to as *exceptions*. The exception-handling section allows programmers to specify what actions should be taken when a specific exception occurs.

In PL/SQL, there are two types of exceptions: *built-in exceptions* and *user-defined exceptions*. In this chapter, you will learn how you can handle certain kind of run-time errors with the help of built-in exceptions. User-defined exceptions are discussed in Chapters 9 and 10.

L A B   6 . 1

HANDLING ERRORS

LAB OBJECTIVES

After this lab, you will be able to:

✔ Understand the Importance of Error Handling

The example shown below will help to illustrate some of the differences between compilation and run-time errors.

■ FOR EXAMPLE

```
DECLARE
    v_num1 INTEGER := &sv_num1;
    v_num2 INTEGER := &sv_num2;
    v_result NUMBER;
BEGIN
    v_result = v_num1 / v_num2;
    DBMS_OUTPUT.PUT_LINE('v_result: '||v_result);
END;
```

The example above is a very simple program. There are two variables, v_num1 and v_num2. A user supplies values for these variables. Next, v_num1 is divided by v_num2, and the result of this division is stored in the third variable, v_result. Finally, the value of v_result is displayed on the screen.

Now, assume that a user supplies values of 3 and 5 for the variables, v_num1 and v_num2, respectively. As a result, the example produces the output shown below:

```
Enter value for sv_num1: 3
old   2:     v_num1 integer := &sv_num1;
new   2:     v_num1 integer := 3;
Enter value for sv_num2: 5
```

```
old   3:     v_num2 integer := &sv_num2;
new   3:     v_num2 integer := 5;
   v_result = v_num1 / v_num2;
               *
ERROR at line 6:
ORA-06550: line 6, column 13:
PLS-00103: Encountered the symbol "=" when expecting
one of the following:
:= . ( @ % ;
ORA-06550: line 7, column 4:
PLS-00103: Encountered the symbol "DBMS_OUTPUT"
ORA-06550: line 7, column 49:
PLS-00103: Encountered the symbol ";" when expecting
one of the following:
. ( * % & - + / mod rem return RETURNING_ an exponent
(**) and or ||
```

You have probably noticed that the example did not execute successfully. A syntax error has been encountered at line 6. Close inspection of the example shows that the statement

```
v_result = v_num1 / v_num2;
```

contains an equal sign operator where an assignment operator should be used. The statement should be rewritten as follows:

```
v_result := v_num1 / v_num2;
```

Once the corrected example is run again, the following output is produced:

```
Enter value for sv_num1: 3
old   2:     v_num1 integer := &sv_num1;
new   2:     v_num1 integer := 3;
Enter value for sv_num2: 5
old   3:     v_num2 integer := &sv_num2;
new   3:     v_num2 integer := 5;
v_result: .6
PL/SQL procedure successfully completed.
```

As you can see, the example now executes successfully because the syntax error has been corrected.

Next, if you change the values of variables v_num1 and v_num2 to 4 and 0, respectively, the following output is produced:

```
Enter value for sv_num1: 4
old    2:     v_num1 integer := &sv_num1;
new    2:     v_num1 integer := 4;
Enter value for sv_num2: 0
old    3:     v_num2 integer := &sv_num2;
new    3:     v_num2 integer := 0;
DECLARE
*
ERROR at line 1:
ORA-01476: divisor is equal to zero
ORA-06512: at line 6
```

Even though this example does not contain syntax errors, it was terminated prematurely because the value entered for v_num2, the divisor, was 0. As you may recall, division by 0 is undefined, and thus leads to an error.

This example illustrates a runtime error that cannot be detected by the compiler. In other words, for some of the values entered for the variables v_num1 and v_num2, this example executes successfully. For other values entered for the variables v_num1 and v_num2, this example cannot execute. As a result, the runtime error occurs. You will recall that the compiler cannot detect runtime errors. In this case, a runtime error occurs because compiler does not know the result of the division of v_num1 by v_num2. This result can be determined only at runtime. Hence, this error is referred to as a runtime error.

In order to handle this type of error in the program, an exception handler must be added. The exception-handling section has the following structure:

```
EXCEPTION
   WHEN EXCEPTION_NAME
   THEN
      ERROR-PROCESSING STATEMENTS;
```

The exception-handling section is placed after the executable section of the block. So, the example given above can be rewritten in the following manner.

■ FOR EXAMPLE

```
DECLARE
   v_num1 integer := &sv_num1;
   v_num2 integer := &sv_num2;
```

```
   v_result number;
BEGIN
   v_result := v_num1 / v_num2;
   DBMS_OUTPUT.PUT_LINE('v_result: '||v_result);
EXCEPTION
   WHEN ZERO_DIVIDE
   THEN
      DBMS_OUTPUT.PUT_LINE
         ('A number cannot be divided by zero.');
END;
```

The section of the example in bold letters shows the exception-handling section of the block. When this version of the example is executed with values of 4 and 0 for variables v_num1 and v_num2, respectively, the following output is produced:

```
Enter value for sv_num1: 4
old     2:      v_num1 integer := &sv_num1;
new     2:      v_num1 integer := 4;
Enter value for sv_num2: 0
old     3:      v_num2 integer := &sv_num2;
new     3:      v_num2 integer := 0;
A number cannot be divided by zero.
PL/SQL procedure successfully completed.
```

This output shows that once an attempt to divide v_num1 by v_num2 was made, the exception-handling section of the block was executed. Therefore, the error message specified by the exception-handling section was displayed on the screen.

This version of the output illustrates several advantages of using an exception-handling section. You have probably noticed that the output looks cleaner compared to the previous version. Even though the error message is still displayed on the screen, the output is more informative. In short, it is oriented more toward a user than a programmer.

It is important for you to realize that in many occasions, a user does not have access to the code. Therefore, references to line numbers and keywords in a program are not significant to most users.

In addition, an exception-handling section allows a program to execute to completion, instead of terminating prematurely. Another advantage offered by the exception-handling section is isolation of error-handling routines. In other words, all error-processing code for a specific block is located in the single section. As a result, the logic of the program becomes easier to follow and understand. Finally, adding an exception-handling section enables event-driven processing of errors. In case of a specific exception event, the exception-handling section is executed. Just like in the example shown earlier, in case of the division by 0, the exception-handling section was executed. In other words, the error message specified by the DBMS_OUTPUT.PUT_LINE statement was displayed on the screen.

LAB 6.1 EXERCISES

6.1.1 UNDERSTANDING THE IMPORTANCE OF ERROR HANDLING

In this exercise, you will calculate the value of the square root of a number and display it on the screen.

Create the following PL/SQL script:

```
-- ch06_1a.sql, version 1.0
  SET SERVEROUTPUT ON;
DECLARE
   v_num NUMBER := &sv_num;
BEGIN
   DBMS_OUTPUT.PUT_LINE
       ('Square root of '||v_num||' is
'||SQRT(v_num));
EXCEPTION
   WHEN VALUE_ERROR THEN
       DBMS_OUTPUT.PUT_LINE('An error has occurred');
END;
```

In the script shown above, the exception VALUE_ERROR is used, an exception raised when conversion or type mismatch errors occur. This exception is covered in greater detail in the Lab 6.2 of this chapter.

In order to test this script fully, execute it two times. For the first run, enter a value of 4 for the variable v_num. For the second run, enter the value of –4 for the variable v_num. Execute the script, then answer the following questions:

a) What output was printed on the screen (for both runs)?

_____

_____

b) Why do you think an error message was generated when the script was run second time?

_____

_____

c) Assume that you are not familiar with the exception VALUE_ ERROR. How would you change this script to avoid this runtime error?

_____

_____

LAB 6.1 EXERCISE ANSWERS

6.1.1 ANSWERS

a) *What* output was printed on the screen (for both runs)?

Answer: *The first version of the output is produced when the value of* v_num *is equal to 4. Your output should look like the following:*

```
Enter value for sv_num: 4
old     2:     v_num NUMBER := &sv_num;
new     2:     v_num NUMBER := 4;
Square root of 4 is 2
PL/SQL procedure successfully completed.
```

The second version of the output is produced when v_num *is equal to −4. Your output should look like the following:*

```
Enter value for sv_num: -4
old     2:     v_num NUMBER := &sv_num;
new     2:     v_num NUMBER := -4;
An error has occurred
PL/SQL procedure successfully completed.
```

b) Why do you think an error message was generated when the script was run second time?

Answer: *Error message "An error has occurred" was generated for the second run of example because a runtime has occurred. The built-in function SQRT is unable to accept a negative number as its argument. Therefore, the exception VALUE_ERROR was raised, and the error message was displayed on the screen.*

c) Assume that you are not familiar with the exception VALUE_ERROR. How would you change this script to avoid this runtime error?

Answer: The new version of the your program should look similar to the program below. All changes are shown in bold letters.

```
-- ch06_1b.sql, version 2.0
  SET SERVEROUTPUT ON;
DECLARE
   v_num NUMBER := &sv_num;
BEGIN
   IF v_num >= 0
   THEN
       DBMS_OUTPUT.PUT_LINE
          ('Square root of '||v_num||' is '||
            SQRT(v_num));
   ELSE
       DBMS_OUTPUT.PUT_LINE
          ('A number cannot be negative');
   END IF;
END;
```

Notice, before you calculate the square root of a number, you can check to see if the number is greater or equal to 0 with the help of the IF-THEN-ELSE statement. If the number is negative, the message "A number cannot be negative" is displayed on the screen. When the value of −4 is entered for the variable v_num, this script produces the output shown below:

```
Enter value for sv_num: -4
old    2:    v_num NUMBER := &sv_num;
new    2:    v_num NUMBER := -4;
A number cannot be negative
PL/SQL procedure successfully completed.
```

LAB 6.1 SELF-REVIEW QUESTIONS

In order to test your progress, you should be able to answer the following questions.

1) A compiler can detect a runtime error.
   a) _____True
   b) _____False

2) Without an exception-handling section, a PL/SQL block cannot be compiled.
   a) _____True
   b) _____False

3) An exception is raised when the following occurs.
   a) _____A compilation error is encountered.
   b) _____A runtime error is encountered.

4) An exception-handling section of a PL/SQL block is placed
   a) _____after the reserved word END.
   b) _____before the reserved word END.
   c) _____before the reserved word BEGIN.

5) The exception ZERO_DIVIDE is raised when number 1 is divided by number 2 and the following occurs:
   a) _____Number 1 is equal to 0.
   b) _____Number 2 is equal to 0.
   c) _____Both numbers are equal to 0.

Quiz answers appear in Appendix A, Section 6.1.

L A B   6 . 2

BUILT-IN EXCEPTIONS

> ## LAB OBJECTIVES
>
> After this lab, you will be able to:
>
> ✔ Use Built-In Exceptions

As mentioned earlier, a PL/SQL block has the following structure:

```
DECLARE
   ...
BEGIN
   EXECUTABLE STATEMENTS;
EXCEPTION
   WHEN EXCEPTION_NAME
   THEN
      ERROR-PROCESSING STATEMENTS;
END;
```

When a built-in exception occurs, it is said to be raised implicitly. In other words, if a program breaks an Oracle rule, the control is passed to the exception-handling section of the block. At this point, the error-processing statements are executed. It is important for you to realize that after the exception-handling section of the block has executed, the block terminates. Control will not return to the executable section of this block. The example shown below illustrates this point.

■ FOR EXAMPLE

```
DECLARE
   v_student_name VARCHAR2(50);
BEGIN
   SELECT first_name||' '||last_name
      INTO v_student_name
      FROM student
```

```
        WHERE student_id = 101;
      DBMS_OUTPUT.PUT_LINE
         ('Student name is '||v_student_name);
   EXCEPTION
      WHEN NO_DATA_FOUND
      THEN
          DBMS_OUTPUT.PUT_LINE('There is no such student');
   END;
```

This example produces the following output:

**There is no such student
PL/SQL procedure successfully completed.**

Because there is no record in the STUDENT table with student ID 101, the SELECT INTO statement does not return any rows. As a result, control passes to the exception-handling section of the block, and the error message "There is no such student" is displayed on the screen. Even though there is a DBMS_OUTPUT.PUT_LINE statement right after the SELECT statement, it will not be executed because control has been transferred to the exception-handling section. Control will never return to the executable section of this block, which contains the DBMS_OUTPUT .PUT_LINE statement.

You have probably noticed that, while every Oracle runtime error has a number associated with it, it must be handled by its name in the exception-handling section. One of the outputs from the example used in the previous lab of this chapter has the following error message:

ORA-01476: divisor is equal to zero

where ORA-01476 stands for error number. This error number refers to the error named ZERO_DIVIDE. So, some common Oracle runtime errors are predefined in the PL/SQL as exceptions.

The list shown below explains some commonly used predefined exceptions and how they are raised:

- NO_DATA_FOUND   This exception is raised when a SELECT INTO statement, which makes no calls to group functions, such as SUM or COUNT, does not return any rows. For example, you issue a SELECT INTO statement against STUDENT table where student ID equals 101. If there is no record in the STUDENT table passing this criteria (student ID equals 101), the NO_DATA_FOUND exception is raised.

When a SELECT INTO statement calls a group function, such as COUNT, the result set is never empty. When used in the SELECT INTO statement against the STUDENT table, function COUNT will return 0 for the value of student ID 123. Hence, any SELECT statement that calls any group function will never raise the NO_DATA_FOUND exception.

- TOO_MANY_ROWS   This exception is raised when a SELECT INTO statement returns more than one row. By definition, a SELECT INTO can return only single row. If a SELECT INTO statement returns more than one row, the definition of the SELECT INTO statement is violated. This causes the TOO_MANY_ROWS exception to be raised.

    For example, you issue a SELECT INTO statement against the STUDENT table for a specific zip code. There is a big chance that this SELECT statement will return more than one row because many students can live in the same zip code area.

- ZERO_DIVIDE   This exception is raised when a division operation is performed in the program and a divisor is equal to zero. An example in the previous lab of this chapter illustrates how this exception is raised.

- LOGIN_DENIED   This exception is raised when a user is trying to login on to Oracle with invalid username or password.

- PROGRAM_ERROR   This exception is raised when a PL/SQL program has an internal problem.

- VALUE_ERROR   This exception is raised when conversion or size mismatch error occurs. For example, you select student's last name into a variable that has been defined as VAR-CHAR2(5). If student's last name contains more than five characters, VALUE_ERROR exception is raised.

- DUP_VALUE_ON_INDEX   This exception is raised when a program tries to store a duplicate value in the column or columns that have a unique index defined on them. For example, you are trying to insert a record into the SECTION table for the course number "25," section 1. If a record for the given course and section numbers already exists in the SECTION table, DUP_VAL_ON_INDEX exception is raised because these columns have a unique index defined on them.

So far, you have seen examples of the programs able to handle a single exception only. For example, a PL/SQL contains an exception-handler with a single exception ZERO_DIVIDE. However, many times in the PL/SQL block you need to handle different exceptions. Moreover, often you need to specify different actions that must be taken when a particular exception is raised, as the following illustrates.

■ FOR EXAMPLE

```
DECLARE
   v_student_id NUMBER := &sv_student_id;
   v_enrolled VARCHAR2(3) := 'NO';
BEGIN
   DBMS_OUTPUT.PUT_LINE
      ('Check if the student is enrolled');
   SELECT 'YES'
     INTO v_enrolled
     FROM enrollment
    WHERE student_id = v_student_id;
   DBMS_OUTPUT.PUT_LINE
      ('The student is enrolled into one course');
EXCEPTION
   WHEN NO_DATA_FOUND
   THEN
      DBMS_OUTPUT.PUT_LINE('The student is not
         enrolled');
   WHEN TOO_MANY_ROWS
   THEN
      DBMS_OUTPUT.PUT_LINE
         ('The student is enrolled into many courses');
END;
```

Notice, this example contains two exceptions in the single exception-handling section. The first exception, NO_DATA_FOUND, will be raised if there are no records in the ENROLLMENT table for a particular student. The second exception, TOO_MANY_ROWS, will be raised if a particular student is enrolled into more than one course.

Consider what happens if you run this example for three different values of student ID: 102, 103, and 319.

First run of the example (student ID is 102) produces the output shown below:

```
Enter value for sv_student_id: 102
old    2:     v_student_id NUMBER := &sv_student_id;
new    2:     v_student_id NUMBER := 102;
Check if the student is enrolled
Student is enrolled into many courses
PL/SQL procedure successfully completed.
```

The first time, a user entered 102 for the value of student ID. Next, the first DBMS_OUTPUT.PUT_LINE statement is executed, and the message "Check if the . . ." is displayed on the screen. Then, the SELECT INTO statement is executed. You have probably noticed that the DBMS_OUT-PUT.PUT_LINE statement following the SELECT INTO statement was not displayed on the screen. When the SELECT INTO statement is executed for the student ID 102, multiple rows are returned. Because the SELECT INTO statement can return only single row, the control is passed to the exception-handling section of the block. Next, your PL/SQL block raises the proper exception. As a result, the message "The student is enrolled into many courses" has been displayed on the screen, and this message is specified by the exception TOO_MANY_ROWS.

 It is important for you to note that built-in exceptions are raised implicitly. Therefore, you only need to specify what action must be taken in case of a particular exception.

A second run of the example (student ID is 103) produces the output shown below:

```
Enter value for sv_student_id: 103
old   2:    v_student_id NUMBER := &sv_student_id;
new   2:    v_student_id NUMBER := 103;
Check if the student is enrolled
The student is enrolled into one course
PL/SQL procedure successfully completed.
```

In this second run, a user entered 103 for the value of student ID. As a result, the first DBMS_OUTPUT.PUT_LINE statement is executed, and the message "Check if the . . ." is displayed on the screen. Then, the SELECT INTO statement is executed. When the SELECT INTO statement is executed for the student ID 103, a single row is returned. Next, the DBMS_OUTPUT.PUT_LINE statement following the SELECT INTO statement is executed. As a result, the message "The student is enrolled into one course" is displayed on the screen. Notice, for this value of the variable student_id no exception has been raised.

A third run of the example (student ID is 319) produces the output shown below:

```
Enter value for sv_student_id: 319
old   2:    v_student_id NUMBER := &sv_student_id;
new   2:    v_student_id NUMBER := 319;
Check if the student is enrolled
```

The student is not enrolled
PL/SQL procedure successfully completed.

This time, a user entered 319 for the value of student ID. The first DBMS_OUTPUT.PUT_LINE statement is executed, and the message "Check if the..." is displayed on the screen. Then, the SELECT INTO statement is executed. When the SELECT INTO statement is executed for the student ID 319, no rows are returned. As a result, control is passed to the exception-handling section of the PL/SQL block, and the proper exception is raised. In this case, the NO_DATA_FOUND exception is raised because the SELECT INTO statement failed to return a single row. So, the message "The student is not enrolled" has been displayed on the screen.

So far, you have seen examples of exception-handling sections that have particular exceptions, such as NO_DATA_FOUND or ZERO_DIVIDE. However, you cannot always predict beforehand what exception might be raised by your PL/SQL block. In cases like this, there is a special exception handler called OTHERS. All predefined Oracle errors (exceptions) can be handled with the help of the OTHERS handler.

Consider the following:

■ FOR EXAMPLE

```
DECLARE
   v_instructor_id NUMBER := &sv_instructor_id;
   v_instructor_name VARCHAR2(50);
BEGIN
   SELECT first_name||' '||last_name
     INTO v_instructor_name
     FROM instructor
    WHERE instructor_id = v_instructor_id;
   DBMS_OUTPUT.PUT_LINE
      ('Instructor name is '||v_instructor_name);
EXCEPTION
   WHEN OTHERS
   THEN
      DBMS_OUTPUT.PUT_LINE('An error has occurred');
END;
```

When run, this example produces the following output:

```
Enter value for sv_instructor_id: 100
old   2:     v_instructor_id NUMBER := &sv_instructor_id;
new   2:     v_instructor_id NUMBER := 100;
```

An error has occurred
PL/SQL procedure successfully completed.

This demonstrates not only the use of the OTHERS exception handler, but also a bad programming practice. The exception OTHERS has been raised because there is no record in the INSTRUCTOR table for instructor ID 100.

This is a simple example, where it is possible to guess what exception handlers should be used. However, in many instances you may find a number of programs that have been written with single exception handler, OTHERS. This is a bad programming practice, because such use of this exception handler does not give you or your user a good feedback. You do not really know what error has occurred. Your user does not know if he or she entered some information incorrectly. There are special error-reporting functions, SQLCODE and SQLERRM, that are very useful when used with OTHERS handler. You will learn about them in Chapter 10.

LAB 6.2 EXERCISES

6.2.1 USING BUILT-IN EXCEPTIONS

In this exercise, you will learn more about some built-in exceptions discussed earlier in the chapter.

Create the following PL/SQL script:

```
-- ch06_2a.sql, version 1.0
SET SERVEROUTPUT ON
DECLARE
    v_exists NUMBER(1);
    v_total_students NUMBER(1);
    v_zip CHAR(5):= '&sv_zip';
BEGIN
    SELECT count(*)
      INTO v_exists
      FROM zipcode
     WHERE zip = v_zip;
    IF v_exists != 0
    THEN
        SELECT COUNT(*)
          INTO v_total_students
          FROM student
         WHERE zip = v_zip;
```

```
            DBMS_OUTPUT.PUT_LINE
                ('There are '||v_total_students||' students');
        ELSE
            DBMS_OUTPUT.PUT_LINE
                (v_zip||' is not a valid zip');
        END IF;
    EXCEPTION
        WHEN VALUE_ERROR OR INVALID_NUMBER
        THEN
            DBMS_OUTPUT.PUT_LINE('An error has occurred');
    END;
```

This script contains two exceptions, VALUE_ERROR and INVALID_NUM-BER. However, only one exception handler is written for both exceptions. You can combine different exceptions in the single exception handler when you want to handle both exceptions in the similar way.

Often the exceptions VALUE_ERROR and INVALID_NUMBER are used in the single exception handler because these Oracle errors refer to the conversion problems that may occur at the runtime.

In order to test this script fully, execute it three times. For the first run enter "07024," for the second run enter "00914," and for the third run enter "12345" for the variable v_zip. Execute the script, then answer the following questions:

a) What output was printed on the screen (for all values of zip)?

_____

_____

b) Explain why no exception has been raised for these values of the variable v_zip?

_____

_____

c) Insert a record into the STUDENT table with zip having the value of "07024." Run the script again for the same value of zip ("07024"). What output was printed on the screen? Why?

_____

_____

d) How would you change the script to display a student's first name and last name instead of displaying the total number of students for any given value of zip? Remember, only one record can be returned by the SELECT INTO statement.

LAB 6.2 EXERCISE ANSWERS

6.2.1 ANSWERS

a) What output was printed on the screen (for all values of zip)?

Answer: The first version of the output is produced when the value of zip is 07024. The second version of the output is produced when the value of zip is 00914. The third version of the output is produced when the value of zip is 12345.

Your output should look like the following:

```
Enter value for sv_zip: 07024
old    4:    v_zip CHAR(5):= '&sv_zip';
new    4:    v_zip CHAR(5):= '07024';
There are 9 students
PL/SQL procedure successfully completed.
```

When "07024" is entered for the variable `v_zip`, the first SELECT INTO statement is executed. This SELECT INTO statement checks if the value of zip is valid, or, in other words, if a record exists the ZIPCODE table for a given value of zip. Next, the value of variable `v_exists` is evaluated with the help of IF statement. For this run of the example, IF statement evaluates to TRUE, and as a result, the SELECT INTO statement against the STUDENT table is evaluated. Next, DBMS_OUTPUT.PUT_LINE following the SELECT INTO statement is executed, and the message "There are 9 students" is displayed on the screen.

```
Enter value for sv_zip: 00914
old    4:    v_zip CHAR(5):= '&sv_zip';
new    4:    v_zip CHAR(5):= '00914';
There are 0 students
PL/SQL procedure successfully completed.
```

For the second run, the value 00914 is entered for the variable v_zip. The SELECT INTO statement against STUDENT table returns one record, and the message "There are 0 students" is displayed on the screen.

Because the SELECT INTO statement against the STUDENT table uses a group function COUNT, there is no reason to use exception NO_ DATA_FOUND because the COUNT function will always return data.

```
Enter value for sv_zip: 12345
old   4:     v_zip CHAR(5):= '&sv_zip';
new   4:     v_zip CHAR(5):= '12345';
12345 is not a valid zip
PL/SQL procedure successfully completed.
```

For the third run, the value 12345 is entered for the variable v_zip. The SELECT INTO statement against ZIPCODE table is executed. Next, the variable v_exists is evaluated with the help of IF statement. Because the value of v_exists equals 0, the IF statement evaluates to FALSE. As a result, ELSE part of the IF statement is executed. So, the message "12345 is not a valid zip" is displayed on the screen.

b) Explain why no exception has been raised for these values of the variable v_zip?

Answer: The exceptions VALUE_ERROR or INVALID_NUMBER have not been raised because there was no conversion or type mismatch error. Both variables, v_exists and v_total_students, have been defined as NUMBER(1).

The group function COUNT used in the SELECT INTO statement returns NUMBER datatype. Moreover, on both occasions, a single digit number is returned by the COUNT function. As a result, neither exception has been raised.

c) Insert a record into the STUDENT table with zip having the value of "07024." Run the script again for the same value of zip ("07024"). What output was printed on the screen? Why?

Answer: After a student has been added, your output should look like the following:

```
 Enter value for sv_zip: 07024
old   4:     v_zip CHAR(5):= '&sv_zip';
new   4:     v_zip CHAR(5):= '07024';
An error has occurred
PL/SQL procedure successfully completed.
```

Once the student has been inserted into the STUDENT table with zip having value "07024," the total number of students changes to 10 (remember, previously this number was 9). As a result, the SELECT INTO statement against the STUDENT table causes an error because the variable `v_total_students` has been defined as NUMBER(1). It means that only single digit number can be stored in this variable. The number 10 is a two-digit number, so the exception INVALID_NUMBER is raised. As a result, the message "An error has occurred" is displayed on the screen.

**LAB
6.2**

d) How would you change the script to display a student's first name and last name instead of displaying the total number of students for any given value of zip? Remember, only one record can be returned by the SELECT INTO statement.

Answer: The new version of your program should look similar to this program. All changes are shown in bold letters.

```
-- ch06_2b.sql, version 2.0
SET SERVEROUTPUT ON
DECLARE
   v_exists NUMBER(1);
   v_student_name VARCHAR2(30);
   v_zip CHAR(5):= '&sv_zip';
BEGIN
   SELECT count(*)
     INTO v_exists
     FROM zipcode
    WHERE zip = v_zip;
   IF v_exists != 0
   THEN
       SELECT first_name||' '||last_name
         INTO v_student_name
         FROM student
        WHERE zip = v_zip
          AND rownum = 1;
       DBMS_OUTPUT.PUT_LINE
           ('Student name is '||v_student_name);
   ELSE
       DBMS_OUTPUT.PUT_LINE
           (v_zip||' is not a valid zip');
   END IF;
EXCEPTION
   WHEN VALUE_ERROR OR INVALID_NUMBER
   THEN
       DBMS_OUTPUT.PUT_LINE('An error has occurred');
   WHEN NO_DATA_FOUND
   THEN
       DBMS_OUTPUT.PUT_LINE
```

```
                ('There are no students for this '||
                 'value of zip code');
    END;
```

This version of the program contains several changes.

The variable `v_total_students`, has been replaced by the variable `v_student_name`. The SELECT INTO statement against the STUDENT table has been changed as well. Another condition has been added to the WHERE clause

```
    rownum = 1
```

You have seen from the previous runs of this program that for any given value of zip there could be multiple records in the STUDENT table. Because SELECT INTO statement returns only a single row, the condition, rownum = 1, has been added to it. Another way to deal with multiple rows returned by the SELECT INTO statement is to add exception, TOO_MANY_ROWS.

Finally, another exception has been added to the program. The SELECT INTO statement against the STUDENT table does not contain any group functions. Therefore, for any given value of zip, the SELECT INTO statement may not return any data, and it causes an error. As a result, the exception NO_DATA_FOUND will be raised.

LAB 6.2 SELF-REVIEW QUESTIONS

In order to test your progress, you should be able to answer the following questions.

1) How does any built-in exception get raised?
    a)_____ Implicitly
    b)_____ Explicitly

2) An Oracle error, exception, is referred to by its
    a)_____ number.
    b)_____ name.
    c)_____ both.

3) When a group function is used in the SELECT INTO statement, exception NO_DATA_FOUND is raised if there are no rows returned.
    a)_____ True
    b)_____ False

4) When an exception is raised and executed, the control is passed back to the PL/SQL block.

    a)_____ True

    b)_____ False

5) An exception-handling section of a PL/SQL block may contain a single exception handler only.

    a)_____ True

    b)_____ False

Quiz answers appear in Appendix A, Section 6.2.

CHAPTER 6

TEST YOUR THINKING

In this chapter you have learned about built-in exceptions. Here are some projects that will help you test the depth of your understanding.

1) Create the following script. Check if there is a record in the STUDENT table for a given student ID. If there is no record for the given student ID, insert a record into the STUDENT table for the given student ID.

2) Create the following script. For a given instructor ID, check if it is a valid instructor. Then check how many sections are taught by this instructor and display this information on the screen.

CHAPTER 7

ITERATIVE CONTROL

Generally, computer programs are written because certain tasks must be executed a number of times. For example, many companies need to process transactions on a monthly basis. A program allows the completion of this task by being executed at the end of each month.

Similarly, programs incorporate instructions that need to be executed repeatedly. For example, a program may need to write a number of records to a table. By using a loop, your program is able to write the desired number of records to a table. In other words, loops are programming facilities that allow a set of instructions to be executed repeatedly.

In PL/SQL, there are four types of loops: simple loops, WHILE loops, numeric FOR loops, and cursor FOR loops. In this chapter, you will explore simple loops, WHILE loops, numeric FOR loops, and nested loops. Cursor FOR loops are discussed later in the book.

L A B 7 . 1

SIMPLE LOOPS

> ## LAB OBJECTIVES
>
> After this lab, you will be able to:
>
> ✔ Use Simple Loops with EXIT conditions
> ✔ Use Simple Loops with EXIT WHEN conditions

A simple loop, as you can see from its name, is the most basic kind of loop and has the following structure:

```
LOOP
    STATEMENT 1;
    STATEMENT 2;
    ...
    STATEMENT N;
END LOOP;
```

The reserved word LOOP marks the beginning of the simple loop. Statements 1 through N are a sequence of statements that is executed repeatedly. These statements consist of one or more of the standard programming structures. END LOOP is a reserved phrase that indicates the end of the loop construct.

The flow of the logic from this structure is illustrated in Figure 7.1.

Every time the loop is iterated, a sequence of statements is executed, then control is passed back to the top of the loop. The sequence of statements will be executed an infinite number of times because there is no statement specifying when the loop must terminate. Hence, a simple loop is called an *infinite loop* because there is no means to exit the loop. As a result, a properly constructed loop needs to have an exit condition that de-

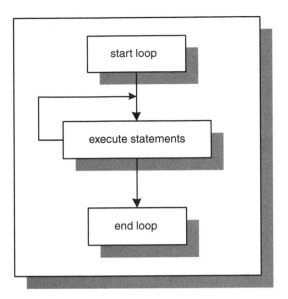

Figure 7.1 ■ Simple loop.

termines when the loop is complete. This exit condition has two forms: *EXIT* and *EXIT WHEN*.

EXIT

The EXIT statement causes a loop to terminate when the *EXIT condition* evaluates to TRUE. The EXIT condition is evaluated with the help of an IF statement. When the EXIT condition is evaluated to TRUE, control is passed to the first executable statement after the END LOOP statement. This is indicated by the following:

```
LOOP
    STATEMENT 1;
    STATEMENT 2;
    IF CONDITION
    THEN
        EXIT;
    END IF;
END LOOP;
STATEMENT 3;
```

In this example, you can see that after the EXIT condition evaluates to TRUE, control is passed to STATEMENT 3, which is the first executable statement after the END LOOP statement.

The EXIT statement is valid only when placed inside of a loop. When placed outside of a loop, it will cause a syntax error. To avoid this error, use the RETURN statement to terminate a PL/SQL block before its normal end is reached.

EXIT WHEN

The EXIT WHEN statement causes a loop to terminate only if the *EXIT WHEN condition* evaluates to TRUE. Control is then passed to the first executable statement after the END LOOP statement. The structure of a loop using an EXIT WHEN clause is as follows:

```
LOOP
    STATEMENT 1;
    STATEMENT 2;
    EXIT WHEN CONDITION;
END LOOP;
STATEMENT 3;
```

This flow of the logic from the EXIT and EXIT WHEN statements is illustrated in Figure 7.2.

Figure 7.2 shows that during each iteration, the loop executes a sequence of statements. Control is then passed to the EXIT condition of the loop. If the EXIT condition evaluates to FALSE, control is passed to the top of the loop. The sequence of statements will be executed repeatedly until the EXIT condition evaluates to TRUE. When the EXIT condition evaluates to TRUE, the loop is terminated, and control is passed to the next executable statement following the loop.

Figure 7.2 also shows that the EXIT condition is included in the body of the loop. Therefore, the decision about loop termination is made inside the body of the loop. *As a result, the body of the loop or a part of it will always be executed at least once. However, the number of iterations of the loop depends on the evaluation of the EXIT condition and is not known until the loop completes.*

As mentioned earlier, Figure 7.2 illustrates that the flow of logic for the structure of EXIT and EXIT WHEN statements is the same even though two different forms of EXIT condition are used. In other words,

```
IF CONDITION
THEN
    EXIT;
END IF;
```

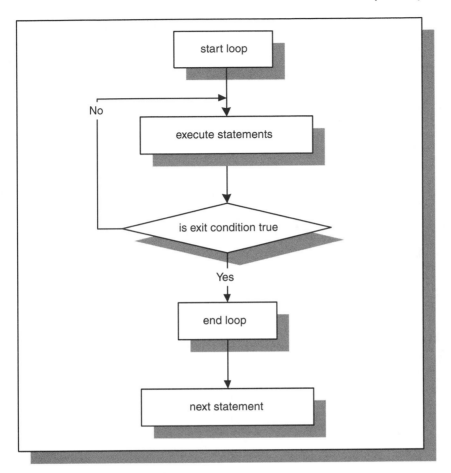

Figure 7.2 ■ Simple loop with the EXIT condition.

is equivalent to

```
EXIT WHEN CONDITION;
```

It is important to note that when the EXIT statement is used without an EXIT condition, the simple loop will execute only once. Consider the following example.

```
DECLARE
   v_counter NUMBER := 0;
BEGIN
   LOOP
      DBMS_OUTPUT.PUT_LINE('v_counter ' =
         ||v_counter);
```

```
        EXIT;
    END LOOP;
END;
This example produces the output:
v_counter = 0
PL/SQL procedure successfully completed.
```

Because the EXIT statement is used without an EXIT CONDITION, the loop is terminated as soon as the EXIT statement is executed.

LAB 7.1 EXERCISES

7.1.1 USING SIMPLE LOOPS WITH EXIT CONDITIONS

In this exercise, you will use the EXIT condition to terminate a simple loop, and a special variable, v_counter, that keeps count of the loop iterations. With each iteration of the loop, the value of v_counter will be incremented and displayed on the screen.

Create the following PL/SQL script:

```
-- ch07_1a.sql, version 1.0
SET SERVEROUTPUT ON
DECLARE
    v_counter BINARY_INTEGER := 0;
BEGIN
    LOOP
        -- increment loop counter by one
        v_counter := v_counter + 1;
        DBMS_OUTPUT.PUT_LINE('v_counter = '||v_counter);
        -- if EXIT condition yields TRUE exit the loop
        IF v_counter = 5
        THEN
            EXIT;
        END IF;
    END LOOP;
    -- control resumes here
    DBMS_OUTPUT.PUT_LINE('Done...');
END;
```

Statement v_counter := v_counter + 1 *is used often when working with a loop. Variable* v_counter *is a loop counter that tracks the number of times the statements in the body of the loop are exe-*

cuted. You will notice that for each iteration of the loop, its value is incremented by 1. However, it is very important to initialize the variable
v_counter *for successful termination of the loop. If* v_counter *is
not initialized, its value is NULL. Then, the statement* v_counter
:= v_counter + 1 *will never increment the value of* v_counter
*by one because NULL + 1 evaluates to NULL. As result, the EXIT condi-
tion will never yield TRUE, and the loop becomes infinite.*

Execute the script, then answer the following questions.

a) What output was printed on the screen?

_____

_____

b) How many times was the loop executed?

_____

_____

c) What is the EXIT condition for this loop?

_____

_____

d) How many times will the value of the variable v_counter be displayed if the DBMS_OUTPUT.PUT_LINE statement is used after the
END IF statement?

_____

_____

e) Why does the number of times the loop counter value is displayed on the screen differ when the DBMS_OUTPUT.PUT_LINE
statement is placed after the END IF statement?

_____

_____

**LAB
7.1**

f) Rewrite this script using the EXIT WHEN condition instead of the EXIT condition, so that it produces the same result.

7.1.2 USING SIMPLE LOOPS WITH *EXIT WHEN* CONDITIONS

In this exercise, you will use the EXIT WHEN condition to terminate the loop. You will add a number of sections for a given course number. Try to answer the questions *before* you run the script. Once you have answered the questions, run the script and check your answers.

Create the following PL/SQL script:

```
-- ch07_2a.sql, version 1.0
SET SERVEROUTPUT ON
DECLARE
   v_course course.course_no%type := 430;
   v_instructor_id instructor.instructor_id%type := 102;
   v_sec_num section.section_no%type := 0;
BEGIN
   LOOP
      -- increment section number by one
      v_sec_num := v_sec_num + 1;
      INSERT INTO section
         (section_id, course_no, section_no,
          instructor_id, created_date, created_by,
          modified_date, modified_by)
      VALUES
         (section_id_seq.nextval, v_course, v_sec_num,
          v_instructor_id, SYSDATE, USER, SYSDATE,
          USER);
      -- if number of sections added is four exit the
      --    loop
      EXIT WHEN v_sec_num = 4;
   END LOOP;
      -- control resumes here
   COMMIT;
EXCEPTION
   WHEN OTHERS
   THEN
```

```
          DBMS_OUTPUT.PUT_LINE('An error has occurred');
END;
```

Notice that the INSERT statement contains an Oracle built-in function called USER. At first glance, this function looks like a variable that has not been declared. This function returns the name of the current user. In other words, it will return the login name that you use when connecting to Oracle.

Try to answer the following questions first, and then execute the script:

a) How many sections will be added for the specified course number?

_____

_____

b) How many times will the loop be executed if the course number is not valid?

_____

_____

c) How would you change this script to add 10 sections for the specified course number?

_____

_____

d) How would you change the script to add only even-numbered sections (maximum section number is 10) for the specified course number?

_____

_____

e) How many times will the loop be executed in this case?

_____

_____

LAB 7.1 EXERCISE ANSWERS

7.1.1 ANSWERS

a) What output was printed on the screen?

Answer: Your output should look like the following:

```
v_counter = 1
v_counter = 2
v_counter = 3
v_counter = 4
v_counter = 5
Done...
PL/SQL procedure successfully completed.
```

Every time the loop is run, the statements in the body of the loop are executed. In this script, the value of v_counter is incremented by 1 and displayed on the screen. EXIT condition is evaluated for each value of v_counter. Once the value of v_counter increases to 5, the loop is terminated. So, for the first iteration of the loop, the value of v_counter is equal to 1, and it is displayed on the screen, and so forth. After the loop has terminated, "Done . . ." is displayed on the screen.

b) How many times was the loop executed?

Answer: The loop was executed five times.

Once the value of v_counter increases to 5, IF statement

```
IF v_counter = 5
THEN
   EXIT;
END IF;
```

evaluates to TRUE, and the loop is terminated.

The loop counter tracks the number of times the loop is executed. You will notice that in this exercise, the maximum value of v_counter is equal to the number of times the loop is iterated.

c) What is the EXIT condition for this loop?

*Answer: The EXIT condition for this loop is **v_counter = 5**.*

The EXIT condition is used as a part of an IF statement. IF statement evaluates the EXIT condition to TRUE or FALSE based on the current value of v_counter.

d) How many times will the value of the variable v_counter be displayed if the DBMS_OUTPUT.PUT_LINE statement is used after the END IF statement?

Answer: The value of v_counter *will be displayed four times.*

```
LOOP
   v_counter := v_counter + 1;
   IF v_counter = 5
   THEN
      EXIT;
   END IF;
   DBMS_OUTPUT.PUT_LINE('v_counter = '||v_counter);
END LOOP;
```

Assume that the loop has iterated four times already. Then the value of v_counter is incremented by 1, so v_counter is equal to 5. Next, the IF statement evaluates the EXIT condition. The EXIT condition yields TRUE, and the loop is terminated. The DBMS_OUTPUT.PUT_LINE statement is not executed for the fifth iteration of the loop because control is passed to the next executable statement after the END LOOP statement. So, only four values of v_counter are displayed on the screen.

e) Why does the number of times the loop counter value is displayed on the screen differ when the DBMS_OUTPUT.PUT_LINE statement is placed after the END IF statement?

Answer: When the DBMS_OUTPUT.PUT_LINE statement is placed before the IF statement, the value of v_counter *is displayed on the screen first. Then it is evaluated by the IF statement. So, for the fifth iteration of the loop "*v_counter = 5*" is displayed first, then the EXIT condition yields TRUE and the loop is terminated.*

When the DBMS_OUTPUT.PUT_LINE statement is placed after the END IF statement, the EXIT condition is evaluated prior to the execution of the DBMS_OUTPUT.PUT_LINE statement. So, for the fifth iteration of the loop, the EXIT condition evaluates to TRUE before the value of v_counter *is displayed on the screen by the DBMS_OUTPUT.PUT_LINE statement.*

f) Rewrite this script using the EXIT WHEN condition instead of the EXIT condition, so that it produces the same result.

Answer: This answer contains only portion of the code that helps to illustrate the changes.

```
-- ch07_1b.sql, version 2.0
SET SERVEROUTPUT ON
...
LOOP

   ...
   DBMS_OUTPUT.PUT_LINE('v_counter = '||v_counter);
   -- if EXIT WHEN condition yields TRUE exit the
loop
   EXIT WHEN v_counter = 5;
END LOOP;
...
```

You have probably noticed that only the IF statement has been replaced by the EXIT WHEN statement. The rest of the statements in the body of the loop do not need to be changed.

7.1.2 ANSWERS

a) How many sections will be added for the specified course number?

Answer: Four sections were added for the given course number.

b) How many times will the loop be executed if the course number is not valid?

Answer: The loop will be executed one time.

If the course number is not valid, INSERT statement

```
INSERT INTO section
   (section_id, course_no, section_no, instructor_id,
    created_date, created_by, modified_date,
    modified_by)
VALUES
   (section_id_seq.nextval, v_course, v_sec_num,
    v_instructor_id, SYSDATE, USER, SYSDATE, USER);
```

will cause an exception to be raised. As soon as an exception is raised, the control is passed out of the loop to the exception handler. Therefore, if the course number is not valid, the loop will be executed only once.

c) How would you change this script to add 10 sections for the specified course number?

Answer: This answer contains only portion of the code that helps to illustrate the changes.

```
-- ch07_2b.sql, version 2.0
SET SERVEROUTPUT ON
...
LOOP
   ...
   -- if number of sections added is ten exit the
loop
   EXIT WHEN v_sec_num = 10;
END LOOP;
...
```

In order to add 10 sections for the given course number, the test value of v_sec_num in the EXIT condition is changed to 10.

d) How would you change the script to add only even-numbered sections (maximum section number is 10) for the specified course number?

Answer: This answer contains only portion of the code that helps to illustrate the changes.

With each iteration of the loop, the value of v_sec_num *should be incremented by two as shown:*

```
-- ch07_2c.sql, version 3.0
SET SERVEROUTPUT ON
LOOP
     -- increment section number by two
     v_sec_num := v_sec_num + 2;
     ...
END LOOP;
...
```

e) How many times will the loop be executed in this case?

Answer: The loop is executed five times when even-numbered sections are added for the given course number.

LAB 7.1 SELF-REVIEW QUESTIONS

In order to test your progress, you should be able to answer the following questions.

1) How many times is simple loop executed if there is no EXIT condition specified?

   a) _____The loop does not execute at all.

   b) _____The loop executes once.

   c) _____The loop executes infinite number of times.

2) How many times is simple loop executed if the EXIT statement is used without an EXIT condition?
   a) _____The loop does not execute at all.
   b) _____The loop executes once.
   c) _____The loop executes infinite number of times.

3) What value must the EXIT condition evaluate to in order for the loop to terminate?
   a) _____TRUE
   b) _____FALSE
   c) _____NULL

4) What statement must be executed before control can be passed from the body of the loop to the first executable statement outside the loop?
   a) _____LOOP statement
   b) _____END LOOP statement
   c) _____EXIT statement
   d) _____RETURN statement

5) A simple loop will execute a minimum of which of the following?
   a) _____Zero times
   b) _____One time
   c) _____Infinite number of times

Quiz answers appear in Appendix A, Section 7.1.

L A B   7 . 2

WHILE LOOPS

```
┌─────────────────────────────────────────────────┐
│              LAB OBJECTIVES                        │
│                                                   │
│  After this Lab, you will be able to:             │
│                                                   │
│  ✔ Use WHILE Loops                                │
└─────────────────────────────────────────────────┘
```

A WHILE loop has the following structure:

```
WHILE CONDITION
LOOP
    STATEMENT 1;
    STATEMENT 2;
    ...
    STATEMENT N;
END LOOP;
```

The reserved word WHILE marks the beginning of a loop construct. The word *CONDITION* is the *test condition* of the loop that evaluates to TRUE or FALSE. The result of this evaluation determines whether the loop is executed. Statements 1 through N are a sequence of statements that is executed repeatedly. The END LOOP is a reserved phrase that indicates the end of the loop construct.

This flow of the logic is illustrated in the Figure 7.3.

Figure 7.3 shows that the test condition is evaluated prior to each iteration of the loop. If the test condition evaluates to TRUE, the sequence of statements is executed, and the control is passed to the top of the loop for the next evaluation of the test condition. If the test condition evaluates to FALSE, the loop is terminated, and the control is passed to the next executable statement following the loop.

As mentioned earlier, before the body of the loop can be executed, the test condition must be evaluated. Therefore, *the decision whether to execute*

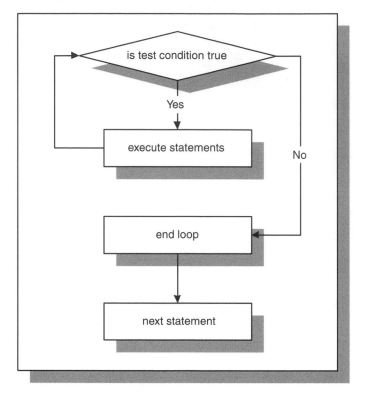

Figure 7.3 ■ WHILE loop.

the statements in the body of the loop is made prior to entering the loop. As a result, the loop will not be executed at all, if the test condition yields FALSE.

■ FOR EXAMPLE

```
DECLARE
    v_counter NUMBER := 5;
BEGIN
    WHILE v_counter < 5
    LOOP
        DBMS_OUTPUT.PUT_LINE('v_counter = '||v_counter);
        -- decrement the value of v_counter by one
        v_counter := v_counter - 1;
    END LOOP;
END;
```

In this example, the body of the loop is not executed at all because the test condition of the loop evaluates to FALSE.

While the test condition of the loop must evaluate to TRUE at least once for the statements in the loop to execute, it is important to insure that the test condition will eventually evaluate to FALSE as well. Otherwise, the WHILE loop will execute continually.

■ FOR EXAMPLE

```
DECLARE
   v_counter NUMBER := 1;
BEGIN
   WHILE v_counter < 5
   LOOP
      DBMS_OUTPUT.PUT_LINE('v_counter = '||v_counter);
      -- decrement the value of v_counter by one
      v_counter := v_counter - 1;
   END LOOP;
END;
```

This is an example of the infinite WHILE loop. The test condition always evaluates to TRUE because the value of `v_counter` is decremented by 1 and is always less than 5.

It is important to note that Boolean expressions can be used to determine when the loop should terminate as well.

```
DECLARE
   v_test BOOLEAN := TRUE;
BEGIN
   WHILE v_test
   LOOP
      STATEMENTS;
      IF TEST_CONDITION
      THEN
         v_test := FALSE;
      END IF;
   END LOOP;
END;
```

When using a Boolean expression as a test condition of a loop, you must make sure that a different value is eventually assigned to the Boolean variable in order to exit the loop. Otherwise, the loop will become infinite.

PREMATURE TERMINATION OF THE LOOP

The EXIT and EXIT WHEN statements can be used inside the body of a WHILE loop. If the EXIT condition evaluates to TRUE before the test condition evaluates to FALSE, the loop is terminated prematurely. If the test condition yields FALSE before the EXIT condition yields TRUE, there is no premature termination of the loop. This is indicated as follows:

```
WHILE TEST_CONDITION
LOOP
    STATEMENT 1;
    STATEMENT 2;
    IF EXIT_CONDITION
    THEN
        EXIT;
    END IF;
END LOOP;
STATEMENT 3;
```

or

```
WHILE TEST_CONDITION
LOOP
    STATEMENT 1;
    STATEMENT 2;
    EXIT WHEN EXIT_CONDITION;
END LOOP;
STATEMENT 3;
```

Consider the following example.

■ *FOR EXAMPLE*

```
DECLARE
    v_counter NUMBER := 1;
BEGIN
    WHILE v_counter <= 5
    LOOP
        DBMS_OUTPUT.PUT_LINE('v_counter = '||v_counter);
        IF v_counter = 2
        THEN
            EXIT;
        END IF;
        v_counter := v_counter + 1;
    END LOOP;
END;
```

Before the statements in the body of the WHILE loop are executed, the test condition

`v_counter <= 5`

must evaluate to TRUE. Then, the value of `v_counter` is displayed on the screen and incremented by one. Next, the EXIT condition

`v_counter = 2`

is evaluated, and as soon as the value of `v_counter` reaches 2, the loop is terminated.

Notice, according to the test condition, the loop should execute five times. However, the loop is executed only twice because the EXIT condition is present inside the body of the loop. So, the loop terminates prematurely.

Now, you'll try to reverse the test condition and EXIT condition.

■ FOR EXAMPLE

```
DECLARE
    v_counter NUMBER := 1;
BEGIN
    WHILE v_counter <= 2
    LOOP
        DBMS_OUTPUT.PUT_LINE('v_counter = '||v_counter);
        v_counter := v_counter + 1;
        IF v_counter = 5
        THEN
            EXIT;
        END IF;
    END LOOP;
END;
```

In this example, the test condition is

`v_counter <= 2`

and the EXIT condition is

`v_counter = 5`

So, in this case, the loop is executed twice as well. However, it does not terminate prematurely because the EXIT condition never evaluates to

TRUE. As soon as the value of v_counter reaches 3, the test condition evaluates to FALSE, and the loop is terminated.

Both examples, when run, produce the following output:

```
v_counter = 1
v_counter = 2
PL/SQL procedure successfully completed.
```

These examples demonstrate not only the use of the EXIT statement inside the body of the WHILE loop, but also a bad programming practice. In the first example, the test condition can be changed so that there is no need to use an EXIT condition, because essentially they both are used to terminate the loop. In the second example, the EXIT condition is useless because its terminal value is never reached. *THEREFORE, YOU SHOULD NEVER USE UNNECESSARY CODE IN YOUR PROGRAM.*

L<small>AB</small> 7.2 E<small>XERCISES</small>

7.2.1 U<small>SING</small> WHILE <small>LOOPS</small>

In this exercise, you will use a WHILE loop to calculate the sum of the integers between 1 and 10.

Create the following PL/SQL script:

```
-- ch07_3a.sql, version 1.0
SET SERVEROUTPUT ON
DECLARE
    v_counter BINARY_INTEGER := 1;
    v_sum NUMBER := 0;
BEGIN
    WHILE v_counter <= 10
    LOOP
        v_sum := v_sum + v_counter;
        DBMS_OUTPUT.PUT_LINE('Current sum is: '||v_sum);
        -- increment loop counter by one
        v_counter := v_counter + 1;
    END LOOP;
    -- control resumes here
    DBMS_OUTPUT.PUT_LINE
        ('The sum of integers between 1 and 10 is: '||
        v_sum);
END;
```

Execute the script, then answer the following questions:

a) What output was printed on the screen?

_____

_____

b) What is the test condition for this loop?

_____

_____

c) How many times was the loop executed?

_____

_____

d) How many times will the loop be executed:

　　if v_counter is not initialized?

　　if v_counter is initialized to 0?

　　if v_counter is initialized to 10?

_____

_____

e) How will the value of v_sum change based on the initial value of v_counter from the previous question?

_____

_____

f) What will be the value of v_sum if it is not initialized?

_____

_____

g) How would you change the script to calculate the sum of even integers between 1 and 100?

LAB 7.2 EXERCISE ANSWERS

7.2.1 ANSWERS

a) What output was printed on the screen?

Answer: Your output should look like the following:

```
Current sum is: 1
Current sum is: 3
Current sum is: 6
Current sum is: 10
Current sum is: 15
Current sum is: 21
Current sum is: 28
Current sum is: 36
Current sum is: 45
Current sum is: 55
The sum of integers between 1 and 10 is: 55
PL/SQL procedure successfully completed.
```

Every time the loop is run, the value of v_counter is checked in the test condition. While the value of v_counter is less than or equal to 10, the statements inside the body of the loop are executed. In this script, the value of v_sum is calculated and displayed on the screen. Next, the value of v_counter is incremented, and control is passed to the top of the loop. Once the value of v_counter increases to 11, the loop is terminated.

So, for the first iteration of the loop, the value of v_sum is equal to one according to the statement

```
v_sum := v_sum + v_counter
```

After the value of v_sum is calculated, the value of v_counter is incremented by 1. Then, for the second iteration of the loop, the value of v_sum is equal to 3 because 2 is added to the old value of v_sum.

After the loop has terminated, "The sum of integers . . ." and "Done . . ." are displayed on the screen.

b) What is the test condition for this loop?

Answer: *The test condition for this loop is* **v_counter <= 10.**

c) How many times was the loop executed?

Answer: *The loop was executed ten times.*

Once the value of v_counter reaches 10, the test condition

    v_counter <= 10

evaluates to FALSE, and the loop is terminated.

As mentioned earlier, the loop counter tracks the number of times the loop is executed. You will notice that in this exercise, the maximum value of v_counter is equal to the number of times the loop is iterated.

d) How many times will the loop be executed:
   i if v_counter is not initialized?
   ii if v_counter is initialized to 0?
   iii if v_counter is initialized to 10?

Answer: *If the value of* v_counter *is not initialized to some value, the loop will not execute at all.*

In order for the loop to execute at least once, the test condition must evaluate to TRUE at least once. If the value of v_counter is only declared and not initialized, it is NULL. *IT IS IMPORTANT TO REMEMBER THAT NULL VARIABLES CANNOT BE COMPARED TO OTHER VARIABLES OR VALUES*. Therefore, the test condition

    v_counter <= 10

never evaluates to TRUE, and the loop is not executed at all.

If v_counter *is initialized to 0, the loop will execute eleven times instead of ten since the minimum value of* v_counter *has decreased by 1.*

When v_counter is initialized to 0, the range of integers for which test condition of the loop evaluates TRUE becomes 0 to 10. The given range of the integers has 11 numbers in it. As a result, the loop will iterate eleven times.

If v_counter *is initialized to 10, the loop will execute once.*

When the initial value of v_counter is equal to 10, the test condition evaluates to TRUE for the first iteration of the loop. Inside the body of the loop, the value of v_counter is incremented by one. As a result, for the second iteration of the loop, the test condition evaluates to FALSE since 11 is not less or equal to 10, and control is passed to the next executable statement after the loop.

e) How will the value of v_sum change based on the initial value of v_counter from the previous question?

Answer: When v_counter *is not initialized, the loop is not executed at all. Therefore, the value of* v_sum *does not change from its initial value, it stays 0.*

When v_counter *is initialized to 0, the loop is executed eleven times. The value of* v_sum *is calculated eleven times as well. However, after the loop completes, the value of* v_sum *is 55 because 0 is added to* v_sum *during first iteration of the loop.*

When v_counter *is initialized to 10, the loop is executed once. As a result, the value of* v_sum *is incremented only once by 10. So, after the loop is complete, the value of* v_sum *is equal to 10.*

f) What will be the value of v_sum if it is not initialized?

Answer: The value of v_sum *will be NULL if is not initialized to some value.*

The value of v_sum in the statement

```
v_sum := v_sum + 1
```

will always be equal to NULL because NULL + 1 is NULL. It was mentioned earlier that NULL variables cannot be compared to other variable or values. *SIMILARLY, CALCULATIONS CANNOT BE PERFORMED ON NULL VARIABLES.*

g) How would you change the script to calculate the sum of even integers between 1 and 100?

Answer: This answer contains only portion of the code that helps to illustrate the changes.

Notice that the value of v_counter *is initialized to 2, and with each iteration of the loop, the value of* v_counter *is incremented by 2 as well.*

```
-- ch07_3b.sql, version 2.0
SET SERVEROUTPUT ON
DECLARE
    v_counter   BINARY_INTEGER := 2;
...
    WHILE v_counter <= 10 LOOP
    ...
```

```
   -- increment loop counter by two
   v_counter := v_counter + 2;
END LOOP;
...
```

LAB 7.2 SELF-REVIEW QUESTIONS

In order to test your progress, you should be able to answer the following questions.

1) How many times is WHILE loop executed if the test condition always evaluates to FALSE?
   a) _____The loop does not execute at all.
   b) _____The loop executes once.
   c) _____The loop executes an infinite number of times.

2) How many times is WHILE loop executed if the test condition always evaluates to TRUE?
   a) _____The loop does not execute at all.
   b) _____The loop executes once.
   c) _____The loop executes an infinite number of times.

3) What value must the test condition evaluate to in order for the loop to terminate?
   a) _____TRUE
   b) _____FALSE
   c) _____NULL

4) What causes a WHILE loop to terminate prematurely?
   a) _____ EXIT condition evaluates to TRUE before test condition evaluates to FALSE.
   b) _____The test condition evaluates to FALSE before EXIT condition evaluates to TRUE.
   c) _____Both test and EXIT conditions evaluate to FALSE.

5) A WHILE loop will execute a minimum of
   a) _____zero times.
   b) _____one time.
   c) _____infinite number of times.

Quiz answers appear in Appendix A, Section 7.2.

L A B   7 . 3

NUMERIC FOR LOOPS

**LAB
7.3**

LAB OBJECTIVES

After this lab, you will be able to:

✔ Use Numeric FOR Loops with the IN Option
✔ Use Numeric FOR Loops with the REVERSE Option

A numeric FOR loop is called numeric because it requires an integer as its terminating value. Its structure is as follows:

```
FOR loop_counter IN[REVERSE] lower_limit..upper_limit
LOOP
    STATEMENT 1;
    STATEMENT 2;
    ...
    STATEMENT N;
END LOOP;
```

The reserved word FOR marks the beginning of a loop construct. The variable, `loop_counter`, is an implicitly defined index variable. So, there is no need to define loop counter in the declaration section of the PL/SQL block. This variable is defined by the loop construct. *Lower_limit* and *upper_limit* are two integer numbers that define the number of iterations for the loop. The values of the `lower_limit` and `upper_limit` are evaluated once, for the first iteration of the loop. At this point, it is determined how many times the loop will iterate. Statements 1 through N are a sequence of statements that is executed repeatedly. END LOOP is a reserved phrase that marks the end of the loop construct.

The reserved word IN or IN REVERSE must be present when defining the loop. If the REVERSE keyword is used, the loop counter will iterate from upper limit to lower limit. However, the syntax for the limit specification does not change. The lower limit is always referenced first. The flow of this logic is illustrated in the Figure 7.4.

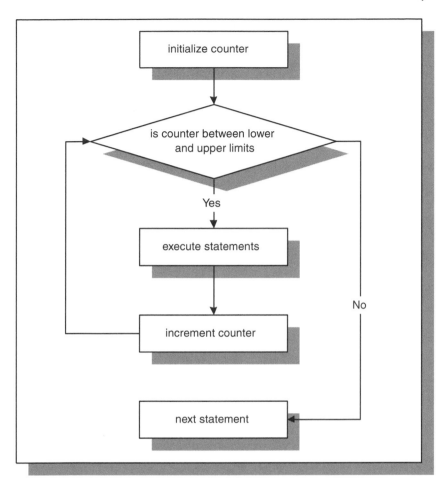

Figure 7.4 ■ Numeric FOR loop.

Figure 7.4 shows that the loop counter is initialized to the lower limit for the first iteration of the loop only. However, the value of the loop counter is tested for each iteration of the loop. As long as the value of v_counter ranges from the lower limit to the upper limit, the statements inside the body of the loop are executed. When the value of the loop counter does not satisfy the range specified by the lower limit and the upper, control is passed to the first executable statement outside the loop.

■ FOR EXAMPLE

```
BEGIN
   FOR v_counter IN 1..5
   LOOP
     DBMS_OUTPUT.PUT_LINE('v_counter = '||v_counter);
   END LOOP;
END;
```

In this example, there is no declaration section for this PL/SQL block because the only variable used, v_counter, is the loop counter. Numbers 1..5 specify the range of the integer numbers for which this loop is executed.

Notice that there is no statement

v_counter := v_counter + 1

anywhere, inside or outside the body of the loop. The value of v_counter is incremented implicitly by the FOR loop itself.

This example produces the following output when run:

```
v_counter = 1
v_counter = 2
v_counter = 3
v_counter = 4
v_counter = 5
PL/SQL procedure successfully completed.
```

As a matter of fact, if you include the statement

v_counter := v_counter + 1

in the body of the loop, PL/SQL script will compile with errors. Consider the following example

■ FOR EXAMPLE

```
BEGIN
    FOR v_counter IN 1..5
    LOOP
        v_counter := v_counter + 1;
        DBMS_OUTPUT.PUT_LINE('v_counter = '|| v_counter);
    END LOOP;
END;
```

When this example is run, the following error message is produced:

```
BEGIN
*
ERROR at line 1:
ORA-06550: line 3, column 7:
PLS-00363: expression 'V_COUNTER' cannot be used as
```

```
an assignment target
ORA-06550: line 3, column 7:
PL/SQL: Statement ignored
```

 It is important to remember the loop counter is implicitly defined and incremented when numeric FOR loop is used. As a result, it cannot be referenced outside the body of the FOR loop. Consider the following example:

```
BEGIN
   FOR v_counter IN 1..5
   LOOP
      DBMS_OUTPUT.PUT_LINE('v_counter = '||v_counter);
   END LOOP;
   DBMS_OUTPUT.PUT_LINE
      ('Counter outside the loop is '||v_counter);
END;
```

When this example is run, the following error message is produced:

```
DBMS_OUTPUT.PUT_LINE ('Counter outside the loop is
'|| v_counter);
                        *
ERROR at line 6:
ORA-06550: line 6, column 53:
PLS-00201: identifier 'V_COUNTER' must be declared
ORA-06550: line 6, column 4:
PL/SQL: Statement ignored
```

Because the loop counter is declared implicitly by the loop, the variable v_counter *cannot be referenced outside the loop. As soon as the loop completes, the loop counter ceases to exist.*

USING THE **REVERSE** OPTION IN THE LOOP

Earlier in this section, you encountered two options that are available when the value of the loop counter is evaluated, IN and IN REVERSE. You have seen examples already that demonstrate the usage of the IN option for the loop. The next example demonstrates the usage of IN REVERSE option for the loop.

■ *FOR EXAMPLE*

```
BEGIN
   FOR v_counter IN REVERSE 1..5
```

```
LOOP
    DBMS_OUTPUT.PUT_LINE('v_counter = '||v_counter);
END LOOP;
END;
```

When this example is run, the following output is produced:

```
v_counter = 5
v_counter = 4
v_counter = 3
v_counter = 2
v_counter = 1
PL/SQL procedure successfully completed.
```

As mentioned before, even though the REVERSE keyword is present, the lower limit of the loop is referenced first. However, it is important to note that the loop counter is evaluated from the upper limit to the lower limit. For the first iteration of the loop, v_counter (in our case it is loop counter) is initialized to 5 (upper limit). Then, its value is displayed on the screen. For the second iteration of the loop, the value of v_counter is *decreased* by 1, and displayed on the screen.

Notice that the number of times the body of the loop is executed is not affected by the option used, IN or IN REVERSE. Only the values assigned to the lower limit and the upper limit determine how many times the body of the loop is executed.

PREMATURE TERMINATION OF THE LOOP

The EXIT and EXIT WHEN statements can be used inside the body of a numeric FOR loop. If the EXIT condition evaluates to TRUE before the loop counter reaches its terminal value, the FOR loop is terminated prematurely. If the loop counter reaches its terminal value before the EXIT condition yields TRUE, there is no premature termination of the FOR loop. Consider the following:

```
FOR LOOP_COUNTER IN LOWER_LIMIT..UPPER_LIMIT
LOOP
    STATEMENT 1;
    STATEMENT 2;
    IF EXIT_CONDITION
    THEN
        EXIT;
    END IF;
```

```
    END LOOP;
    STATEMENT 3;
```

or

```
    FOR LOOP_COUNTER IN LOWER_LIMIT..UPPER_LIMIT
    LOOP
        STATEMENT 1;
        STATEMENT 2;
        EXIT WHEN EXIT_CONDITION;
    END LOOP;
    STATEMENT 3;
```

Consider the following example of the FOR loop that uses EXIT WHEN condition. This condition is causing the loop to terminate prematurely.

■ FOR EXAMPLE

```
    BEGIN
        FOR v_counter IN 1..5
        LOOP
            DBMS_OUTPUT.PUT_LINE('v_counter = '||v_counter);
            EXIT WHEN v_counter = 3;
        END LOOP;
    END;
```

Notice that according to the range specified, the loop should execute five times. However, the loop is executed only three times because the EXIT condition is present inside the body of the loop. So, the loop terminates prematurely.

LAB 7.3 EXERCISES

7.3.1 USING NUMERIC FOR LOOPS WITH THE IN OPTION

In this exercise, you will use numeric FOR loop to calculate a factorial of 10 (10! = 1*2*3...*10).

Create the following PL/SQL script:

```
    -- ch07_4a.sql, version 1.0
    SET SERVEROUTPUT ON
    DECLARE
        v_factorial NUMBER := 1;
```

```
BEGIN
   FOR v_counter IN 1..10
   LOOP
      v_factorial := v_factorial * v_counter;
   END LOOP;
   -- control resumes here
   DBMS_OUTPUT.PUT_LINE
      ('Factorial of ten is: '||v_factorial);
END;
```

LAB 7.3

Execute the script, then answer the following questions:

a) What output was printed on the screen?

_____

_____

b) How many times was the loop executed?

_____

_____

c) What is the value of the loop counter before the loop?

_____

_____

d) What is the value of the loop counter after the loop?

_____

_____

e) How many times will the loop be executed if the value of v_counter is incremented by 5 inside the body of the loop?

_____

_____

f) Rewrite this script using the REVERSE option. What will the value of `v_factorial` be after the loop is completed?

_____

_____

7.3.2 USING NUMERIC *FOR* LOOPS WITH THE *REVERSE* OPTION

In this exercise, you will use the REVERSE option to specify the range of numbers used by the loop to iterate. You will display a list of even numbers starting from 10 going down to 0. Try to answer the questions *before* you run the script. Once you have answered the questions, run the script and check your results.

Create the following PL/SQL script:

```
-- ch07_5a.sql, version 1.0
SET SERVEROUTPUT ON
BEGIN
   FOR v_counter IN REVERSE 0..10
   LOOP
      -- if v_counter is even, display its value on
      -- screen
      IF MOD(v_counter, 2) = 0
      THEN
         DBMS_OUTPUT.PUT_LINE
            ('v_counter = '||v_counter);
      END IF;
   END LOOP;
   -- control resumes here
   DBMS_OUTPUT.PUT_LINE('Done...');
END;
```

As in the previous exercises, answer the following questions first, and then execute the script:

a) What output will be printed on the screen?

_____

_____

b) How many times will the body of the loop be executed?

_____

_____

c) How many times will the value of `v_counter` be displayed on the screen?

_____

_____

d) How would you change this script to start the list from 0 and go up to 10?

_____

_____

e) How would you change the script to display only odd numbers on the screen?

_____

_____

f) How many times will the loop be executed in this case?

_____

_____

LAB 7.3 EXERCISE ANSWERS

7.3.1 ANSWERS

a)   What output was printed on the screen?

Answer: Your output should look like the following:

```
Factorial of ten is :3628800
Done...
PL/SQL procedure successfully completed.
```

Every time the loop is run, the value of v_counter is incremented by one implicitly, and the current value of the factorial is calculated. Once the value of v_counter increases to 10, the loop is run for the last time. At this point, the final value of the factorial is calculated, and the loop is terminated. After the loop has terminated, control is passed to the first statement outside the loop—in this case, DBMS_OUTPUT.PUT_LINE.

b) How many times was the loop executed?

Answer: The loop was executed ten times according to the range specified by the lower limit and the upper limit of the loop. In this example, lower limit is equal to 1, and upper limit is equal to 10.

c) What is the value of the loop counter before the loop?

Answer: The loop counter is defined by the loop implicitly. Therefore, before the loop, the loop counter is undefined and has no value.

d) What is the value of the loop counter after the loop?

Answer: Similarly, after the loop completed, the loop counter is undefined again and can hold no value.

e) How many times will the loop be executed if the value of v_counter is incremented by 5 inside the body of the loop?

Answer: If the value of v_counter is incremented by 5 inside the body of the loop, the PL/SQL block will not compile successfully. As a result, it will not execute at all.

In this example, variable v_counter is a loop counter. Therefore, its value can be incremented only by the loop implicitly. Any executable statement that causes v_counter to change its current value leads to compilation errors.

f) Rewrite this script using the REVERSE option. What will the value of v_factorial be after the loop is completed?

Answer: This answer contains only portion of the code that helps to illustrate the changes.

The value of v_factorial will be equal to 3628800 after the loop is completed.

```
-- ch07_4b.sql, version 2.0
SET SERVEROUTPUT ON
...
FOR v_counter IN REVERSE 1..10
LOOP
   ...
```

LAB
7.3

```
END LOOP;
...
```

The script above produces the following output:

```
Factorial of ten is :3628800
Done...
PL/SQL procedure successfully completed.
```

The value of v_factorial computed by this loop is equal to the value of v_factorial computed by the original loop. You will notice that in some cases it does not matter which option, IN or REVERSE, you are using to obtain the final result. You will also notice that in other cases, the result produced by the loop can differ significantly.

7.3.2 ANSWERS

a) What output will be printed on the screen?

Answer: Your output should look like the following:

```
v_counter = 10
v_counter = 8
v_counter = 6
v_counter = 4
v_counter = 2
v_counter = 0
Done...
PL/SQL procedure successfully completed.
```

Notice that the values of v_counter are displayed in the decreasing order from 10 to 0 because the REVERSE option is used. Remember that regardless of the option used, the lower limit is referenced first.

b) How many times will the body of the loop be executed?

Answer: The body of the loop will be executed eleven times since the range of the integer numbers specified varies from 1 to 10.

c) How many times will the value of v_counter be displayed on the screen?

Answer: The value of v_counter will be displayed on the screen six times, since the IF statement will evaluate to TRUE only for even integers.

d) How would you change this script to start the list from 0 and go up to 10?

Answer: This answer contains only portion of the code that helps to illustrate the changes.

To start the list of integers from 0 and go up to 10, the IN option needs to be used in the loop.

```
-- ch07_5b.sql, version 2.0
SET SERVEROUTPUT ON
...
FOR v_counter IN 0..10 LOOP
   ...
END LOOP;
...
```

LAB
7.3

This example produces the following output:

```
v_counter = 0
v_counter = 2
v_counter = 4
v_counter = 6
v_counter = 8
v_counter = 10
Done...
PL/SQL procedure successfully completed.
```

Notice that when the IN option is used, the value of v_counter is initialized to 0, and, with each iteration of the loop, it is incremented by 1. When the REVERSE option is used, v_counter is initialized to 10, and its value is decremented by 1 with each iteration of the loop.

e) How would you change the script to display only odd numbers on the screen?

Answer: This answer contains only portion of the code that helps to illustrate the changes.

```
-- ch07_5c.sql, version: 3.0
SET SERVEROUTPUT ON
...
FOR v_counter IN REVERSE 0..10 LOOP
     -- if v_counter is even, display its value on
screen
   IF MOD(v_counter, 2) != 0
   THEN
```

```
    ...
END LOOP;
...
```

Notice that only test condition of the IF statement is changed in order to display the list of odd integers, and the following output is produced:

```
v_counter = 9
v_counter = 7
v_counter = 5
v_counter = 3
v_counter = 1
Done...
PL/SQL procedure successfully completed.
```

f)   How many times will the loop be executed in this case?

Answer: In this case loop will be executed eleven times.

Based on the test condition used in the IF statement, even or odd integers are displayed on the screen. Depending on the test condition, the number of times v_counter is displayed on the screen varies. However, the loop is executed eleven times as long as the number range specified is 0 to 10.

LAB 7.3 SELF-REVIEW QUESTIONS

In order to test your progress, you should be able to answer the following questions.

1)   How many times is numeric FOR loop executed if the value of the lower limit is equal to the value of the upper limit?
a) _____The loop does not execute at all.
b) _____The loop executes once.
c) _____The loop executes an infinite number of times.

2)   How many times is the numeric FOR loop executed if the value of the lower limit is greater than the value of the upper limit?
a) _____The loop does not execute at all.
b) _____The loop executes once.
c) _____The loop executes an infinite number of times.

3)   What is the value of the loop counter prior to entering the loop?
a) _____0
b) _____1
c) _____Undefined

4) What is the value of the loop counter after termination of the loop?
   a) _____Same as upper limit
   b) _____Same as lower limit
   c) _____Undefined

5) When the REVERSE option is used, the value of `v_counter` is initialized to which of the following?
   a) _____Lower limit
   b) _____Upper limit
   c) _____NULL

Quiz answers appear in Appendix A, Section 7.3.

L A B   7 . 4

NESTED LOOPS

LAB OBJECTIVES

After this lab, you will be able to:

✔ Use Nested Loops

You have explored three types of loops: simple loops, WHILE loops, and numeric FOR loop. Any of these three types of loops can be nested inside of another. For example, a simple loop can be nested inside a WHILE loop and vice versa. Consider the following example.

■ FOR EXAMPLE

```
DECLARE
    v_counter1 INTEGER := 0;
    v_counter2 INTEGER;
BEGIN
    WHILE v_counter1 < 3
    LOOP
        DBMS_OUTPUT.PUT_LINE('v_counter1: '||v_counter1);
        v_counter2 := 0;
        LOOP
            DBMS_OUTPUT.PUT_LINE
                ('v_counter2: '||v_counter2);
            v_counter2 := v_counter2 + 1;
            EXIT WHEN v_counter2 >= 2;
        END LOOP;
        v_counter1 := v_counter1 + 1;
    END LOOP;
END;
```

In this example, the WHILE loop is called an *outer loop* because it encompasses the simple loop. The simple loop is called an *inner loop* because it is enclosed by the body of the WHILE loop.

The outer loop is controlled by the loop counter, `v_counter1`, and it will execute providing the value of `v_counter1` is less than 3. With each iteration of the loop, the value of `v_counter1` is displayed on the screen. Next, the value of `v_counter2` is initialized to 0. It is important to note that `v_counter2` is not initialized at the time of the declaration. The simple loop is placed inside the body of the WHILE loop, and the value of `v_counter2` must be initialized every time before control is passed to the simple loop.

Once control is passed to the inner loop, the value of `v_counter2` is displayed on the screen, and incremented by 1. Next, the EXIT WHEN condition is evaluated. If the EXIT WHEN condition evaluates to FALSE, control is passed back to the top of the simple loop. If the EXIT WHEN condition evaluates to TRUE, the control is passed to the first executable statement outside the loop. In our case, control is passed back to the outer loop, and the value of `v_counter1` is incremented by 1, and the TEST condition of the WHILE loop is evaluated again.

**LAB
7.4**

This logic is demonstrated by the output produced by the example:

```
v_counter1: 0
v_counter2: 0
v_counter2: 1
v_counter1: 1
v_counter2: 0
v_counter2: 1
v_counter1: 2
v_counter2: 0
v_counter2: 1
PL/SQL procedure successfully completed.
```

Notice that for each value of `v_counter1`, there are two values of `v_counter2` displayed. For the first iteration of the outer loop, the value of `v_counter1` is equal to 0. Once control is passed to the inner loop, the value of `v_counter2` is displayed on the screen twice, and so forth.

LOOP LABELS

Earlier in the book, you read about labeling of PL/SQL blocks. Loops can be labeled in the similar manner as well, as follows:

```
<<label_name>>
FOR LOOP_COUNTER IN LOWER_LIMIT..UPPER_LIMIT
LOOP
```

```
        STATEMENT 1;
        ...
        STATEMENT N;
    END LOOP label_name;
```

The label must appear right before the beginning of the loop. This syntax example shows that the label can be optionally used at the end of the loop statement. It is very helpful to label nested loops because labels improve readability. Consider the following example.

■ *FOR EXAMPLE*

LAB
7.4

```
    BEGIN
        <<outer_loop>>
        FOR i IN 1..3
        LOOP
            DBMS_OUTPUT.PUT_LINE('i = '||i);
            <<inner_loop>>
            FOR j IN 1..2
            LOOP
                DBMS_OUTPUT.PUT_LINE('j = '||j);
            END LOOP inner_loop;
        END LOOP outer_loop;
    END;
```

For both outer and inner loops, the statement END LOOP must be used. If the loop label is added to each END LOOP statement, it becomes easier to understand which loop is being terminated.

Loop labels can also be used when referencing loop counters.

■ *FOR EXAMPLE*

```
    BEGIN
        <<outer>>
        FOR v_counter IN 1..3
        LOOP
            <<inner>>
            FOR v_counter IN 1..2
            LOOP
                DBMS_OUTPUT.PUT_LINE
                    ('outer.v_counter '||outer.v_counter);
                DBMS_OUTPUT.PUT_LINE
                    ('inner.v_counter '||inner.v_counter);
            END LOOP inner;
```

```
    END LOOP outer;
END;
```

In this example, both inner and outer loops use the same loop counter, v_counter. In order to reference both the outer and inner values of v_counter, the loop labels are used. This example produces the following output:

outer.v_counter 1
inner.v_counter 1
outer.v_counter 1
inner.v_counter 2
outer.v_counter 2
inner.v_counter 1
outer.v_counter 2
inner.v_counter 2
outer.v_counter 3
inner.v_counter 1
outer.v_counter 3
inner.v_counter 2
PL/SQL procedure successfully completed.

**LAB
7.4**

Your program is able to differentiate between two variables having the same name because loop labels are used when the variables are referenced. If no loop labels are used when v_counter is referenced, the output produced by this script will change significantly. Basically, once control is passed to the inner loop, the value of the v_counter from outer loop is unavailable. When control is passed back to the outer loop, the value of v_counter becomes available again.

In this example, the same name for two different loop counters is used to demonstrate another use of the loop labels. However, it is not considered a good programming practice. *You should avoid using the same name for different variables.*

LAB 7.4 EXERCISES

7.4.1 USING NESTED LOOPS

In this exercise, you will use nested numeric FOR loops.

Create the following PL/SQL script:

```
-- ch07_6a.sql, version 1.0
SET SERVEROUTPUT ON
DECLARE
   v_test NUMBER := 0;
BEGIN
   <<outer_loop>>
   FOR i IN 1..3
   LOOP
      DBMS_OUTPUT.PUT_LINE('Outer Loop');
      DBMS_OUTPUT.PUT_LINE('i = '||i);
      DBMS_OUTPUT.PUT_LINE('v_test = '||v_test);
      v_test := v_test + 1;
      <<inner_loop>>
      FOR j in 1..2
      LOOP
         DBMS_OUTPUT.PUT_LINE('Inner Loop');
         DBMS_OUTPUT.PUT_LINE('j = '||j);
         DBMS_OUTPUT.PUT_LINE('i = '||i);
         DBMS_OUTPUT.PUT_LINE('v_test = '||v_test);
      END LOOP inner_loop;
   END LOOP outer_loop;
END;
```

Execute the script, then answer the following questions:

a) What output was printed on the screen?

_____

_____

b) How many times was the outer loop executed?

_____

_____

c) How many times was the inner loop executed?

_____

_____

d) What are the values of the loop counters, i and j, after both loops terminate?

_____

_____

e) Rewrite this script using the REVERSE option for both loops. How many times will each loop be executed in this case?

_____

_____

LAB 7.4 EXERCISE ANSWERS

7.4.1 ANSWERS

a) What output was printed on the screen?

Answer: Your output should look like the following:

```
Outer Loop
i = 1
v_test = 0
Inner Loop
j = 1
i = 1
v_test = 1
Inner Loop
j = 2
i = 1
v_test = 1
Outer Loop
i = 2
v_test = 1
Inner Loop
j = 1
i = 2
v_test = 2
Inner Loop
j = 2
i = 2
v_test = 2
```

```
Outer Loop
i = 3
v_test = 2
Inner Loop
j = 1
i = 3
v_test = 3
Inner Loop
j = 2
i = 3
v_test = 3
PL/SQL procedure successfully completed.
```

Every time the outer loop is run, the value of the loop counter is incremented by 1 implicitly and displayed on the screen. In addition, the value of v_test is displayed on the screen and is incremented by 1 as well. Next, control is passed to the inner loop.

Every time the inner loop is run, the value of the inner loop counter is incremented by 1 and displayed on the screen along with the value of the outer loop counter and variable v_test.

b)   How many times was the outer loop executed?

Answer: The outer loop was executed three times according to the range specified by the lower limit and the upper limit of the loop. In this example, lower limit is equal to 1, and upper limit is equal to 10.

c)   How many times was the inner loop executed?

Answer: The inner loop was executed six times.

For each iteration of the outer loop, the inner loop is executed twice. However, the outer loop is executed three times. So, overall the inner loop was executed six times.

d)   What are the values of the loop counters, i and j, after both loops terminate?

Answer: After both loops terminated, both loop counters are undefined again and can hold no values. As I have mentioned earlier, the loop counter ceases to exist once the numeric FOR loop is terminated.

e)   Rewrite this script using the REVERSE option for both loops. How many times will each loop be executed in this case?

Answer: This answer contains only portion of the code that helps to illustrate the changes.

The outer loop will execute three times, and the inner loop will execute six times.

```
-- ch07_6b.sql, version 2.0
SET SERVEROUTPUT ON
...
<<outer_loop>>
FOR i IN REVERSE 1..3
LOOP
    <<inner_loop>>
      FOR j IN REVERSE 1..2
      LOOP
          ...
      END LOOP inner_loop;
END LOOP outer_loop;
...
```

This script produces the following output:

```
Outer Loop
i = 3
v_test = 0
Inner Loop
j = 2
i = 3
v_test = 1
Inner Loop
j = 1
i = 3
v_test = 1
Outer Loop
i = 2
v_test = 1
Inner Loop
j = 2
i = 2
v_test = 2
Inner Loop
j = 1
i = 2
v_test = 2
Outer Loop
i = 1
v_test = 2
Inner Loop
j = 2
```

**LAB
7.4**

```
i = 1
v_test = 3
Inner Loop
j = 1
i = 1
v_test = 3
PL/SQL procedure successfully completed.
```

Notice that the output produced by this example has changed significantly. The values of the loop counters are decremented because the REVERSE option is used. However, the value of the variable v_test was not affected by using the REVERSE option.

LAB 7.4 SELF-REVIEW QUESTIONS

In order to test your progress, you should be able to answer the following questions.

1) What types of PL/SQL loop can be nested one inside another?
   a) _____A simple loop can only be nested inside WHILE loop.
   b) _____A WHILE loop can only be nested inside simple loop.
   c) _____Any loop can be nested inside another loop.

2) When nested loops are used, you must use loop labels.
   a) _____True
   b) _____False

3) When a loop label is defined, you must use it with an END LOOP statement.
   a) _____True
   b) _____False

4) When nested loops are used, it is recommended that you use the same name for the loop counters.
   a) _____True
   b) _____False

5) If the loop label is defined, you must use it when the loop counter is referenced.
   a) _____True
   b) _____False

Quiz answers appear in Appendix A, Section 7.4.

CHAPTER 7

TEST YOUR THINKING

In this chapter you have learned about simple loops, WHILE loops, and numeric FOR loops. You also learned that all these loops can be nested one inside another. Here are some projects that will help you test the depth of your understanding.

1) Rewrite the script `ch07_1a.sql` using WHILE loop instead of the simple loop. Make sure that the output produced by this script does not differ from the output produced by the script `ch07_1a.sql`.

2) Rewrite the script `ch07_4a.sql` using a simple loop instead of the numeric FOR loop. Make sure that the output produced by this script does not differ from the output produced by the script `ch07_4a.sql`.

3) Rewrite the script `ch07_6a.sql`. A simple loop should be used as the outer loop, and a WHILE loop should be used as the inner loop.

**LAB
7.4**

INTRODUCTION TO CURSORS

Cursors are memory areas that allow you to allocate an area of memory and access the information retrieved from a SQL statement. For example, you use a cursor to operate on all the rows of the STUDENT table for those students taking a particular course (having associated entries in the ENROLLMENT table). In this chapter, you will learn to declare an explicit cursor that enables a user to process many rows returned by a query and allows the user to write code that will process each row one at a time.

L A B 8 . 1

CURSOR MANIPULATION

LAB OBJECTIVES

After this lab, you will be able to:

✔ Process an Explicit Cursor
✔ Make Use of Cursor Attributes
✔ Put It All Together

In order for Oracle to process an SQL statement, it needs to create an area of memory known as the *context area*; this will have the information needed to process the statement. This information includes the number of rows processed by the statement, a pointer to the parsed representation of the statement (parsing an SQL statement is the process whereby information is transferred to the server, at which point the SQL statement is evaluated as being valid). In a query, the active set refers to the rows that will be returned.

A cursor is a handle, or pointer, to the context area. Through the cursor, a PL/SQL program can control the context area and what happens to it as the statement is processed. Two important features about the cursor are

1. Cursors allow you to fetch and process rows returned by a SE-LECT statement, one row at a time.
2. A cursor is named so that it can be referenced.

TYPES OF CURSORS

There are two types of cursors: (1) An *IMPLICIT* cursor is automatically declared by Oracle every time an SQL statement is executed. The user will not be aware of this happening and will not be able to control or process the information in an implicit cursor. (2) An *EXPLICIT* cursor is defined by the program for any query that returns more than one row of data.

That means the programmer has declared the cursor within the PL/SQL code block. This declaration allows for the application to sequentially process each row of data as it is returned by the cursor.

IMPLICIT CURSOR

In order to better understand the capabilities of an explicit cursor, you first need to run through the process of an implicit cursor. The process is as follows:

- Any given PL/SQL block issues an implicit cursor whenever an SQL statement is executed, as long as an explicit cursor does not exist for that SQL statement.
- A cursor is automatically associated with every DML (Data Manipulation) statement (UPDATE, DELETE, INSERT).
- All UPDATE and DELETE statements have cursors that identify the set of rows that will be affected by the operation.
- An INSERT statement needs a place to receive the data that is to be inserted in the database; the implicit cursor fulfills this need.
- The most recently opened cursor is called the "SQL%" Cursor.

THE PROCESSING OF AN IMPLICIT CURSOR

The implicit cursor is used to process INSERT, UPDATE, DELETE, and SELECT INTO statements. During the processing of an implicit cursor, Oracle automatically performs the OPEN, FETCH, and CLOSE operations.

An implicit cursor cannot tell you how many rows were affected by an update.

SQL%ROWCOUNT returns numbers of rows updated. It can be used as follows:

```
SET SERVEROUTPUT ON
BEGIN
    UPDATE student
       SET first_name = 'B'
     WHERE first_name LIKE 'B%';
    DBMS_OUTPUT.PUT_LINE(SQL%ROWCOUNT);
END;
```

EXPLICIT CURSOR

The only means of generating an explicit cursor is for the cursor to be named in the DECLARE section of the PL/SQL Block.

The advantages of declaring an explicit cursor over the indirect implicit cursor are that the explicit cursor gives more programmatic control to the programmer. Implicit cursors are less efficient than explicit cursors and thus it is harder to trap data errors.

The process of working with an explicit cursor consists of the following steps:

1. DECLARING the cursor. This initializes the cursor into memory.
2. OPENING the cursor. The previously declared cursor can now be opened; memory is allotted.
3. FETCHING the cursor. The previously declared and opened cursor can now retrieve data; this is the process of fetching the cursor.
4. CLOSING the cursor. The previously declared, opened, and fetched cursor must now be closed to release memory allocation.

DECLARING A CURSOR

Declaring a cursor defines the name of the cursor and associates it with a SELECT statement. The first step is to Declare the Cursor with the following syntax:

```
CURSOR c_cursor_name IS select statement
```

The naming conventions that are used in the Oracle Interactive Series advise you to always name a cursor as c_cursorname. *By using a* c_ *in the beginning of the name, it will always be clear to you that the name is referencing a cursor.*

It is not possible to make use of a cursor unless the complete cycle of (1) declaring, (2) opening, (3) fetching, and finally, (4) closing have been performed. In order to explain these four steps, the following examples will have code fragments for each step and then will show you the complete process.

■ *FOR EXAMPLE:*

This is a PL/SQL fragment that demonstrates the first step of declaring a cursor. A cursor named `C_MyCursor` is declared as a select statement of all the rows in the zipcode table that have the item state equal to "NY."

```
DECLARE
    CURSOR C_MyCursor IS
        SELECT *
          FROM zipcode
         WHERE state = 'NY';
...
    <code would continue here with opening, fetching,
and closing of the cursor>
```

Cursor names follow the same rules of scope and visibility that apply to the PL/SQL identifiers. Because the name of the cursor is a PL/SQL identifier, it must be declared before it is referenced. Any valid select statement can be used to define a cursor, including joins and statements with the UNION or MINUS clause.

RECORD TYPES

A record is a composite data structure, which means that it is composed of more than one element. Records are very much like a row of a database table, but each element of the record does not stand on its own. PL/SQL supports three kinds of records: (1) table based, (2) cursor_based, (3) programmer-defined.

A table-based record is one whose structure is drawn from the list of columns in the table. A cursor-based record is one whose structure matches the elements of a predefined cursor. To create a table-based or cursor_based record use the %ROWTYPE attribute.

```
<record_name>   <table_name or cursor_name>%ROWTYPE
```

■ *FOR EXAMPLE*

```
-- ch08_1a.sql
DECLARE
    vr_student student%ROWTYPE;
BEGIN
    SELECT *
        INTO vr_student
```

```
        FROM student
         WHERE student_id = 156;
        DBMS_OUTPUT.PUT_LINE (vr_student.first_name||' '
            ||vr_student.last_name||' has an ID of 156');
EXCEPTION
     WHEN no_data_found
         THEN
              RAISE_APPLICATION_ERROR(-2001,'The Student '||
                 'is not in the database');
     END;
```

The variable `vr_student` is a record type of the existing database table student. That is, it has the same components as a row in the student table. A cursor-based record is much the same, except that it is drawn from the select list of an explicitly declared cursors. When referencing elements of the record, you use the same syntax that you use with tables.

```
record_name.item_name
```

In order to define a variable that is based on a cursor record, the cursor must first be declared. In the following lab, you will start by declaring a cursor and then proceed with the process of opening the cursor, fetching from the cursor, and finally closing the cursor.

LAB 8.1 EXERCISES

8.1.1 PROCESSING AN EXPLICIT CURSOR

a) Write the declarative section of a PL/SQL block that defines a cursor named `c_student`, based on the student table with the `last_name` and the `first_name` concatenated into one item called name, and leaving out the `created_by` and `modified_by` columns. Then declare a record based on this cursor.

_____

_____

OPENING A CURSOR

The next step in controlling an explicit cursor is to open it. When the Open cursor statement is processed, the following four actions will take place automatically:

1. The variables (including bind variables) in the WHERE clause are examined.
2. Based on the values of the variables, the active set is determined and the PL/SQL engine executes the query for that cursor. Variables are examined at cursor open time only.
3. The PL/SQL engine identifies the active set of data—the rows from all involved tables that meet the WHERE clause criteria.
4. The active set pointer is set to the first row.

The syntax for opening a cursor is:

```
OPEN cursor_name;
```

 A pointer into the active set is also established at the cursor open time. The pointer determines which row is the next to be fetched by the cursor. More than one cursor can be open at a time.

b) Add the necessary lines to the PL/SQL block that you just wrote to open the cursor.

_____

_____

FETCHING ROWS IN A CURSOR

After the cursor has been declared and opened, you can then retrieve data from the cursor. The process of getting the data from the cursor is referred to as *fetching* the cursor. There are two methods of fetching a cursor, done with the following command:

```
FETCH cursor_name INTO PL/SQL variables;
```

or

```
FETCH cursor_name INTO PL/SQL record;
```

When the cursor is fetched the following occurs:

1. The fetch command is used to retrieve one row at a time from the active set. This is generally done inside a loop. The values of each row in the active set can then be stored into the corresponding variables or PL/SQL record one at a time, performing operations on each one successively.

2. After each FETCH, the active set pointer is moved forward to the next row. Thus, each fetch will return successive rows of the active set, until the entire set is returned. The last FETCH will not assign values to the output variables; they will still contain their prior values.

■ *FOR EXAMPLE*

```
-- ch08_2a.sql
DECLARE
    CURSOR c_zip IS
        SELECT *
          FROM zipcode;
    vr_zip c_zip%ROWTYPE;
BEGIN
    OPEN c_zipcode;
    LOOP
        FETCH c_zip INTO vr_zip;
        EXIT WHEN c_zip%NOTFOUND;
        DBMS_OUTPUT.PUT_LINE(vr_zip.zipcode||
            ' '||vr_zip.city||' '||vr_zip.state);
    END LOOP;
    ...
```

The lines in italics have not yet been covered but are essential for the code to run correctly. They will be explained later on in the chapter.

c) In Chapter 3 you learned how to construct a loop. For the PL/SQL block that you have been writing, add a loop. Inside the loop FETCH the cursor into the record. Include a DBMS_OUTPUT line inside the loop so that each time the loop iterates all the information in the record are displayed in a SQL*Plus session.

CLOSING A CURSOR

Once all of the rows in the cursor have been processed (retrieved), the cursor should be closed. This tells the PL/SQL engine that the program is finished with the cursor, and the resources associated with it can be freed. The syntax for closing the cursor is:

```
CLOSE cursor_name;
```

Once a cursor is closed, it is no longer valid to fetch from it. Likewise, it is not possible to close an already closed cursor (either one will result in an Oracle error).

d) Continue with the code you have developed by adding a close statement to the cursor. Is your code complete now?

_____

_____

8.1.2 MAKING USE OF CURSOR ATTRIBUTES

Table 8.1 lists the attributes of a cursor, which are used to determine the result of a cursor operation when fetched or opened.

a) Now that you know cursor attributes, you can use one of these to exit the loop within the code you developed in the previous example. Are you able to make a fully executable block now? If not, explain why.

Cursor attributes can be used with implicit cursors by using the prefix SQL, for example: SQL%ROWCOUNT.

Table 8.1 ■ Explicit Cursor Attributes

Cursor Attribute	Syntax	Explanation
%NOTFOUND	cursor_name%NOTFOUND	A Boolean attribute that returns TRUE if the previous FETCH did not return a row, and FALSE if it did.
%FOUND	cursor_name%FOUND	A Boolean attribute that returns TRUE if the previous FETCH returned a row, and FALSE if it did not.
%ROWCOUNT	cursor_name%ROWCOUNT	# of records fetched from a cursor at that point in time.
%ISOPEN	cursor_name%ISOPEN	A Boolean attribute that returns TRUE if cursor is open, FALSE if it is not.

If you use a SELECT INTO syntax in your PL/SQL block, you will be creating an implicit cursor. You can then use these attributes on the implicit cursor.

■ *FOR EXAMPLE*

```
-- ch08_3a.sql
SET SERVEROUTPUT ON
DECLARE
    v_city zipcode.city%type;
BEGIN
    SELECT city
      INTO v_city
      FROM zipcode
     WHERE zip = 07002;
    IF SQL%ROWCOUNT = 1
    THEN
      DBMS_OUTPUT.PUT_LINE(v_city ||' has a '||
          'zipcode of 07002');
    ELSIF SQL%ROWCOUNT = 0
    THEN
       DBMS_OUTPUT.PUT_LINE('The zipcode 07002 is '||
           ' not in the database');
    ELSE
       DBMS_OUTPUT.PUT_LINE('Stop harassing me');
    END IF;
END;
```

_____

_____

b) What will happen if this code is run? Describe what is happening in each phase of the example.

_____

_____

c) Rerun this block changing 07002 to 99999. What do you think will happen? Explain.

_____

_____

d) Now try running this file. Did it run as you expected? Why or why not? What could be done to improve the way it handles a possible error condition?

_____

_____

8.1.3 PUTTING IT ALL TOGETHER

Here is an example of the complete cycle of declaring, opening, fetching, and closing a cursor including use of cursor attributes.

```
-- ch08_4a.sql
1> DECLARE
2>    v_sid        student.student_id%TYPE;
3>    CURSOR c_student IS
4>       SELECT student_id
5>         FROM student
6>         WHERE student_id < 110;
7> BEGIN
8>    OPEN c_student;
9>    LOOP
10>      FETCH c_student INTO v_sid;
11>      EXIT WHEN c_student%NOTFOUND;
12>      DBMS_OUTPUT.PUT_LINE('STUDENT ID : '||v_sid);
13>    END LOOP;
14>    CLOSE c_student;
15> EXCEPTION
16>    WHEN OTHERS
17>    THEN
18>      IF c_student%ISOPEN
19>      THEN
20>         CLOSE c_student;
21>      END IF;
22> END;
```

a) Describe what is happening in each phase of example ch08_4a.sql. Use the line numbers to reference the example.

_____

_____

b) Modify the example to make use of the cursor attributes %FOUND and %ROWCOUNT.

_____

_____

c) Fetch a cursor that has data from the student table into a %ROWTYPE. Only select students with a `student_id` under 110. The columns are the STUDENT_ID, LAST_NAME, FIRST_NAME, and a count of the number of classes each student is enrolled in (using the enroll table). Fetch the cursor with a loop and then output all the columns. You will have to use an alias for the enrollment count.

LAB 8.1 EXERCISE ANSWERS

8.1.1 ANSWERS

a) Write the declarative section of a PL/SQL block that defines a cursor named `c_student` based on the student table with the `last_name` and the `first_name` concatenated into one item called `name` and leaving out the `created_by` and `modified_by` columns. Then declare a record based on this cursor.

Answer:

```
DECLARE
   CURSOR c_student is
      SELECT first_name||'  '||Last_name name
        FROM student;
   vr_student c_student%ROWTYPE;
```

b) Add the necessary lines to the PL/SQL block that you just wrote to open the cursor.

Answer: The following lines should be added to the lines in a).

```
BEGIN
   OPEN c_student;
```

c) In Chapter 3 you learned how to construct a loop. For the PL/SQL block that you have been writing add a loop, and inside the loop FETCH the cursor into the record. Include a DBMS_OUTPUT line inside the loop so that each time the loop iterates all the information in the record is displayed in a SQL*Plus session.

Answer: the following lines should be added:

```
LOOP
    FETCH c_student INTO vr_student;
    DBMS_OUTPUT.PUT_LINE(vr_student.name);
```

d) Continue with the code you have developed by adding a close statement to the cursor. Is your code complete now?

Answer: The following lines should be added:

```
CLOSE c_student;
```

The code is not complete since there is not a proper way to exit the loop.

8.1.2 ANSWERS

a) Now that you know cursor attributes, you can use one of these to exit the loop within the code you developed in the previous example. Are you able to make a fully executable block now? If not explain why.

Answer: You can make use of attribute %NOTFOUND to close the loop. It would also be a wise idea to add an exception clause to the end of the block to close the cursor if it is still open. If you add the following statements to the end of your block it will be complete.

```
        EXIT WHEN c_student%NOTFOUND;
    END LOOP;
    CLOSE c_student;
EXCEPTION
    WHEN OTHERS
    THEN
        IF c_student%ISOPEN
        THEN
            CLOSE c_student;
        END IF;
END;
```

b) What will happen if this code is run? Describe what is happening in each phase of example

Answer: The PL/SQL block ch08_3a *would display the following output:*

```
Bayonne has a zipcode of 07002
PL/SQL procedure successfully completed.
```

The declaration section declares a variable, `v_city`, anchored to the datatype of the city item in the zipcode table. The SELECT statement causes an implicit cursor to be opened, fetched, and then closed. The IF clause makes use of the attribute %ROW-COUNT to determine if the implicit cursor has a rowcount of 1 or not. If it does have a row count of 1, then the first `DBMS_OUTPUT` line will be displayed. You should notice that this example does not handle a situation where the rowcount is greater than 1. Since the zipcode table's primary key is the zipcode, this could happen.

c) Rerun this block changing 07002 to 99999. What do you think will happen? Explain.

Answer: The PL/SQL block would display the following:

```
DECLARE
ERROR at line 1:
ORA-01403: no data found
ORA-06512: at line 4
```

A select statement in a PL/SQL block that does not return any rows will raise a no data found exception. Since there was no exception handler, the above error would be displayed.

d) Now, try running this file. Did it run as you expected? Why or why not? What could be done to improve the way it handles a possible error condition?

Answer: You may have expected the second and third condition of the IF statement to capture the instance of a %ROWCOUNT equal to 0. Now that you understand that a SELECT statement that returns no rows will raise a NO_DATA_FOUND exception, it would be a good idea to handle this by adding a <%WHEN NO_DATA_FOUND> exception to the existing block. You can add a %ROWCOUNT in the exception, either to display the rowcount in a DBMS_OUTPUT or to put an IF statement to display various possibilities.

8.1.3 ANSWERS

a) Describe what is happening in each phase of example `ch08_4a.sql`. Use the line numbers to reference the example.

Answer: The example illustrates a cursor fetch loop, in which multiple rows of data are returned from the query. The cursor is declared in the declaration section of the block (1-6) just like other identifiers. In the executable section of the block (7-15), a cursor is opened using the OPEN (8) statement. Because the cursor returns multiple rows, a loop is used to assign returned data to the variables with a FETCH statement (10). Because the loop statement has no other means of termination, there must be an exit condition specified. In this case, one of the attributes for the cursor is, %NOTFOUND

(12). The cursor is then closed to free the memory allocation (14). Additionally, if the exception handler is called, there is a check to see if the cursor is open (18) and if it is closed (20).

b) Modify the example to make use of the cursor attributes %FOUND and %ROWCOUNT .

Answer: Your modification should look like this:

```
-- ch08_5a.sql
DECLARE
    v_sid        student.student_id%TYPE;
    CURSOR c_student IS
       SELECT student_id
         FROM student
        WHERE student_id < 110;
  BEGIN
    OPEN c_student;
    LOOP
       FETCH c_student INTO v_sid;
       IF c_student%FOUND THEN
       DBMS_OUTPUT.PUT_LINE
          ('Just FETCHED row '
             ||TO_CHAR(c_student%ROWCOUNT)||
             ' Student ID: '||v_sid);
       ELSE
          EXIT;
       END IF;
    END LOOP;
    CLOSE c_student;
  EXCEPTION
    WHEN OTHERS
    THEN
       IF c_student%ISOPEN
       THEN
          CLOSE c_student;
       END IF;
  END;
```

There has been a modification to the loop structure. Instead of having an exit condition, an IF statement is being used. The IF statement is making use of the cursor attribute %FOUND. This attribute returns true when a row has been "found" in the cursor and false when it has not. The next attribute %ROWCOUNT returns a number, which is the current row number of the cursor.

c)   Fetch a cursor that has a data from the Student table into a %ROW-TYPE. The columns are the student_id, last_name, first_name, and a count of the number of classes each student is enrolled in (using the ENROLL table). Fetch the cursor with a loop and then output all the columns. You will have to use an alias for the enrollment count.

Answer: One method of doing this would be as follows:

```
-- ch08_6a.sql
DECLARE
    CURSOR c_student_enroll IS
        SELECT s.student_id, first_name, last_name,
               COUNT(*) enroll
          FROM student s, enrollment e
         WHERE s.student_id = e.student_id
           AND s.student_id <110
         GROUP BY s.studid, slname, sfname;
    r_student_enroll    c_student_enroll%ROWTYPE;
BEGIN
    OPEN c_student_enroll;
    LOOP
       FETCH c_student_enroll INTO r_student_enroll;
       EXIT WHEN c_student_enroll%NOTFOUND;
       DBMS_OUTPUT.PUT_LINE('Student INFO: '||
           r_student_enroll.student_id||' is '||
           r_student_enroll.first_name|| ' ' ||
           r_student_enroll.last_name||
           ' '||r_student_enroll.enroll||'.');
    END LOOP;
    CLOSE c_student_enroll;
EXCEPTION
    WHEN OTHERS
    THEN
     IF c_student_enroll %ISOPEN
       THEN
     CLOSE c_student_enroll;
END;
```

In the declarative section, a cursor c_student_enroll *is defined as well as a record, which is the type of a row of the cursor. The cursor loop structure makes use of an exit condition with the %NOTFOUND cursor attribute. When there are no more rows, the %NOTFOUND will be false and will cause the loop to exit. While the cursor is open and loop is processing, it will fetch a row of the cursor in a record one at a time. The DBMS output will cause each row to be displayed to the screen. Finally, the cursor is closed and an exception clause will also close the cursor it any error is raised.*

Go to the Companion Web site for this book, located at
`http://www.phptr.com/phptrinteractive/`*... for more examples and exercises on cursors.*

Assorted Tips on Cursors

Cursor SELECT List

Match the SELECT list with PL/SQL variables or PL/SQL record components.

The number of variables must be equal to the number of columns or expressions in the SELECT list.

The number of the components of a record must match the columns or expressions in the SELECT list.

Cursor Scope

The scope of a cursor declared in the main block (or an enclosing block) extends to the sub-blocks.

Expressions in a Cursor SELECT List

PL/SQL variables, expressions, and even functions can be included in the cursor SELECT list.

Column Aliases in Cursors

An alternative name you provide to a column or expression in the SELECT list is called an alias.

In an explicit cursor column, aliases are required for calculated columns when:

- You FETCH into a record declared with %ROWTYPE declaration against that cursor.
- You want to reference the calculated column in the program.

LAB 8.1 SELF-REVIEW QUESTIONS

In order to test your progress, you should be able to answer the following questions.

1)   Implicit cursors are the only way to fetch and manage data from the database.
    a)_____ True
    b)_____ False

2) What are cursor attributes used for?
   a)_____ Controlling cursors
   b)_____ Populating cursors
   c)_____ Ordering pizza
   d)_____ Closing cursors

3) Number the following steps in processing a cursor.
   a)_____ Fetch
   b)_____ Declare
   c)_____ Close
   d)_____ Open
   e)_____ Dance

4) What is the difference between an implicit and an explicit cursor?
   a)_____ An implicit cursor is easier to manage.
   b)_____ Cursor attributes can only be used on explicit cursors.
   c)_____ It is easier to trap errors with implicit cursors.
   d)_____ Explicit cursors give the programmer greater control.

5) What must be done to place a cursor in memory?
   a)_____ It must be fetched.
   b)_____ It must be pinned.
   c)_____ It must be memorized verbatim.
   d)_____ It must be declared.

Quiz answer appear in Appendix A, Section 8.2.

L A B   8 . 2

USING CURSOR FOR LOOPS AND NESTING CURSORS

LAB OBJECTIVES

After this lab, you will be able to:

✔ Use a Cursor FOR LOOP
✔ Process Nested Cursors

There is an alternative method of handling cursors. It is called the cursor FOR LOOP because of the simplified syntax that is used. When using the cursor FOR LOOP, the process of opening, fetching, and closing are implicitly handled. This makes the blocks much simpler to code and easier to maintain.

The cursor FOR LOOP specifies a sequence of statements to be repeated once for each row returned by the cursor. Use the cursor FOR LOOP if you need to FETCH and PROCESS each and every record from a cursor.

■ FOR EXAMPLE

Assume the existence of a table called log with one column

```
(description VARCHAR2(250)).
-- ch08_7a.sql
DECLARE
   CURSOR c_student IS
       SELECT student_id, last_name, first_name
         FROM student
```

```
                    WHERE student_id < 110;
BEGIN
    FOR r_student IN c_student
    LOOP
        INSERT INTO table_log
            VALUES(r_student.last_name);
    END LOOP;
END;
```

LAB 8.2 EXERCISES

8.2.1 USING CURSOR FOR LOOPS

a) Write a PL/SQL block that will reduce the cost of all courses by 5% for courses having an enrollment of 8 students or more. Use a cursor for loop that will update the COURSE table.

_____

_____

8.2.2 PROCESSING NESTED CURSORS

Cursors can be nested inside each other. Although this may sound complex, it is really just a loop inside a loop, much like nested loops covered in the previous chapter. If you had one parent cursor and two child cursors, then each time the parent cursor makes a single loop, it will loop through each child cursor once and then begin a second round. In the following two examples, you will encounter a nested cursor with a single child cursor.

■ FOR EXAMPLE

```
-- ch08_8a.sql
1   DECLARE
2       v_zip zipcode.zip%TYPE;
3       CURSOR c_zip IS
4           SELECT zip, city, state
5             FROM zipcode
6            WHERE state = 'CT';
7       CURSOR c_student IS
8           SELECT first_name, last_name
```

```
 9              FROM student
10             WHERE zip = v_zip;
11  BEGIN
12     FOR r_zip IN c_zip
13     LOOP
14        v_zip := r_zip.zip;
15        DBMS_OUTPUT.PUT_LINE(CHR(10));
16        DBMS_OUTPUT.PUT_LINE('Students living in '||
17           r_zip.city);
18        FOR r_student in c_student
19        LOOP
20           DBMS_OUTPUT.PUT_LINE(
                 r_student.first_name||
21               ' '||r_student.last_name);
22        END LOOP;
23     END LOOP;
24* END;
```

There are two cursors in the previous example. The first is a cursor of the zipcodes and the second cursor is a list of students. The variable v_zip is initialized in line 14 to be the zipcode of the current record of the c_zip cursor. The c_student cursor ties in c_zip cursor by means of this variable. Thus, when the cursor is processed in lines 18–22, it is retrieving students that have the zipcode of the current record for the parent cursor. The parent cursor is processed from lines 12–23. Each iteration of the parent cursor will only execute the DBMS_OUTPUT in lines 16 and 17 once. The DBMS_OUTPUT in line 20 will be executed once for each iteration of the child loop, producing a line of output for each student.

a) Write a PL/SQL block with two cursor FOR LOOPS. The parent cursor will call the student_id, first_name, and last_name from the student table for student with a student_id less than 110 and output one line with this information. For each student, the child cursor will loop through all the courses that the student is enrolled in, outputting the course_no and the description.

The following is an example of a nested cursor. Review the code.

■ FOR EXAMPLE

```
-- ch08_9a.sql
DECLARE
   v_amount course.cost%TYPE;
   v_instructor_id  instructor.instructor_id%TYPE;
   CURSOR c_inst IS
      SELECT first_name, last_name, instructor_id
        FROM instructor;
   CURSOR c_cost IS
      SELECT c.cost
        FROM course c, section s, enrollment e
       WHERE s.instructor_id = v_instructor_id
         AND c.course_no = s.course_no
         AND s.section_id = e.section_id;
BEGIN
   FOR r_inst IN c_inst
   LOOP
      v_instructor_id := r_inst.instructor_id;
      v_amount := 0;
      DBMS_OUTPUT.PUT_LINE(
         'Generated by instructor '||
         r_inst.first_name||'  '||r_inst.last_name);
      FOR r_cost IN c_cost
      LOOP
         v_amount := v_amount + NVL(r_cost.cost, 0);
      END LOOP;
      DBMS_OUTPUT.PUT_LINE
      (TO_CHAR(v_amount,'$999,999'));
   END LOOP;
END;
```

b) Before you run the code above, analyze what it is doing and determine what you think the result would be. Explain what is happening in each phase of the PL/SQL block and what is happening to the variables as control is passing through parent and child cursor.

_____

_____

c) Run the code and see what the result is. Is it what you expected? Explain the difference.

_____

_____

LAB 8.2 EXERCISE ANSWERS

8.2.1 ANSWERS

a) Write a PL/SQL block that will reduce the cost of all courses by 5% for courses having an enrollment of 8 students or more. Use a cursor for loop that will update the course table.

Answer: Your block should look like this:

```
-- ch08_10a.sql
DECLARE
    CURSOR c_group_discount IS
        SELECT DISTINCT s.course_no
          FROM section s, enrollment e
         WHERE s.section_id = e.section_id
         GROUP BY s.course_no, e.section_id, s.section_id
         HAVING COUNT(*)>=8;
BEGIN
    FOR r_group_discount IN c_group_discount    LOOP
        UPDATE course
           SET cost = cost * .95
         WHERE cnumber = r_group_discount.cnumber;
    END LOOP;
    COMMIT;
END;
```

The cursor `c_group_discount` *is declared in the declarative section. The proper SQL is used to generate the select statement to answer the question given. The cursor is processed in a FOR LOOP—in each iteration of the loop the SQL update statement will be executed. This means it does not have to be opened, fetched and closed. Also, it means that a cursor attribute does not have to be used to create an exit condition for the loop that is processing the cursor.*

8.2.2 ANSWERS

a) Write a PL/SQL block with two cursors for loops. The parent cursor will call the `student_id`, `first_name`, and `last_name` from the student table for students with a `student_id` less than 110 and output one line with this information. For each student, the child cursor will loop through all the courses that the student is enrolled in, outputting the `course_no` and the description.

Answer: Your block should look like this:

```
-- ch08_11a.sql
DECLARE
    v_sid student.student_id%TYPE;
    CURSOR c_student IS
        SELECT student_id, first_name, last_name
          FROM student
         WHERE student_id < 110;
    CURSOR c_course IS
        SELECT c.course_no, c.description
          FROM course c, section s, enrollment e
         WHERE c.course_no = s.course_no
           AND s.section_id = e.section_id
           AND e.student_id = v_sid;
BEGIN
    FOR r_student IN c_student
    LOOP
        v_sid := r_student.student_id;
        DBMS_OUTPUT.PUT_LINE(chr(10));
        DBMS_OUTPUT.PUT_LINE(' The Student '||
            r_student.student_id||' '||
            r_student.first_name||' '||
            r_student.last_name);
        DBMS_OUTPUT.PUT_LINE(' is enrolled in the '||
            'following courses: ');
        FOR r_course IN c_course
        LOOP
            DBMS_OUTPUT.PUT_LINE(r_course.course_no||
                '   '||r_course.description);
        END LOOP;
    END LOOP;
END;
```

The select statements for the two cursors are defined in the declarative section of the PL/SQL block. A variable to store the student_id *from the parent cursor is also declared. The course cursor is the child cursor, and, since it makes use of the variable* v_sid, *the variable must be declared first. Both cursors are processed with a FOR LOOP, which eliminates the need for OPEN, FETCH, and CLOSE. When the parent student loop is processed, the first step is to initialize the variable* v_sid, *the value is then used when the child loop is processed. DBMS_OUTPUT is used so that display is generated for each cursor loop. The parent cursor will display the student name once, and the child cursor will display the name of each course in which the student is enrolled.*

b) Before you run the code above, analyze what it is doing and determine what you think the result would be. Explain what is happening in each phase of the PL/SQL block and what is happening to the variables as control is passing through parent and child cursor.

Answer: The declaration section contains a declaration for two variables. The first is v_amount *of the datatype matching that of the cost in the course table; the second is the* v_instructor_id *of the datatype matching the* instructor_id *in the instructor table. There are also two declarations for two cursors. The first is for* c_inst, *which is comprised of the* first_name, last_name, *and* instructor_id *for an instructor from the instructor table. The second cursor,* c_cost, *will produce a result set of the cost of the course taken for each student enrolled in a course by the instructor that matches the variable* v_instructor_id. *These two cursors will be run in nested fashion. First, the cursor* c_inst *is opened in a FOR LOOP. The value of the variable* v_instructor_id *is initialized to match the* instructor_id *of the current row of the* c_inst *cursor. The variable* v_amount *is initialized to 0. The second cursor is open within the loop for the first cursor. This means that for each iteration of the cursor* c_inst, *the second cursor will be opened, fetched, and closed. The second cursor will loop through all the cost generated by each student enrolled in a course for the instructor, which is current of the* c_inst *cursor. Each time the nest loop iterates, it will increase the variable* v_amount *by adding the current cost in the* c_cost *loop. Prior to opening the* c_cost *loop, there is a DBMS_OUTPUT to display the instructor name. After the* c_cost *cursor loop is closed, it will display the total amount generated by all the enrollments of the current instructor.*

c) Run the code and see what the result is. Is it what you expected? Explain the difference.

Answer: The result set would be as follows:

```
Generated by instructor Fernand   Hanks
$16,915
Generated by instructor Tom   Wojick
$18,504
Generated by instructor Nina   Schorin
$30,137
Generated by instructor Gary   Pertez
$24,044
Generated by instructor Anita   Morris
$13,389
Generated by instructor Todd   Smythe
$14,940
Generated by instructor Rick   Chow
$0
Generated by instructor Charles   Lowry
$12,175
```

```
Generated by instructor Marilyn   Frantzen
$13,224
PL/SQL procedure successfully completed.
```

In this example, the nested cursor is tied to the current row of the outer cursor by means of the variable v_instructor_id. A more common way of doing this is to pass a parameter to a cursor. You will learn more about how to achieve this in the next section.

LAB 8.2 SELF-REVIEW QUESTIONS

In order to test your progress, you should be able to answer the following questions.

1) In a cursor FOR LOOP, cursor and loop handling is carried out implicitly.
   a) _____ True
   b) _____ False

2) In a cursor FOR LOOP, it is necessary to declare the rowtype for the cursor.
   a) _____ True
   b) _____ False

3) Is it necessary to open, fetch, and close a cursor in a cursor FOR LOOP?
   a) _____ Yes
   b) _____ No

4) The Child loop in a nested cursor is passed through how many times for each cycle of the parent?
   a) _____ Three
   b) _____ One or more
   c) _____ Two
   d) _____ It depends on the individual code

5) If the SELECT statement of the cursor makes use of a variable, when should the variable be declared?
   a) _____ It is a bind variable and therefore does not need to be declared.
   b) _____ In the declarative section.
   c) _____ Before the cursor that is using it.
   d) _____ It will be self-declared upon initialization.

Quiz answers appear in Appendix A, Section 8.2.

LAB 8.3

USING PARAMETERS WITH CURSORS AND FOR UPDATE CURSORS

LAB OBJECTIVES

After this lab, you will be able to:

✔ Use Parameters in a Cursor
✔ Use a FOR UPDATE Cursor

CURSORS WITH PARAMETERS

A cursor can be declared with parameters. This enables a cursor to generate a specific result set, which is, on the one hand, more narrow, but on the other hand, reusable. A cursor of all the data from the zipcode table may be very useful, but it would be more useful for certain data processing if it held information for only one state. Up to now, you know how to create such a cursor. But, wouldn't it be more useful if you could create a cursor that could accept a parameter or a state and then run through only the data for that state?

■ *FOR EXAMPLE*

```
CURSOR c_zip (p_state IN zipcode.state%TYPE) IS
    SELECT zip, city, state
       FROM zipcode
      WHERE state = p_state;
```

The main points to keep in mind for parameters in cursors are as follows:

- Cursor parameters make the cursor more reusable.
- Cursor parameters can be assigned default values.
- The scope of the cursor parameters is local to the cursor.
- The mode of the parameters can only be IN.

When a cursor has been declared as taking a parameter, it must be called with a value for that parameter. The `c_zip` cursor that was just declared is called as follows:

```
OPEN c_zip (parameter_value)
```

The same cursor could be opened with a FOR cursor loop as follows:

```
FOR r_zip IN c_zip('NY')
LOOP  ...
```

LAB 8.3 EXERCISES

8.3.1 USING PARAMETERS IN A CURSOR

a) Complete the code for the parameter cursor that was begun above. Have a DBMS_OUTPUT line the displays the zipcode, city, and state. This is identical to the process you have already used in a FOR CURSOR loop, only now, when you OPEN the cursor, you pass a parameter.

_____

_____

b) The following PL/SQL is fairly complex. It involves all the topics covered in so far this chapter. There is a nested cursor with three levels, meaning a grandparent cursor, a parent cursor, and a child cursor. Before running this script, review the code and identify the levels of nesting in the code. When you describe each level of the code, explain what parameters are being passed into the cursor and why. What do you think the result will be from running this statement?

```
-- ch08_12a.sql
1  DECLARE
2     CURSOR c_student IS
3        SELECT first_name, last_name, student_id
```

```
  4            FROM student
  5           WHERE last_name LIKE 'J%';
  6        CURSOR c_course
  7              (p_studid IN student.student_id%TYPE)
           IS
  8            SELECT c.description, s.section_id sec_id
  9              FROM course c, section s, enrollment e
 10             WHERE e.student_id = p_studid
 11               AND c.course_no = s.course_no
 12               AND s.section_id = e.section_id;
 13        CURSOR c_grade(p_sid IN section.section_id%TYPE,
 14                       p_stuid IN student.student_id%TYPE)
 15           IS
 16           SELECT gt.description grd_desc,
 17               TO_CHAR (AVG(g.numeric_grade), '999') num_grd
 18             FROM enrollment e,
 19                  grade g, grade_type gt
 20            WHERE e.section_id = p_section_id
 21              AND e.student_id = g.student_id
 22              AND e.student_id = p_student_id
 23              AND e.section_id = g.section_id
 24              AND g.grade_type_code = gt.grade_type_code
 25            GROUP BY gt.description ;
 26   BEGIN
 27      FOR r_student IN c_student
 28      LOOP
 29        DBMS_OUTPUT.PUT_LINE(CHR(10));
 30        DBMS_OUTPUT.PUT_LINE(r_student.first_name||
 31           ' '||r_student.last_name);
 32        FOR r_course IN c_course(r_student.student_id)
 33        LOOP
 34          DBMS_OUTPUT.PUT_LINE('Grades for course :'||
 35             r_course.description);
 36          FOR r_grade IN c_grade(r_course.sec_id,
 37                               r_st.student_id)
 38          LOOP
 39            DBMS_OUTPUT.PUT_LINE(r_grade.num_grd||
 40               ' '||r_grade.grd_desc);
 41          END LOOP;
 42        END LOOP;
 43      END LOOP;
 44   END;
```

c) Now run the code and see if you were correct. Analyze the code line by line and explain what is being processed and then displayed for each line.

_____

_____

8.3.2 USING A *FOR UPDATE* CURSOR

The CURSOR FOR UPDATE clause is only used with a cursor when you want to update tables in the database. Generally, when you execute a SELECT statement, you are not locking any rows. The purpose of using the FOR UPDATE clause is to lock the rows of the tables that you want to update, so that another user cannot perform an update until you perform your update and release the lock. The next COMMIT or ROLLBACK statement releases the lock. The FOR UPDATE clause will change the manner in which the cursor operates in only a few respects. When you open a cursor, all rows that meet the restriction criteria are identified as considered part of the active set. Using the FOR UPDATE clause will lock these rows that have been identified in the active set. If the FOR UPDATE clause is used, then rows may not be fetched from the cursor after a commit has been issued. It is important for you to consider where to place the commit. Be careful to consider issues covered in the Transaction Management topic covered in Chapter 3.

The syntax is simply to add FOR UPDATE to the end of the cursor definition. If there are multiple items being selected, but you only want to lock one of them, then end the cursor definition with the following syntax:

```
FOR UPDATE OF <item_name>
```

■ *FOR EXAMPLE*

```
-- ch08_13a.sql
DECLARE
  CURSOR c_course IS
    SELECT course_no, cost
      FROM course FOR UPDATE;
BEGIN
  FOR r_course IN c_course
  LOOP
    IF r_course.cost < 2500
    THEN
        UPDATE course
```

BARNES&NOBLE
BOOKSELLERS

GotBooks Inc
c/o Alibris
475 Lillard Drive, #102
Sparks, NV 89434-8926 USA

To: LEENA SHRESTHA
STRAYER UNIVERSITY
9435 MIRROR POND DRIVE
FAIRFAX, VA 22032

Packing Slip

✂ Your Barnes & Noble Booksellers Order – – – – – Ship via USPS Priority or UPS Ground –

Shipping Instructions:

- Print this Packing Slip by clicking the Print button, above.
- Clip out the mailing label portion and affix to the package.
- Enclose Packing Slip in package (Packing Slip is the remainder of the page after you've clipped out the mailing label).

Please ship this item via **USPS Priority or UPS Ground** no later than two business days from Sat Apr 29, 2006. Please note that UPS Ground does not ship to P.O. Boxes, APO/FPO, or U.S. Protectorates.

Shipped to:
Leena Shrestha
Strayer University
9435 Mirror Pond Drive

Ordered by	Order date	Customer order No
Leena Shrestha	Apr 29, 2006	78528703001
Seller		**Item #**

Alibris PN
15569717-1

Description
Oracle Pl/Sql Interactive Workbook
Benjamin Rosenzweig Elena Silvestrova Benjamin
Ros

{Dealer Book ID: 337814}

**Used and Out-of-Print Books brought to you
by our Authorized Sellers.**

Return Instructions

If you are dissatisfied for any reason, return your purchase within 30 days of receipt for a full refund of the purchase price.
Include the packing slip and indicate the reason for return for fastest processing.
(Please note that we can refund shipping costs only if the return is the result of our error.)

Ship your returns to:

Alibris Distribution Center - Returns
475 Lillard Drive #102
Sparks, NV 89434 USA

Reason for Return:
☐ Item not as described
☐ Item different than expected
☐ Incorrect item received
☐ Other

Problems? Questions? Suggestions? Contact Barnes & Noble Customer Service at
http://www.barnesandnoble.com/help/cds2.asp?PID=8133

http://sellers.alibris.com/ops/podisplay.cfm?order_nbr=15569717-1

5/3/2006

```
                SET crsecost = r_course.cost + 10
              WHERE course_no = r_course.course_no;
         END IF;
      END LOOP;
   END;
```

This example shows how to update the cost of all courses with a cost under $2500. It will increment them by 10.

a) In the example given above, where should the commit be placed? What are the issues involved in deciding where to place a commit in this example?

LAB 8.3

_____

_____

■ FOR EXAMPLE

```
-- ch08_14a.sql
DECLARE
   CURSOR c_grade(
      p_student_id IN student.student_id%TYPE,
      p_section_id IN section.section_id%TYPE)
   IS
      SELECT final_grade
        FROM enrollment
       WHERE student_id = p_student_id
         AND section_id = p_section_id
       FOR UPDATE;
   CURSOR c_enrollment IS
      SELECT e.student_id, e.section_id
        FROM enrollment e, section s
       WHERE s.course_no = 135
         AND e.section_id = s.section_id;
BEGIN
   FOR r_enroll IN c_enrollment
   LOOP
      FOR r_grade IN c_grade(r_enroll.student_id,
                             r_enroll.section_id)
      LOOP
         UPDATE enrollment
            SET final_grade  = 90
          WHERE student_id = r_enroll.student_id
            AND section_id = r_enroll.section_id
```

```
      END LOOP;
   END LOOP;
END;
```

b) What do you think will happen if you run the code in this example? After making your analysis, run the code, and then perform a SELECT statement to determine if your guess is correct.

_____

_____

c) Where should the commit go in the above example? Explain the considerations.

_____

_____

FOR UPDATE OF can be used when creating a cursor for update that is based on multiple tables. FOR UPDATE OF locks the rows of a table that both contain one of the specified columns and are members of the active set. In other words, it is the means of specifying which table you want to lock. If the FOR UPDATE OF clause is used, then rows may not be fetched from the cursor after a commit has been issued.

■ FOR EXAMPLE

```
-- ch08_15a.sql
DECLARE
   CURSOR c_stud_zip IS
      SELECT s.student_id, z.city
        FROM student s, zipcode z
       WHERE z.city = 'Brooklyn'
         AND s.zip = z.zip
       FOR UPDATE OF phone;
BEGIN
  FOR r_stud_zip IN c_stud_zip
  LOOP
     UPDATE student
        SET phone = '718'||SUBSTR(sphone,4)
      WHERE studid = r_stud_zip.studid;
  END LOOP;
END;
```

d) What changes to the database will take place if the example given above example is run? Explain specifically what is being locked as well as when it is locked and when it is released.

_____

_____

8.3.3 WHERE CURRENT OF Clause

Use WHERE CURRENT OF when you want to update the most recently fetched row. WHERE CURRENT OF can only be used with a FOR UPDATE OF cursor. The advantage of the WHERE CURRENT OF clause is that it enables you to eliminate the WHERE clause in the UPDATE statement.

■ FOR EXAMPLE

```
-- ch08_16a.sql
DECLARE
    CURSOR c_stud_zip IS
        SELECT s.studid, z.city
          FROM student s, zipcode z
         WHERE z.city = 'Brooklyn'
           AND s.szip = z.zip
          FOR UPDATE OF sphone;
BEGIN
    FOR r_stud_zip IN c_stud_zip
    LOOP
        DBMS_OUTPUT.PUT_LINE(r_stud_zip.studid);
        UPDATE student
           SET sphone = '718'||SUBSTR(sphone,4)
         WHERE CURRENT OF c_stud_zip;
    END LOOP;
END;
```

a) Compare the last two examples. Explain their similarities and differences. What has been altered by using the WHERE CURRENT OF clause? What is the advantage of doing this?

_____

_____

The FOR UPDATE and WHERE CURRENT OF syntax can be used with cursors that are performing a delete as well as an update.

LAB 8.3 EXERCISE ANSWERS

8.3.1 ANSWERS

**LAB
8.3**

a) Complete the code for the parameter cursor that was begun above. Have a DBMS_OUTPUT line the displays the zipcode, city, and state. This is identical to the process you have already used in a FOR CURSOR loop, only now, when you open the cursor, you pass a parameter.

Answer: Your block should look like this:

```
-- ch08_17a.sql
DECLARE
    CURSOR c_zip (p_state IN zipcode.state%TYPE) IS
        SELECT zip, city, state
          FROM zipcode
         WHERE state = p_state
BEGIN
    FOR r_zip IN c_zip('NJ')
    LOOP  ...
       DBMS_OUTPUT.PUT_LINE(r_zip.city||
          ' '||r_zip.zip');
    END LOOP;
END;
```

To complete the block, the cursor declaration must be surrounded by DECLARE and BEGIN. The cursor is opened by passing the parameter "NJ," and then, for each iteration of the cursor loop, the zipcode and the city are displayed by using the built-in package DBMS_OUTPUT.

b) The following PL/SQL is fairly complex. It involves all the topics covered in this chapter so far. There is a nested cursor with three levels, meaning a grandparent cursor, a parent cursor, and a child cursor. Before running this script, review the code and identify the levels of nesting in the code. When you describe each level of the code, explain what parameters are being passed into the cursor and why. What do you think the result will be from running this statement?

Answer: The grandparent cursor c_student *is declared in lines 2–5. It takes no parameters and is a collection of students with a last name beginning with J. The parent* cursor is declared in lines *6–12*. The parent cursor `c_course` takes in the parameter of the `student_ID` to generate a list of courses taken by that student. The child cursor `c_grade` is declared in lines *13–25*. It takes in two parameters, both the `section_id` and the `student_id`. In this way it can generate an average of the different grade types for that student for that course. The parent cursor loop begins on line *27*, and only the student name is displayed with DBMS_OUTPUT. The parent cursor loop begins on line *32*. It takes the parameter of the `student_id` from the grandparent cursor. Only the description of the course is displayed. The child cursor loop begins on line *36*. It takes in the parameter of the `section_id` from the parent cursor and the `student_id` from the grandparent cursor. The grades are then displayed. The grandparent cursor loop ends on line *41*, the parent cursor on line *42*, and finally the child on line *43*.

c) Now run the code and see if you are correct. Analyze the code line by line and explain what is being processed and displayed for each line.

Answer: The output will be a student name, followed by the courses he or she is taking and the average grade he or she has earned for each grade type. If you did not get the correct answer, try commenting out different sections of the block and see what will happen. This will help you to understand what is happening in each step.

8.3.2 ANSWERS

a) In the example given above, where should the commit be placed? What are the issues involved in deciding where to place a commit in this example?

Answer: Placing a commit after each update can be costly. But, if there are a lot of updates, and the commit comes after the block loop, then there is a risk of a rollback segment being not large enough. Normally, the commit would go after the loop, except when the transaction count is high, and then you might want to code something that does a commit for each 10000 records. If this were part of a large procedure, you may want to put a SAVEPOINT after the loop. Then, if you need to rollback this update at a later point, it would an easy task.

b) What do you think will happen if you run the code in this example? After making your analysis, run the code and then perform a SELECT statement to determine if your guess is correct.

Answer: The `final_grade` *for all students enrolled in course 135 will be updated to 90. There are two cursors here. One cursor captures the students who are enrolled in course 135 into the active set. The other cursor takes the* `student_id` *and the* `section_id` *from this active set and selects the corresponding* `final_grade` *from the enrollment table and locks the entire enrollment table. The enrollment cursor loop is begun first, and then it passes the* `student_id` *and the* `section_id` *as an IN parameter for the second cursor loop of the* `c_grade` *cursor, which performs the update.*

c) Where should the commit go in the above example? Explain the considerations.

Answer: The commit should go immediately after the update to insure that each update is committed into the database.

d) What changes to the database will take place if the example given above example is run? Explain specifically what is being locked as well as when it is locked and when it is released.

Answer: The phone numbers of students living in Brooklyn are being updated to change the area code to 718. The cursor declaration is only locking the phone column of the student table. The lock is never released because there is no commit or rollback statement.

LAB 8.3

8.3.3 Answers

a) Compare the last two examples. Explain their similarities and differences. What has been altered by using the WHERE CURRENT OF clause? What is the advantage of doing this?

Answer: These two statements perform the same update. The WHERE CURRENT OF clause allows you to eliminate a match in the UPDATE statement because the update is being performed for the current record of the cursor only.

LAB 8.3 SELF-REVIEW QUESTIONS

In order to test your progress, you should be able to answer the following questions.

1) The main benefit of using parameter with cursors is that it makes the cursor reusable.
   a) _____ True
   b) _____ False

2) The following are acceptable types of parameters to be used with cursors.
   a) _____ IN
   b) _____ OUT
   d) _____ %ROWTYPE
   e) _____ IN OUT

3) By adding the key work FOR UPDATE at the end of a cursor you are
   a) _____ simply alerting the DBA that you are updating a table.
   b) _____ freeing up rollback segments for the update.
   c) _____ locking the indicated rows for an update.
   d) _____ creating a bind variable.

4) Adding the key words WHERE CURRENT OF to a FOR UDATE cursor causes the following to take place:

   a) _____ The DBA gets annoyed.

   b) _____ Rows are locked and unlocked one at a time.

   c) _____ The update occurs for the current record in the cursor.

   d) _____ The scope of the cursor is increased.

5) The principal difference between a FOR UPDATE cursor without a WHERE CURRENT OF clause and one with a WHERE CURRENT OF clause is:

   a) _____ Without the clause the update needs to have a where clause.

   b) _____ Rows are only locked with the extra clause present.

   c) _____ Only the items specified in the WHERE CURRENT OF clause are locked.

   d) _____ Processing will only occur for the current row of the cursor.

Quiz answers appear in Appendix A, Section 8.3.

CHAPTER 8

TEST YOUR THINKING

In the chapter discussion, you learned how to process data with a cursor. Additionally, you learned how to simplify the code by using a cursor FOR LOOP. You also encountered the more complex example of nesting cursors within cursors.

1) Write a nested cursor where the parent cursor calls information about each section of a course. The child cursor counts the enrollment. The only output is one line for each course with the course name, section number, and the total enrollment.

2) Write an anonymous PL/SQL block that finds all the courses that have at least one section that is at its maximum enrollment. If there are no courses that meet that criterion, then pick two courses and create that situation for each.

   a) For each of those courses, add another section. The instructor for the new section should be taken from the existing records in the instructor table. Use the instructor who is signed up to teach the least number of courses. Handle the fact that, during the execution of your program, the instructor teaching the most courses may change.

   b) Use an exception handling techniques to capture error conditions.

CHAPTER 9

EXCEPTIONS

In Chapter 6, you explored the concept of error handling and built-in exceptions. In this chapter you will continue by examining whether an exception can catch a run-time error occurring in the declaration, executable, or exception-handling section of a PL/SQL block. You will also learn how to define your own exception and how to reraise an exception.

L A B   9 . 1

EXCEPTION SCOPE

> ## LAB OBJECTIVES
>
> After this lab, you will be able to:
>
> ✔ Understand the Scope of an Exception

You are already familiar with the term *scope*—for example, the scope of a variable. Even though variables and exceptions serve different purposes, the same scope rules apply to them. Now examine the scope of an exception by the means of an example.

■ FOR EXAMPLE

```
DECLARE
    v_student_id = &sv_student_id;
    v_name VARCHAR2(30);
BEGIN
    SELECT RTRIM(first_name)||' '||RTRIM(last_name)
      INTO v_name
      FROM student
     WHERE student_id = v_student_id;
    DBMS_OUTPUT.PUT_LINE('Student name is '||v_name);
EXCEPTION
    WHEN NO_DATA_FOUND
    THEN
        DBMS_OUTPUT.PUT_LINE('There is no such student');
END;
```

In this example, you display the student's name on the screen. If there is no record in the STUDENT table corresponding to the value of v_student_id provided by the user, the exception NO_DATA_FOUND is raised.

Therefore, you can say that the exception NO_DATA_FOUND covers this block, or this block is the scope of this exception. In other words, *the scope of an exception is the portion of the block that is covered by this exception.*

Now, you can expand on that:

■ FOR EXAMPLE

```
DECLARE
    v_student_id NUMBER := &sv_student_id;
    v_name VARCHAR2(30);
    v_total NUMBER(1);
-- outer block
BEGIN
    SELECT RTRIM(first_name)||' '||RTRIM(last_name)
      INTO v_name
      FROM student
     WHERE student_id = v_student_id;
    DBMS_OUTPUT.PUT_LINE('Student name is '||v_name);
    -- inner block
    BEGIN
        SELECT COUNT(*)
          INTO v_total
          FROM enrollment
         WHERE student_id = v_student_id;
        DBMS_OUTPUT.PUT_LINE
            ('Student is registered for '||v_total||
             ' course(s)');
    EXCEPTION
        WHEN VALUE_ERROR OR INVALID_NUMBER
        THEN
            DBMS_OUTPUT.PUT_LINE
                ('An error has occurred');
    END;
EXCEPTION
    WHEN NO_DATA_FOUND
    THEN
        DBMS_OUTPUT.PUT_LINE('There is no such student');
END;
```

The part of the example shown in bold letters has been added to the original version of the example. The new version of the example has an inner block added to it. This block has structure similar to the outer block. It has a SELECT INTO statement and an exception section to handle errors.

When VALUE_ERROR or INVALID_NUMBER error occurs in the inner block, the exception is raised.

It is important that you realize that exceptions VALUE_ERROR and INVALID_NUMBER have been defined for the inner block only. Therefore, they can be raised in the inner block only. If one of these errors occurs in the outer block, this program will be unable to terminate successfully.

On the other hand, the exception NO_DATA_FOUND has been defined in the outer block; therefore, it is global to the inner block. This version of the example will never raise the exception NO_DATA_FOUND in the inner block. Why do you think this is the case?

It is important to note that if you define an exception in a block, it is local to that block. However, it is global to any blocks enclosed by that block. In other words, in the case of nested blocks, any exception defined in the outer block becomes global to its inner blocks.

Note what happens when the example is changed so that the exception NO_DATA_FOUND can be raised by the inner block.

■ *FOR EXAMPLE*

```
DECLARE
    v_student_id NUMBER := &sv_student_id;
    v_name VARCHAR2(30);
    v_registered CHAR;
-- outer block
BEGIN
    SELECT RTRIM(first_name)||' '||RTRIM(last_name)
      INTO v_name
      FROM student
     WHERE student_id = v_student_id;
    DBMS_OUTPUT.PUT_LINE('Student name is '||v_name);
    -- inner block
    BEGIN
        SELECT 'Y'
          INTO v_registered
          FROM enrollment
         WHERE student_id = v_student_id;
        DBMS_OUTPUT.PUT_LINE('Student is registered');
    EXCEPTION
        WHEN VALUE_ERROR OR INVALID_NUMBER
        THEN
```

```
            DBMS_OUTPUT.PUT_LINE('An error has occurred');
      END;
EXCEPTION
   WHEN NO_DATA_FOUND
   THEN
         DBMS_OUTPUT.PUT_LINE('There is no such student');
END;
```

The part of the example shown in bold letters has been added to the original version of the example. The new version of the example has a different SELECT INTO statement. To answer the question posted earlier, the exception NO_DATA_FOUND can be raised by the inner block because the SELECT INTO statement does not contain group function, COUNT(). This function always returns a result, so when no rows are returned by the SELECT INTO statement, the value returned by the COUNT(*) equals to zero.

Now, run this example with the value of 284 for student ID. As a result, the following output is produced:

```
Enter value for sv_student_id: 284
old    2:      v_student_id NUMBER := &sv_student_id;
new    2:      v_student_id NUMBER := 284;
Student name is Salewa Lindeman
There is no such student
PL/SQL procedure successfully completed.
```

You have probably noticed that this example produces only a partial output. Even though you are able to see the student's name, the error message is displayed saying that this student does not exist. This error message is displayed because the exception NO_DATA_FOUND is raised in the inner block.

The SELECT INTO statement of the outer block returns student name, and it is displayed on the screen by the DBMS_OUTPUT.PUT_LINE statement. Next, the control is passed to the inner block. The SELECT INTO statement of the inner block does not return any rows. As a result, the error occurs.

Next, PL/SQL tries to find a handler for the exception NO_DATA_FOUND in the inner block. Because there is no such handler in the inner block, the control is transferred to the exception section of the outer block. The exception section of the outer block contains the handler for the exception NO_DATA_FOUND. So, this handler executes, and the message "There is no such student" is displayed on the screen. The process is called *exception propagation*, and it will be discussed in the detail in the Lab 3 of this chapter.

It is important to realize that this example has been shown for illustrative purposes only. In its current version, it is not very useful. The SELECT INTO statement of the inner block is prone to another exception, TOO_MANY_ROWS, that is not handled by this example. In addition, the error message "There is no such student" is not very descriptive when the exception NO_DATA_FOUND is raised by the inner block.

LAB 9.1 EXERCISES

9.1.1 UNDERSTANDING THE SCOPE OF AN EXCEPTION

In this exercise, you will display how many students there are for each zip-code (we still use the first 50 zipcodes only). You will use nested PL/SQL blocks to achieve the desired results. The original PL/SQL script will not contain any exception handlers. So, you will be asked to identify possible errors that may occur and define exception handlers for them.

Create the following PL/SQL script:

```
-- ch09_1a.sql, version 1.0
SET SERVEROUTPUT ON
DECLARE
   CURSOR zip_cur IS
      SELECT zip
        FROM zipcode
       WHERE rownum <= 50
     ORDER BY zip;
   v_total NUMBER(1);
-- outer block
BEGIN
   FOR zip_rec IN zip_cur LOOP
      -- inner block
      BEGIN
         SELECT count(*)
           INTO v_total
           FROM student
          WHERE zip = zip_rec.zip;
         IF v_total != 0
```

```
        THEN
            DBMS_OUTPUT.PUT_LINE
                ('There is(are) '||v_total||
                 ' student(s) for zipcode '||
                  zip_rec.zip);
            END IF;
        END;
    END LOOP;
    DBMS_OUTPUT.PUT_LINE('Done...');
END;
```

Answer the following questions:

a) What output was printed on the screen?

_____

_____

b) The first run of this example was successful. The output produced by the example shows that there are 9 students for zip code 07024. What will happen if there are 10 students with zip code 07024? What output will be produced?

_____

_____

c) Based on the error message produced by the example in the previous question, what exception handler must be added to the script?

_____

_____

d) How would you change this script so that when an error occurs, the cursor loop does not terminate prematurely?

_____

_____

LAB 9.1 EXERCISE ANSWERS

9.1.1 ANSWERS

a) What output was printed on the screen?

Answer:

```
There is(are) 1 student(s) for zipcode 01247
There is(are) 1 student(s) for zipcode 02124
There is(are) 1 student(s) for zipcode 02155
There is(are) 1 student(s) for zipcode 02189
There is(are) 1 student(s) for zipcode 02563
There is(are) 1 student(s) for zipcode 06483
There is(are) 1 student(s) for zipcode 06605
There is(are) 1 student(s) for zipcode 06798
There is(are) 3 student(s) for zipcode 06820
There is(are) 3 student(s) for zipcode 06830
There is(are) 1 student(s) for zipcode 06850
There is(are) 1 student(s) for zipcode 06851
There is(are) 1 student(s) for zipcode 06853
There is(are) 1 student(s) for zipcode 06870
There is(are) 1 student(s) for zipcode 06877
There is(are) 2 student(s) for zipcode 06880
There is(are) 1 student(s) for zipcode 06902
There is(are) 2 student(s) for zipcode 06903
There is(are) 1 student(s) for zipcode 06905
There is(are) 1 student(s) for zipcode 06907
There is(are) 2 student(s) for zipcode 07003
There is(are) 1 student(s) for zipcode 07008
There is(are) 6 student(s) for zipcode 07010
There is(are) 2 student(s) for zipcode 07011
There is(are) 2 student(s) for zipcode 07012
There is(are) 2 student(s) for zipcode 07016
There is(are) 1 student(s) for zipcode 07023
There is(are) 9 student(s) for zipcode 07024
There is(are) 1 student(s) for zipcode 07029
There is(are) 2 student(s) for zipcode 07036
There is(are) 1 student(s) for zipcode 07040
There is(are) 5 student(s) for zipcode 07042
There is(are) 1 student(s) for zipcode 07044
There is(are) 5 student(s) for zipcode 07047
Done…
PL/SQL procedure successfully completed.
```

b) The first run of this example was successful. The output produced by the example shows that there are 9 students for zip code 07024. What will happen if there are 10 students with zip code 07024? What output will be produced?

Answer: The example will produce a partial output only. When the total number of students is calculated for the zip code 07024, the error occurs.

The SELECT INTO statement returns a value of 10. However, the variable `v_total` has been defined so that it is able to hold only single digit numbers. Because 10 is a two-digit number, the error occurs during the execution of the SELECT INTO statement. As a result, the error message is displayed on the screen.

The output shown below contains only a portion of the output produced by the example.

```
There is(are) 1 student(s) for zipcode 01247
...
There is(are) 1 student(s) for zipcode 07023
DECLARE
*
ERROR at line 1:
ORA-06502: PL/SQL: numeric or value error
ORA-06512: at line 19
```

Notice, as soon as the error occurs, the example terminates because there is no exception handler for this error.

c) Based on the error message produced by the example in the previous question, what exception handler must be added to the script?

Answer: The error message produced by this example in the previous question referred to numeric or value error. Therefore, an exception VALUE_ERROR or INVALID_NUMBER must be added to the script.

This answer contains only portion of the code that helps to illustrate the changes.

```
-- ch09_1b.sql, version 2.0
SET SERVEROUTPUT ON
DECLARE
    ...
-- outer block
BEGIN
    FOR zip_rec IN zip_cur LOOP
        ...
    END LOOP;
    DBMS_OUTPUT.PUT_LINE('Done...');
```

```
EXCEPTION
    WHEN VALUE_ERROR OR INVALID_NUMBER
    THEN
        DBMS_OUTPUT.PUT_LINE('An error has occurred');
END;
```

When run, this version of the example produces the following output (only a portion of the output is shown below).

```
There is(are) 1 student(s) for zipcode 01247
...
There is(are) 1 student(s) for zipcode 07023
An error has occurred
PL/SQL procedure successfully completed.
```

Notice, because an exception handler has been added to the script, it was able to terminate successfully.

d) How would you change this script so that when an error occurs, the cursor loop does not terminate prematurely?

Answer: This answer contains only portion of the code that helps to illustrate the changes.

```
-- ch09_1c.sql, version 3.0
SET SERVEROUTPUT ON
DECLARE
    ...
-- outer block
BEGIN
    FOR zip_rec IN zip_cur LOOP
        BEGIN
        ...
        EXCEPTION
            WHEN VALUE_ERROR OR INVALID_NUMBER
            THEN
                DBMS_OUTPUT.PUT_LINE
                    ('An error has occurred');
        END;
    END LOOP;
    DBMS_OUTPUT.PUT_LINE('Done...');
END;
```

In order for the cursor loop to be able to execute even after an exception has occurred, the exception handler must be moved inside the loop in the inner block. In this case, once an exception has occurred, the control is transferred to the exception handler of the block. Once the exception is raised, the control is passed to the next executable statement of the outer block. That statement is END LOOP. If the end of the loop has not been reached and there are more records to process, the control is passed to the top of the loop, and the inner block is executed again. As a result, this version of the script produces the following output (again, only a portion of the output is shown).

```
There is(are) 1 student(s) for zipcode 01247
...
There is(are) 1 student(s) for zipcode 07023
An error has occurred
There is(are) 1 student(s) for zipcode 07029
There is(are) 2 student(s) for zipcode 07036
There is(are) 1 student(s) for zipcode 07040
There is(are) 5 student(s) for zipcode 07042
There is(are) 1 student(s) for zipcode 07044
There is(are) 5 student(s) for zipcode 07047
Done...
PL/SQL procedure successfully completed.
```

LAB 9.1 SELF-REVIEW QUESTIONS

In order to test your progress, you should be able to answer the following questions.

1) An exception defined in the inner block can be raised in
   a) _____both inner and outer blocks.
   b) _____the outer block only.
   c) _____the inner block only.

2) If an exception has been raised in the inner block and has been handled in the outer block, the control is transferred back to inner block for the further execution of the script.
   a) _____True
   b) _____False

3) If an exception has been raised in the outer block, and its handler is defined in the inner block, the following will occur:
   a) _____The control will be passed to the inner block to handle the raised exception.
   b) _____The script will terminate due to exception that is not handled.

4) An exception defined inside the body of the loop
   a) _____terminates this loop after it has been raised.
   b) _____allows loop to proceed with next iteration.
   c) _____causes an error.

5) A WHEN clause of the exception-handling section of a PL/SQL block can reference a single exception only.
   a) _____True
   b) _____False

Quiz answers appear in Appendix A, Section 9.1.

LAB 9.2

USER-DEFINED EXCEPTIONS

LAB OBJECTIVES

After this lab, you will be able to:

✔ Use User-Defined Exceptions

Often in your programs you may need to handle problems that are specific to the program you write. For example, your program asks a user to enter a value for student_id. This value is then assigned to the variable v_student_id that is used later in the program. Generally, you want a positive number for an id. By mistake, the user enters a negative number. However, no error has occurred because student_id has been defined as a number, and the user has supplied a legitimate numeric value. Therefore, you may want to implement your own exception to handle this situation.

This type of an exception is called a *user-defined exception* because it is defined by the programmer. As a result, before the exception can be used, it must be declared. A user-defined exception is declared in the declarative part of a PL/SQL block as shown below:

```
DECLARE
  exception_name EXCEPTION;
```

Notice that this declaration looks similar to the variable declaration. You specify an exception name followed by the keyword EXCEPTION. Consider the following code fragment.

■ *FOR EXAMPLE*

```
DECLARE
    e_invalid_id EXCEPTION;
```

In the example, the name of the exception is prefixed by the letter "e." This is not a required syntax; rather, it allows you to differentiate among variable names and exception names.

Once an exception has been declared, the executable statements associated with this exception are specified in the exception-handling section of the block. The format of the exception-handling section is the same as for built-in exceptions. Consider the example shown below.

■ *FOR EXAMPLE*

```
DECLARE
    e_invalid_id EXCEPTION;
BEGIN
    ...
EXCEPTION
    WHEN e_invalid_id
    THEN
        DBMS_OUTPUT.PUT_LINE
            ('An id cannot be negative');
END;
```

You already know that built-in exceptions are raised implicitly. In other words, when a certain error occurs, a built-in exception associated with this error is raised. Of course, you are assuming that you have included this exception in the exception-handling section of your program. For example, TOO_MANY_ROWS exception is raised when a SELECT INTO statement returns multiple rows. Next, you will explore how a user-defined exception is raised.

A user-defined exception must be raised explicitly. In other words, you need to specify in your program under which circumstances an exception must be raised as shown below:

```
DECLARE
    exception_name EXCEPTION;
BEGIN
    ...
    IF CONDITION
    THEN
```

```
                RAISE exception_name;
        ELSE
            ...
        END IF;
     EXCEPTION
        WHEN exception_name
        THEN
            ERROR-PROCESSING STATEMENTS;
     END;
```

In the structure shown above, the circumstances under which a user-defined exception must be raised are determined with the help of the IF-THEN-ELSE statement. If *CONDITION* evaluates to TRUE, a user-defined exception is raised. If *CONDITION* evaluates to FALSE, the program proceeds with its normal execution. In other words, the statements associated with the ELSE part of the IF-THEN-ELSE statement are executed. Any form of the IF statement can be used to check when a user-defined exception must be raised.

In the next modified example used in this lab, you will see the exception `e_invalid_id`, when a negative number is entered for the variable `v_student_id`.

■ FOR EXAMPLE

```
DECLARE
    v_student_id STUDENT.STUDENT_ID%TYPE :=
        &sv_student_id;
    v_total_courses NUMBER;
    e_invalid_id EXCEPTION;
BEGIN
    IF v_student_id < 0
    THEN
        RAISE e_invalid_id;
    ELSE
        SELECT COUNT(*)
          INTO v_total_courses
          FROM enrollment
        WHERE student_id = v_student_id;
        DBMS_OUTPUT.PUT_LINE
            ('The student is registered for '||
              v_total_courses||' courses');
    END IF;
    DBMS_OUTPUT.PUT_LINE('No exception has been raised');
```

```
EXCEPTION
   WHEN e_invalid_id
   THEN
       DBMS_OUTPUT.PUT_LINE('An id cannot be negative');
END;
```

In the example shown above, the exception `e_invalid_id` is raised with the help of IF-THEN-ELSE statement. Once a user supplies a value for the `student_id`, the sign of this numeric value is checked. If the value is less than zero, the IF-THEN-ELSE statement evaluates to TRUE, and the exception `e_invalid_id` is raised. Therefore, the control transfers to the exception-handling section of the block. Next, statements associated with this exception are executed. In this case, the message "An id cannot be negative" is displayed on the screen. If the value entered for the `student_id` is positive, the IF-THEN-ELSE statement yields FALSE, and the ELSE part of the IF-THEN-ELSE statement is executed.

Run this example for two values of `student_id`: 102 and −102.

First run of the example (`student_id` is 102) produces the output shown below:

```
Enter value for sv_student_id: 102
old   2:     v_student_id STUDENT.STUDENT_ID%TYPE :=
&sv_student_id;
new   2:     v_student_id STUDENT.STUDENT_ID%TYPE := 102;
The student is registered for 2 courses
No exception has been raised
PL/SQL procedure successfully completed.
```

For this run, you entered a positive value for the variable `v_student_id`. As a result, the IF-THEN-ELSE statement evaluates to FALSE, and the ELSE part of the statement executes. The SELECT INTO statement determines how many records are in the ENROLLMENT table for a given `student_id`. Next, the message "The student is registered for 2 courses" statement is displayed on the screen. At this point, IF-THEN-ELSE statement is complete. So, the control is transferred to the DBMS_OUTPUT.PUT_LINE statement that follows END IF. As a result, another message is displayed on the screen.

A second run of the example (student ID is −102) produces the following output :

```
Enter value for sv_student_id: -102
old   2:     v_student_id STUDENT.STUDENT_ID%TYPE :=
&sv_student_id;
```

```
new    2:     v_student_id STUDENT.STUDENT_ID%TYPE
:= -102;
An id cannot be negative
PL/SQL procedure successfully completed.
```

For the second run, a negative value was entered for the variable `v_student_id`. The IF-THEN-ELSE statement evaluates to TRUE, and the exception `e_invalid_id` is raised. As a result, the control is transferred to the exception-handling section of the block, and the error message "An id cannot be negative" is displayed on the screen.

 It is important for you to note that RAISE statement must be used in conjunction with an IF statement. Otherwise, the control of the execution will be transferred to the exception-handling section of the block for every single execution. Consider the following example:

```
DECLARE
    e_test_exception EXCEPTION;
BEGIN
    DBMS_OUTPUT.PUT_LINE('Exception has not been raised');
    RAISE e_test_exception;
    DBMS_OUTPUT.PUT_LINE('Exception has been raised');
EXCEPTION
    WHEN e_test_exception
    THEN
        DBMS_OUTPUT.PUT_LINE('An error has occurred');
END;
```

Every time this example is run, the output shown below is produced:

```
Exception has not been raised
An error has occurred
PL/SQL procedure successfully completed.
```

Even though no error has occurred, the control is transferred to the exception-handling section. So, it is important for you to check to see if the error has occurred before raising the exception associated with that error.

The same scope rules apply to the user-defined exceptions. An exception declared in the inner block must be raised in the inner block and defined in the exception-handling section of the inner block. Consider the following example.

■ *FOR EXAMPLE*

```
-- outer block
BEGIN
    DBMS_OUTPUT.PUT_LINE('Outer block');
    -- inner block
    DECLARE
        e_my_exception EXCEPTION;
    BEGIN
        DBMS_OUTPUT.PUT_LINE('Inner block');
    EXCEPTION
        WHEN e_my_exception
        THEN
            DBMS_OUTPUT.PUT_LINE('An error has occurred');
    END;
    IF 10 > &sv_number
    THEN
        RAISE e_my_exception;
    END IF;
END;
```

In this example, the exception, `e_my_exception`, has been declared in the inner block. However, you are trying to raise this exception in the outer block. This example causes a syntax error because the exception declared in the inner block ceases to exists once the inner block terminates. As a result, this example produces the following output:

```
Enter value for sv_number: 11
old   13:     IF 10 > &sv_number
new   13:     IF 10 > 11
        RAISE e_my_exception;
              *
ERROR at line 15:
ORA-06550: line 15, column 13:
PLS-00201: identifier 'E_MY_EXCEPTION' must be declared
ORA-06550: line 15, column 7:
PL/SQL: Statement ignored
```

Notice, the error message

PLS-00201: identifier 'E_MY_EXCEPTION' must be declared

is the same error message you get when trying to use a variable that has not been declared.

LAB 9.2 EXERCISES

9.2.1 USING USER-DEFINED EXCEPTIONS

In this exercise, you will define an exception that will allow you to raise an error if instructor teaches ten or more sections.

Create the following PL/SQL script:

```
-- ch09_2a.sql, version 1.0
SET SERVEROUTPUT ON
DECLARE
   CURSOR instruct_cur IS
       SELECT instructor_id, COUNT(*) tot_sec
         FROM section
       GROUP BY instructor_id;

   v_name VARCHAR2(30);
   e_too_many_sections EXCEPTION;
BEGIN
   FOR instruct_rec IN instruct_cur LOOP
      IF instruct_rec.tot_sec >= 10
      THEN
         RAISE e_too_many_sections;
      ELSE
          SELECT RTRIM(first_name)||' '||RTRIM(last_name)
            INTO v_name
            FROM instructor
           WHERE instructor_id =
                  instruct_rec.instructor_id;
          DBMS_OUTPUT.PUT_LINE
             ('Instructor, '||v_name||', teaches '||
              instruct_rec.tot_sec||' sections');
      END IF;
   END LOOP;
EXCEPTION
   WHEN e_too_many_sections
   THEN
      DBMS_OUTPUT.PUT_LINE
         ('This instructor teaches too much');
END;
```

Execute the script, then answer the following questions:

a) What output was printed on the screen?

_____

_____

b) What is the condition that causes the user-defined exception to be raised?

_____

_____

c) How would you change the script so that the cursor FOR LOOP processes all records returned by the cursor? In other words, once an exception is raised, the cursor FOR LOOP should not terminate.

_____

_____

d) How would you change the script to display an instructor's name in the error message as well?

_____

_____

LAB 9.2 EXERCISE ANSWERS

9.2.1 ANSWERS

a) What output was printed on the screen?

Answer: Your output should look like the following:

```
Instructor, Fernand Hanks, teaches 9 sections
This instructor teaches too much
PL/SQL procedure successfully completed.
```

b) What is the condition that causes the user-defined exception to be raised?

Answer: The user-defined exception is raised if the condition,

```
instruct_rec.tot_sec >= 10
```

evaluates to TRUE. In other words, if instructor teaches ten or more sections, the exception `e_too_many_sections` *is raised.*

c) How would you change the script so that the cursor FOR LOOP processes all records returned by the cursor? In other words, once an exception is raised, the cursor FOR LOOP should not terminate.

Answer: This answer contains only a portion of the program affected by changes. All changes are shown in bold letters.

```
-- ch09_2b.sql, version 2.0
SET SERVEROUTPUT ON
DECLARE
    ...
BEGIN
    FOR instruct_rec IN instruct_cur LOOP
        BEGIN
            IF instruct_rec.tot_sec >= 10
              THEN
                ...
              END IF;
        EXCEPTION
            WHEN e_too_many_sections
            THEN
                DBMS_OUTPUT.PUT_LINE
                    ('This instructor teaches too much');
        END;
    END LOOP;
END;
```

There are several changes in the new version of this script. First, the inner block has been created inside the body of the cursor FOR LOOP. Next, the exception-handling section has been moved from the outer block to the inner block.

In this script, the exception has been declared in the outer block, but it is raised in the inner block. This does not cause any errors because the exception, `e_too_many_sections`, is global to the inner block. Hence, it can be raised anywhere in this script.

The new version of this script produces the output shown below:

```
Instructor, Fernand Hanks, teaches 9 sections
This instructor teaches too much
```

```
This instructor teaches too much
This instructor teaches too much
This instructor teaches too much
This instructor teaches too much
This instructor teaches too much
Instructor, Charles Lowry, teaches 9 sections
PL/SQL procedure successfully completed.
```

d) How would you change the script to display an instructor's name in the error message as well?

Answer: Your script should look similar to the script shown below. All changes are shown in bold letters.

```
-- ch09_2c.sql, version 3.0
SET SERVEROUTPUT ON
DECLARE
   CURSOR instruct_cur IS
      SELECT instructor_id, COUNT(*) tot_sec
        FROM section
     GROUP BY instructor_id;

   v_name VARCHAR2(30);
   e_too_many_sections EXCEPTION;
BEGIN
   FOR instruct_rec IN instruct_cur LOOP
      BEGIN
         SELECT RTRIM(first_name)||' '||
                RTRIM(last_name)
           INTO v_name
           FROM instructor
          WHERE instructor_id =
                instruct_rec.instructor_id;
         IF instruct_rec.tot_sec >= 10
         THEN
            RAISE e_too_many_sections;
         ELSE
            DBMS_OUTPUT.PUT_LINE
               ('Instructor, '||v_name||', teaches '||
                  instruct_rec.tot_sec||' sections');
         END IF;
      EXCEPTION
      WHEN e_too_many_sections
      THEN
```

```
            DBMS_OUTPUT.PUT_LINE
               ('Instructor, '||v_name||
                ', teaches too much');
        END;
     END LOOP;
  END;
```

In order to achieve the desired result, the SELECT INTO statement has been moved outside the IF-THEN-ELSE statement. This change allows you to get an instructor's name regardless of the number of sections he or she teaches. As a result, you are able to include an instructor's name in the error message, thus improving the error message itself.

The new version of the output is shown below:

```
Instructor, Fernand Hanks, teaches 9 sections
Instructor, Tom Wojick, teaches too much
Instructor, Nina Schorin, teaches too much
Instructor, Gary Pertez, teaches too much
Instructor, Anita Morris, teaches too much
Instructor, Todd Smythe, teaches too much
Instructor, Marilyn Frantzen, teaches too much
Instructor, Charles Lowry, teaches 9 sections
PL/SQL procedure successfully completed.
```

This version of the output is oriented more toward a user compared to the previous versions because it displays the name of the instructor in every message. The previous versions of the output were confusing because it was not clear what instructor caused this error. For example, consider the output produced by the first version of this script.

```
Instructor, Fernand Hanks, teaches 9 sections
This instructor teaches too much
```

It is not clear to a user if the message "This instructor teaches too much" is caused by the fact that Fernand Hanks teaches nine sections, or that another instructor teaches more than nine sections.

Remember, you have created this script, and you know the exception that you have defined. However, as mentioned earlier, most of the time, a user does not have access to your program. Therefore, it is important for you to have clear error messages in your programs.

LAB 9.2 SELF-REVIEW QUESTIONS

In order to test your progress, you should be able to answer the following questions.

1) In order to use a user-defined exception, it must be
   a) _____declared.
   b) _____declared and raised.

2) How does any user-defined exception get raised?
   a) _____Implicitly
   b) _____Explicitly

3) If a user-defined exception has been declared in the inner block, it can be raised in the outer block.
   a) _____True
   b) _____False

4) When a user-defined exception is raised and executed, the control is passed back to the PL/SQL block.
   a) _____True
   b) _____False

5) A user-defined exception is raised with the help of the following:
   a) _____IF-THEN and RAISE statements
   b) _____IF-THEN statement only
   c) _____RAISE statement only

Quiz answers appear in Appendix A, Section 9.2.

L A B 9 . 3

EXCEPTION PROPAGATION

LAB OBJECTIVES

After this lab, you will be able to:

✔ Understand How Exceptions Propagate
✔ Reraise Exceptions

You already have seen how different types of exceptions are raised when a runtime error occurs in the executable portion of the PL/SQL block. However, a runtime error may occur in the declaration section of the block or in the exception-handling section of the block. The rules that govern how exceptions are raised in these situations are referred to as *exception propagation.*

Consider the first case: A runtime error occurred in the executable section of the PL/SQL block. This case should be treated as a review because the examples that you have seen earlier in this chapter show how an exception is raised when an error occurs in the executable section of the block.

If there is an exception specified associated with a particular error, the control is passed to the exception-handling section of the block. Once the statements associated with the exception are executed, the control is passed to the host environment or to the enclosing block. If there is no exception handler for this error, the exception is propagated to the enclosing block (outer block). Then, the steps described above are repeated again. If no exception handler is found, the execution of the program halts, and the control is transferred to the host environment.

Next, take a look at a second case: A runtime error occurred in the declaration section of the block. If there is no outer block, the execution of the program halts, and the control is passed to the host environment. Consider the following script.

■ FOR EXAMPLE

```
DECLARE
    v_test_var CHAR(3):= 'ABCDE';
BEGIN
    DBMS_OUTPUT.PUT_LINE('This is a test');
EXCEPTION
    WHEN INVALID_NUMBER OR VALUE_ERROR
    THEN
        DBMS_OUTPUT.PUT_LINE('An error has occurred');
END;
```

When executed, this example produces the output shown below:

```
DECLARE
*
ERROR at line 1:
ORA-06502: PL/SQL: numeric or value error
ORA-06512: at line 2
```

As you can see, the assignment statement in the declaration section of the block causes an error. Even though there is an exception handler for this error, the block is not able to execute successfully. So, based on this example you may conclude that *when a runtime error occurs in the declaration section of the PL/SQL block, the exception-handling section of this block is not able to catch the error.*

Next, let's consider an example with nested PL/SQL blocks.

■ FOR EXAMPLE

```
--outer block
BEGIN
    -- inner block
    DECLARE
       v_test_var CHAR(3):= 'ABCDE';
    BEGIN
       DBMS_OUTPUT.PUT_LINE('This is a test');
    EXCEPTION
       WHEN INVALID_NUMBER OR VALUE_ERROR
       THEN
           DBMS_OUTPUT.PUT_LINE
```

```
                        ('An error has occurred in the inner '||
                        'block');
        END;
EXCEPTION
    WHEN INVALID_NUMBER OR VALUE_ERROR
    THEN
        DBMS_OUTPUT.PUT_LINE
            ('An error has occurred in the program');
END;
```

When executed, this example produces the output shown below:

An error has occurred in the program
PL/SQL procedure successfully completed.

In this example, the PL/SQL block is enclosed by another block, and the program is able to complete. This is possible because the exception defined in the outer block is raised when the error occurs in the declaration section of the inner block. Therefore, you can conclude *that when a runtime error occurs in the declaration section of the inner block, the exception immediately propagates to the enclosing (outer) block.*

Finally, consider a third case: A runtime error occurred in the exception-handling section of the block. Just like in the previous case, if there is no outer block, the execution of the program halts, and the control is passed to the host environment. Consider the following script.

■ FOR EXAMPLE

```
DECLARE
    v_test_var CHAR(3) := 'ABC';
BEGIN
    v_test_var := '1234';
    DBMS_OUTPUT.PUT_LINE('v_test_var: '||v_test_var);
EXCEPTION
    WHEN INVALID_NUMBER OR VALUE_ERROR
    THEN
        v_test_var := 'ABCD';
        DBMS_OUTPUT.PUT_LINE('An error has occurred');
END;
```

When executed, this example produces the output shown below:

```
DECLARE
*
ERROR at line 1:
ORA-06502: PL/SQL: numeric or value error
ORA-06512: at line 9
ORA-06502: PL/SQL: numeric or value error
```

As you can see, the assignment statement in the executable section of the block causes an error. Therefore, the control is transferred to the exception-handling section of the block. However, the assignment statement in the exception-handling section of the block raises the same error. As a result, the output of this example contains the same error message twice. The first message is generated by the assignment statement in the executable section of the block, and the second message is generated by the assignment statement of the exception-handling section of this block. So, based on this example one may conclude that *when a runtime error occurs in the exception-handling section of the PL/SQL block, the exception-handling section of this block is not able to prevent the error.*

Next, consider an example with nested PL/SQL blocks.

■ FOR EXAMPLE

```
--outer block
BEGIN
   -- inner block
   DECLARE
      v_test_var CHAR(3) := 'ABC';
   BEGIN
      v_test_var := '1234';
      DBMS_OUTPUT.PUT_LINE('v_test_var: '||v_test_var);
   EXCEPTION
      WHEN INVALID_NUMBER OR VALUE_ERROR
      THEN
         v_test_var := 'ABCD';
         DBMS_OUTPUT.PUT_LINE
            ('An error has occurred in the inner '||
            'block');
   END;
EXCEPTION
   WHEN INVALID_NUMBER OR VALUE_ERROR
   THEN
      DBMS_OUTPUT.PUT_LINE
         ('An error has occurred in the program');
END;
```

When executed, this example produces the output shown below:

An error has occurred in the program
PL/SQL procedure successfully completed.

In this example, the PL/SQL block is enclosed by another block, and the program is able to complete. This is possible because the exception defined in the outer block is raised when the error occurs in the exception-handling section of the inner block. Therefore, you can conclude that *when a runtime error occurs in the exception-handling section of the inner block, the exception immediately propagates to the enclosing block.*

In the previous two examples, an exception is raised implicitly by a runtime error in the exception-handling section of the block. However, an exception can be raised in the exception-handling section of the block explicitly by the RAISE statement. Consider the following example.

■ FOR EXAMPLE

```
--outer block
DECLARE
    e_exception1 EXCEPTION;
    e_exception2 EXCEPTION;
BEGIN
    -- inner block
    BEGIN
        RAISE e_exception1;
    EXCEPTION
        WHEN e_exception1
        THEN
            RAISE e_exception2;
        WHEN e_exception2
        THEN
            DBMS_OUTPUT.PUT_LINE
                ('An error has occurred in the inner '||
                'block');
    END;
EXCEPTION
    WHEN e_exception2
    THEN
        DBMS_OUTPUT.PUT_LINE
            ('An error has occurred in the program');
    END;
```

This example produces the output shown below:

```
An error has occurred in the program
PL/SQL procedure successfully completed.
```

Here two exceptions are declared: e_exception1 and e_exception2. The exception e_exception1 is raised in the inner block via statement RAISE. In the exception-handling section of the block, the exception e_exception1 tries to raise e_exception2. Even though there is an exception handler for the exception e_exception2, the control is transferred to the outer block. This happens because only one exception can be raised in the exception-handling section of the block. *Only after one exception has been handled, another can be raised, but two or more exceptions cannot be raised simultaneously.*

When a PL/SQL block is not enclosed by another block, the control is transferred to the host environment, and the program is not able to complete successfully. Then, the error message shown below is displayed.

```
DECLARE
*
ERROR at line 1:
ORA-06510: PL/SQL: unhandled user-defined exception
ORA-06512: at line 9
ORA-06510: PL/SQL: unhandled user-defined exception
```

RERAISING AN EXCEPTION

On some occasions you may want to be able to stop your program if a certain type of error occurs. In other words, you may want to handle an exception in the inner block and then pass it to the outer block. This process is called *reraising an exception*. The example shown below helps to illustrate this point.

■ FOR EXAMPLE

```
-- outer block
DECLARE
    e_exception EXCEPTION;
BEGIN
    -- inner block
    BEGIN
        RAISE e_exception;
    EXCEPTION
        WHEN e_exception
```

```
          THEN
               RAISE;
          END;
     EXCEPTION
          WHEN e_exception
          THEN
               DBMS_OUTPUT.PUT_LINE('An error has occurred');
     END;
```

In the example shown above, the exception, `e_exception`, is declared in the outer block. Then it is raised in the inner block. As a result, the control is transferred to the exception handling section of the inner block. The statement RAISE in the exception-handling section of the block causes the exception to propagate to the exception-handling section of the outer block. Notice that *when the RAISE statement is used in the exception-handling section of the inner block, it is not followed by the exception name.*

When run, this example produces the output shown below:

**The error has occurred
PL/SQL procedure successfully completed.**

It is important to note that when an exception is reraised in the block that is not enclosed by any other block, the program is unable to complete successfully. Consider the following example:

```
DECLARE
     e_exception EXCEPTION;
BEGIN
     RAISE e_exception;
EXCEPTION
     WHEN e_exception
     THEN
          RAISE;
END;
```

When run, this example produces the following output:

```
DECLARE
*
ERROR at line 1:
ORA-06510: PL/SQL: unhandled user-defined exception
ORA-06512: at line 8
```

LAB 9.3 EXERCISES

9.3.1 UNDERSTANDING HOW EXCEPTIONS PROPAGATE

In this exercise, you will use nested PL/SQL blocks to practice exception propagation. You will be asked to experiment with the script via exceptions. Try to answer the questions *before* you run the script. Once you have answered the questions, run the script and check your answers.

Create the following PL/SQL script:

```
-- ch09_3a.sql, version 1.0
SET SERVEROUTPUT ON
DECLARE
   v_my_name VARCHAR2(15) := 'ELENA SILVESTROVA';
BEGIN
   DBMS_OUTPUT.PUT_LINE('My name is '||v_my_name);
   DECLARE
      v_your_name VARCHAR2(15);
   BEGIN
      v_your_name := '&sv_your_name';
      DBMS_OUTPUT.PUT_LINE
         ('Your name is '||v_your_name);
   EXCEPTION
      WHEN VALUE_ERROR
      THEN
         DBMS_OUTPUT.PUT_LINE
            ('Error in the inner block');
         DBMS_OUTPUT.PUT_LINE('This name is too long');
   END;
EXCEPTION
   WHEN VALUE_ERROR
   THEN
      DBMS_OUTPUT.PUT_LINE('Error in the outer block');
      DBMS_OUTPUT.PUT_LINE('This name is too long');
END;
```

Answer the following questions first, and then execute the script:

a) What exception is raised by the assignment statement in the declaration section of the outer block?

_____

_____

b) Once this exception (based on the previous question) is raised, will the program terminate successfully? You should explain your answer.

_____

_____

c) How would you change this script so that the exception is able to handle an error caused by the assignment statement in the declaration section of the outer block?

_____

_____

d) Change the value of the variable from "Elena Silvestrova" to "Elena." Then change the script so that if there is an error caused by the assignment statement of the inner block, it is handled by the exception-handling section of the outer block.

_____

_____

9.3.2 RERAISING EXCEPTIONS

In this exercise, you will check how many sections there are for each course. If a course does not have any section associated with it, you will raise an exception, `e_no_sections`. Again, try to answer the questions *before* you run the script. Once you have answered the questions, run the script and check your answers.

Create the following PL/SQL script:

```
-- ch09_4a.sql, version 1.0
SET SERVEROUTPUT ON
DECLARE
    CURSOR course_cur IS
        SELECT course_no
        FROM course;
```

```
        v_total NUMBER;
        e_no_sections EXCEPTION;
BEGIN
    FOR course_rec in course_cur
    LOOP
        BEGIN
            SELECT COUNT(*)
              INTO v_total
              FROM section
             WHERE course_no = course_rec.course_no;
            IF v_total = 0
            THEN
                RAISE e_no_sections;
            ELSE
                DBMS_OUTPUT.PUT_LINE
                    ('Course, '||course_rec.course_no||
                     ' has '||v_total||' sections');
            END IF;
        EXCEPTION
            WHEN e_no_sections
            THEN
                DBMS_OUTPUT.PUT_LINE
                    ('There are no sections for course '||
                     course_rec.course_no);
        END;
    END LOOP;
END;
```

Answer the following questions first, and then execute the script:

a) What exception will be raised if there are no sections for a given course number?

_____

_____

b) If the exception `e_no_sections` is raised, will the cursor FOR LOOP terminate? You should explain your answer.

_____

_____

c) Change this script so that the exception `e_no_sections` is reraised in the outer block.

LAB 9.3 EXERCISE ANSWERS

9.3.1 ANSWERS

a) What exception is raised by the assignment statement in the declaration section of the outer block?

Answer: The exception VALUE_ERROR is raised by the assignment statement of the outer block.

The variable `v_my_name` is declared as VARCHAR2(15). However, the value that is assigned to this variable contains seventeen letters. As a result, the assignment statement causes a runtime error.

b) Once this exception (based on the previous question) is raised, will the program terminate successfully? You should explain your answer.

Answer: When that exception VALUE_ERROR is raised, the script is not able to complete successfully because the error occurred in the declaration section of the outer block. Since the outer block is not enclosed by any other block, the control is transferred to the host environment. As a result, the error message will be generated when this example is run.

c) How would you change this script so that the exception is able to handle an error caused by the assignment statement in the declaration section of the outer block?

Answer: In order for the exception to handle the error generated by the assignment statement in the declaration section of the outer block, the assignment statement must be moved to the executable section of this block. This answer shown below contains only a portion of the program affected by changes. All changes are shown in bold letters.

```
-- ch09_3b.sql, version 2.0
DECLARE
   v_my_name VARCHAR2(15);
BEGIN
   v_my_name := 'ELENA SILVESTROVA';
   ...
END;
```

The new version of this script produces the output shown below:

```
Enter value for sv_your_name: TEST A NAME
old    9:        v_your_name := '&sv_your_name';
new    9:        v_your_name := 'TEST A NAME';
Error in the outer block
This name is too long
PL/SQL procedure successfully completed.
```

d) Change the value of the variable from "Elena Silvestrova" to "Elena." Then change the script so that if there is an error caused by the assignment statement of the inner block, it is handled by the exception-handling section of the outer block.

Answer: This answer shown below contains only a portion of the program affected by changes. All changes are shown in bold letters.

```
-- ch09_3c.sql, version 3.0
SET SERVEROUTPUT ON
DECLARE
   v_my_name VARCHAR2(15) := 'ELENA';
BEGIN
   DBMS_OUTPUT.PUT_LINE('My name is '||v_my_name);
   DECLARE
      v_your_name VARCHAR2(15) := '&sv_your_name';
   BEGIN
      DBMS_OUTPUT.PUT_LINE
          ('Your name is '||v_your_name);
   ...
END;
```

In this version of the example, the assignment statement was moved from the executable section of the inner block to the declaration section of this block. As a result, if an exception is raised by the assignment statement of the inner block, the control is transferred to the exception section of the outer block.

You can modify this example in a different manner that allows you to achieve the same result.

```
-- ch09_3c.sql, version 3.0
SET SERVEROUTPUT ON
DECLARE
   v_my_name VARCHAR2(15) := 'ELENA';
BEGIN
   DBMS_OUTPUT.PUT_LINE('My name is '||v_my_name);
   DECLARE
```

```
        v_your_name VARCHAR2(15);
    BEGIN
        v_your_name := := '&sv_your_name';
        DBMS_OUTPUT.PUT_LINE
            ('Your name is '||v_your_name);
    EXCEPTION
        WHEN VALUE_ERROR
        THEN
            RAISE;
    ...
END;
```

In this version of example, the RAISE statement was used in the exception-handling section of the inner block. As a result, the exception is reraised in the outer block.

Both versions of this example produce very similar output. The first output is generated by the third version of the example, and the second output is generated by the fourth version of the example.

```
Enter value for sv_your_name: THIS NAME MUST BE REALLY
LONG
old    6:          v_your_name VARCHAR2(15) :=
'&sv_your_name';
new    6:          v_your_name VARCHAR2(15) := 'THIS NAME
MUST BE REALLY LONG';
My name is ELENA
Error in the outer block
This name is too long
PL/SQL procedure successfully completed.


Enter value for sv_your_name: THIS NAME MUST BE
REALLY LONG
old    8:        v_your_name := '&sv_your_name';
new    8:        v_your_name := 'THIS NAME MUST BE REALLY
LONG';
My name is ELENA
Error in the outer block
This name is too long
PL/SQL procedure successfully completed.
```

Notice, the only difference between two versions of output is the line number of the bind variable. In the first version of the output, the assignment statement takes place in the declaration section of the inner block. In the second version of the output, the assignment statement occurs in the executable section of the inner block. However, all messages displayed on the screen are identical in both versions of the output.

9.3.2 ANSWERS

a) What exception will be raised if there are no sections for a given course number?

Answer: If there are no sections for a given course number, the exception e_no_sections *is raised.*

b) If the exception e_no_sections is raised, will the cursor FOR LOOP terminate? You should explain your answer.

Answer: If the exception e_no_sections *is raised, the cursor FOR LOOP will continue its normal execution. This is possible because the inner block, in which this exception is raised and handled, is located inside the body of the loop.*

c) Change this script so that the exception e_no_sections is reraised in the outer block.

Answer: Your script should look similar to the script shown below. All changes are shown in bold letters.

```
-- ch09_4b.sql, version 2.0
SET SERVEROUTPUT ON
DECLARE
   ...
BEGIN
   FOR course_rec in course_cur
   LOOP
      BEGIN
         ...
      EXCEPTION
         WHEN e_no_sections
         THEN
            RAISE;
      END;
   END LOOP;
EXCEPTION
   WHEN e_no_sections
   THEN
      DBMS_OUTPUT.PUT_LINE('There are no sections '||
                           'for the course');
END;
```

In this version of the example, the exception-handling section of the inner block was modified. The DBMS_OUTPUT.PUT_LINE statement has been replaced by the RAISE statement. In addition, the exception-handling section was included in the outer block.

Notice, the error message has been modified as well. There is no course number displayed by the error message. This change is necessary because the exception-handling section of the outer block is located outside the cursor FOR loop. Therefore, the course number is not visible by the exception.

LAB 9.3 SELF-REVIEW QUESTIONS

In order to test your progress, you should be able to answer the following questions.

1) When an exception is raised in the declaration section of the inner block, it propagates to the
a) _____exception-handling section of this block.
b) _____exception-handling section of the enclosing (outer) block.
c) _____host environment and causes a syntax error.

2) When an exception is raised in the declaration section of the outer block, it propagates to the
a) _____exception-handling section of this block.
b) _____ host environment and causes a syntax error.

3) When an exception is raised in the executable section of the inner block, it propagates to the
a) _____exception-handling section of this block.
b) _____exception-handling section of the enclosing block.
c) _____host environment and causes a syntax error.

4) When an exception is reraised in the inner block, the control is transferred to the
a) _____exception-handling section of this block.
b) _____exception-handling section of the enclosing block.

5) To reraise an exception one must issue the following statement:
a) _____RAISE *exception_name*
b) _____RAISE
c) _____There is no need to issue any statements.

Quiz answers appear in Appendix A, Section 9.3.

**LAB
9.3**

C H A P T E R   9

TEST YOUR THINKING

In this chapter you have learned about built-in exceptions. Here are some projects that will help you test the depth of your understanding.

1) Create the following script. For each section determine the number of students registered. If this number is equal or greater than 15, raise user-defined exception `e_too_many_students` and display the error message. Otherwise, display how many students are there for a section. Make sure that your program is able to process all sections.

2) Modify the script you created in the previous exercise. Once the exception `e_too_many_students` has been raised in the inner block, reraise it in the outer block.

CHAPTER 10

EXCEPTIONS: ADVANCED CONCEPTS

In Chapters 6 and 9, you encountered the concept of error handling, built-in exceptions, and user-defined exceptions. You also learned about the scope of an exception, and how to reraise an exception.

In this chapter you will conclude your exploration of error handling and exceptions with advanced topics. After working through this chapter, you will be able to associate an error number with an error message. You also will be able to trap a runtime error having an Oracle error number but no name by which it can be referenced.

LAB 10.1

RAISE_APPLICATION_ ERROR

> ### LAB OBJECTIVES
>
> After this lab, you will be able to:
>
> ✔ Use RAISE_APPLICATION_ERROR

RAISE_APPLICATION_ERROR is a special built-in procedure provided by Oracle. This procedure allows programmers to create meaningful error messages for a specific application. Therefore, the RAISE_ APLICATION_ERROR procedure works with user-defined exceptions. The syntax of the RAISE_APPLICATION_ERROR is:

```
RAISE_APPLICATION_ERROR(error_number, error_message);
or
RAISE_APPLICATION_ERROR(error_number, error_message,
                        keep_errors);
```

As you can see, there are two forms of the RAISE_APPLICATION_ERROR procedure. The first form contains only two parameters: *error_number* and *error_message*. The *error_number* is a number of the error that a programmer associates with a specific error message. This error number can be any number between –20,999 and –20,000. The *error_message* is the text of the error, and it can contain up to 512 characters.

The second form of the RAISE_APPLICATION_ERROR contains one additional parameter: *keep_errors*. *Keep_errors* is an optional Boolean parameter. If *keep_errors* is set to TRUE, the new error will be added to the list of errors that has been raised already. If *keep_errors* is set to FALSE, the new error replaces the list of errors that has been raised already. The default value for the parameter *keep_errors* is FALSE.

It is important for you to note that the RAISE_APPLICATION_ERROR procedure works with *unnamed user-defined exceptions*. It associates the number of the error with the text of the error. Therefore, the user-defined exception does not have a name associated with it.

Consider the following example used in Chapter 9. This example illustrates the use of the named user-defined exception and the RAISE statement. Within the example you will be able to compare a modified version using the unnamed user-defined exception and the RAISE_APPLICATION_ERROR procedure.

■ FOR EXAMPLE

First, view the original example from Chapter 9. Notice, the named user-defined exception and the RAISE statement are shown in bold letters.

```
DECLARE
    v_student_id STUDENT.STUDENT_ID%TYPE :=
                 &sv_student_id;
    v_total_courses NUMBER;
    e_invalid_id EXCEPTION;
BEGIN
    IF v_student_id < 0
    THEN
        RAISE e_invalid_id;
    ELSE
        SELECT COUNT(*)
          INTO v_total_courses
          FROM enrollment
         WHERE student_id = v_student_id;
        DBMS_OUTPUT.PUT_LINE
            ('The student is registered for '||
              v_total_courses||' courses');
    END IF;
    DBMS_OUTPUT.PUT_LINE('No exception has been raised');
EXCEPTION
    WHEN e_invalid_id
    THEN
        DBMS_OUTPUT.PUT_LINE('An id cannot be negative');
END;
```

Now, compare the modified example as follows (changes are shown in bold letters):

```
DECLARE
   v_student_id STUDENT.STUDENT_ID%TYPE :=
                   &sv_student_id;
   v_total_courses NUMBER;
BEGIN
   IF v_student_id < 0
   THEN
      RAISE_APPLICATION_ERROR
          (-20000, 'An id cannot be negative');
   ELSE
      SELECT COUNT(*)
        INTO v_total_courses
        FROM enrollment
       WHERE student_id = v_student_id;
      DBMS_OUTPUT.PUT_LINE
          ('The student is registered for '||
            v_total_courses||' courses');
   END IF;
END;
```

The second version of the example does not contain the name of the exception, the RAISE statement, and the error-handling section of the PL/SQL block. Instead, it has a single RAISE_APPLICATION_ERROR statement.

Even though the RAISE_APPLICATION_ERROR is a built-in procedure, it is can be referred to as a statement when used in the PL/SQL block.

Both versions of the example achieve the same result: The processing stops if a negative number is provided for the v_student_id. However, the second version of this example produces the output that has the look and feel of an error message. Now, run both versions of the example with the value of –4 for the variable v_student_id.

The first version of the example produces the following output:

```
Enter value for sv_student_id: -4
old   3: v_student_id STUDENT.STUDENT_ID%TYPE :=
&sv_student_id;
new   3: v_student_id STUDENT.STUDENT_ID%TYPE := -4;
An id cannot be negative
PL/SQL procedure successfully completed.
```

The second version of the example produces the following output:

```
Enter value for sv_student_id: -4
old    3: v_student_id STUDENT.STUDENT_ID%TYPE :=
&sv_student_id;
new    3: v_student_id STUDENT.STUDENT_ID%TYPE := -4;
DECLARE
*
ERROR at line 1:
ORA-20000: An id cannot be negative
ORA-06512: at line 8
```

The output produced by the first version of the example contains the error message "An id cannot be negative" and the message "PL/SQL completed . . .". The error message "An id cannot . . ." in the output generated by the second version of the example looks like the error message generated by the system because the error number ORA-20000 precedes the error message.

The RAISE_APPLICATION_ERROR procedure can work with built-in exceptions as well. Consider the following example:

■ FOR EXAMPLE

```
DECLARE
    v_student_id STUDENT.STUDENT_ID%TYPE :=
                &sv_student_id;
    v_name VARCHAR2(50);
BEGIN
    SELECT first_name||' '||last_name
      INTO v_name
      FROM student
     WHERE student_id = v_student_id;
     DBMS_OUTPUT.PUT_LINE(v_name);
EXCEPTION
   WHEN NO_DATA_FOUND
   THEN
       RAISE_APPLICATION_ERROR
           (-20001, 'This ID is invalid');
END;
```

When the value of 100 is entered for the student ID, the example produces the output shown below:

```
Enter value for sv_student_id: 100
old    3: v_student_id STUDENT.STUDENT_ID%TYPE :=
&sv_student_id;
```

```
new    3: v_student_id STUDENT.STUDENT_ID%TYPE := 100;
DECLARE
*
ERROR at line 1:
ORA-20001: This ID is invalid
ORA-06512: at line 14
```

The built-in exception NO_DATA_FOUND is raised because there is no record in the STUDENT table corresponding to this value of the student ID. However, the number of the error message does not refer to the exception NO_DATA_FOUND. It refers to the error message "This ID is invalid."

The RAISE_APPLICATION_ERROR procedure allows programmers to return error messages in a manner that is consistent with Oracle errors. However, it is important for you to note that it is up to a programmer to maintain the relationship between the error numbers and the error messages. For example, you have designed an application to maintain the enrollment information on students. In this application you have associated the error text "This ID is invalid" with the error number ORA-20001. This error message can be used by your application for any invalid ID. Once you have associated the error number (ORA-20001) with a specific error message (This ID is invalid), you should not assign this error number to another error message. If you do not maintain the relationship between error numbers and error messages, the error-handling interface of your application might become very confusing to the users and to yourself.

LAB 10.1 EXERCISES

10.1.1 USING RAISE_APPLICATION_ERROR

In this exercise, you calculate how many students are registered for each course. You then display a message on the screen that contains the course number and the number of students registered for it. The original PL/SQL script will not contain any exception handlers. So, you will be asked to add the RAISE_APPLICATION_ERROR statement.

Create the following PL/SQL script:

```
-- ch10_1a.sql, version 1.0
SET SERVEROUTPUT ON
DECLARE
```

```
         CURSOR course_cur IS
            SELECT course_no, section_id
              FROM section
            ORDER BY course_no, section_id;
         v_cur_course SECTION.COURSE_NO%TYPE := 0;
         v_students NUMBER(3) := 0;
         v_total NUMBER(3) := 0;
     BEGIN
         FOR course_rec IN course_cur LOOP
            IF v_cur_course = 0
            THEN
               v_cur_course := course_rec.course_no;
            END IF;
            SELECT COUNT(*)
            INTO v_students
            FROM enrollment
            WHERE section_id = course_rec.section_id;
            IF v_cur_course = course_rec.course_no
            THEN
               v_total := v_total + v_students;
            ELSE
               DBMS_OUTPUT.PUT_LINE
                  ('Course '||v_cur_course||' has
                  '||v_total||
                   ' student(s)');
               v_cur_course := course_rec.course_no;
               v_total := 0;
            END IF;
         END LOOP;
         DBMS_OUTPUT.PUT_LINE('Done...');
     END;
```

Take a closer look this script. As you learned earlier, this script determines the number of students registered for each course. It then displays the course number and the number of students on the screen. In order to achieve these results, the cursor needs to be defined on the SECTION table. This cursor retrieves the course numbers and section IDs. It also now defines three variables: v_cur_course, v_students, and v_total.

The variable v_cur_course holds the number of the current course. There are duplicate course numbers in the SECTION table because a course can have multiple sections. In order to display the number of students for each course rather than each section, you need to store the number of the current course. For example, course 10 has three sections: 1, 2, and 3. Section 1 has 3 students, section 2 has 5 students, and section 3 has 10 students. Therefore, course 10 has 18 students. Once this number is calculated, the message "10 has 18 student(s)" can be displayed on the screen. As a result, you need to compare the variable `v_cur_course` to the course number returned by the cursor.

The variable `v_students` holds the number of students registered for a specific section of a course. As long as the value of the variable `v_cur_course` equals to the value of the `course_rec.course_no`, the variable `v_students` is added to the current value of the variable `v_total`. The variable `v_total` holds the total number of students registered for a given course.

Notice that in the body of the cursor FOR LOOP, there are two IF statements. The first IF statement

```
IF v_cur_course = 0
THEN
    v_cur_course := course_rec.course_no;
END IF;
```

is executed only once, for the first iteration of the cursor FOR LOOP only. This IF statement guarantees that the value of course_rec.course_no is assigned to the variable v_cur_course before any further processing.

The second IF statement

```
IF v_cur_course = course_rec.course_no
THEN
    v_total := v_total + v_students;
ELSE
    DBMS_OUTPUT.PUT_LINE
        ('Course '||v_cur_course||' has '||v_total||
        ' student(s)');
    v_cur_course := course_rec.course_no;
    v_total := 0;
END IF;
```

compares the value of the `v_cur_course` to the value of the `course_rec.course_no`. For the first iteration of the cursor FOR LOOP, this condition of the IF statement evaluates to TRUE, and the value of `v_students` is added to the current value of the `v_total`. For the next iteration of the cursor FOR LOOP, the IF statement evaluates to TRUE if the course number has not changed. However, if the course number has changed, this IF statement evaluates to FALSE, and the ELSE part of the IF statement is executed. Therefore, the DBMS_OUTPUT.PUT_LINE statement displays the course information on the screen, the value of the `course_rec.course_no` is assigned to the variable `v_cur_course`, and the value of the variable `v_total` is set to 0 again. Why do you think the variable `v_total` must be set to 0?

Execute the script and answer the following questions:

a) What output was printed on the screen?

_____

_____

b) Modify this script so that if a course has more than 20 students enrolled in it, an error message is displayed indicating that this course has too many students enrolled.

_____

_____

c) Execute the new version of the script. What output was printed on the screen?

_____

_____

d) Generally, when an exception is raised and handled inside a loop, the loop does not terminate prematurely. Why do you think the cursor FOR LOOP terminates as soon as RAISE_APPLICATION_ERROR executes?

_____

_____

LAB 10.1 EXERCISE ANSWERS

10.1.1 ANSWERS

a) What output was printed on the screen?

Answer:

```
Course 10 has 1 student(s)
Course 10 has 1 student(s)
Course 20 has 6 student(s)
Course 25 has 40 student(s)
Course 100 has 7 student(s)
Course 120 has 19 student(s)
Course 122 has 20 student(s)
Course 124 has 3 student(s)
Course 125 has 6 student(s)
Course 130 has 6 student(s)
Course 132 has 0 student(s)
Course 134 has 2 student(s)
Course 135 has 2 student(s)
Course 140 has 7 student(s)
Course 142 has 3 student(s)
Course 144 has 0 student(s)
Course 145 has 0 student(s)
Course 146 has 1 student(s)
Course 147 has 0 student(s)
Course 204 has 0 student(s)
Course 210 has 0 student(s)
Course 220 has 0 student(s)
Course 230 has 2 student(s)
Course 240 has 1 student(s)
Course 310 has 0 student(s)
Course 330 has 0 student(s)
Course 350 has 9 student(s)
Course 420 has 0 student(s)
Done...
PL/SQL procedure successfully completed.
```

Notice that each course number is displayed a single time only.

b) Modify this script so that if a course has more than 20 students enrolled in it, an error message is displayed indicating that this course has too many students enrolled.

Answer: This answer contains a portion of the code that is needed to illustrate the changes. All changes are shown in bold letters.

```
-- ch10_1b.sql, version 2.0
SET SERVEROUTPUT ON
DECLARE
   ...
BEGIN
   FOR course_rec IN course_cur LOOP
```

```
...
IF v_cur_course = course_rec.course_no
THEN
    v_total := v_total + v_students;
    IF v_total > 20
    THEN
        RAISE_APPLICATION_ERROR
            (-20002, 'Course '||v_cur_course||
            ' has too many students');
    END IF;
ELSE
    ...
END IF;
END LOOP;
DBMS_OUTPUT.PUT_LINE('Done...');
END;
```

Consider the result if you were to add another IF statement to this script, one in which the IF statement checks if the value of the variable exceeds 20. If the value of the variable does exceed 20, the RAISE_APPLICA-TION_ERROR statement executes, and the error message is displayed on the screen.

c) Execute the new version of the script. What output was printed on the screen?

Answer: Your output should look similar to the following:

```
Course 10 has 1 student(s)
Course 20 has 7 student(s)
DECLARE
*
ERROR at line 1:
ORA-20002: Course 25 has too many students
ORA-06512: at line 32
```

Course 25 has 40 students enrolled. As a result, the IF statement

```
IF v_total > 20
THEN
    RAISE_APPLICATION_ERROR
        (-20002, 'Course '||v_cur_course||
        ' has too many students');
END IF;
```

evaluates to TRUE, and the unnamed user-defined error is displayed on the screen.

d) Generally, when an exception is raised and handled inside a loop, the loop does not terminate prematurely. Why do you think the cursor FOR LOOP terminates as soon as RAISE_APPLICATION_ERROR- executes?

Answer: When the RAISE_APPLICATION_ERROR procedure is used to handle a user-defined exception, the control is passed to the host environment as soon as the error is handled. Therefore, the cursor FOR LOOP terminates prematurely. In this case, it terminates as soon as the course that has more than 20 students registered for it is encountered.

When a user-defined exception is used with the RAISE statement, the exception propagates from the inner block to the outer block. For example,

```
-- outer block
BEGIN
    FOR record IN cursor
    LOOP
        -- inner block
        BEGIN
            RAISE my_exception;
        EXCEPTION
            WHEN my_exception
            THEN
                    DBMS_OUTPUT.PUT_LINE
                        ('An error has occurred');
        END;
    END LOOP;
END;
```

In this example, the exception my_exception is raised and handled in the inner block. So, the control of the execution is passed to the outer block once the exception my_exception is raised. As a result, the cursor FOR LOOP will not terminate prematurely.

When the RAISE_APPLICATION_ERROR procedure is used, the control is always passed to the host environment. The exception does not propagate from the inner block to the outer block. Therefore, any loop defined in the outer block will terminate prematurely if an error has been raised in the inner block with the help of the RAISE_APPLICATION_ERROR procedure.

LAB 10.1 SELF-REVIEW QUESTIONS

In order to test your progress, you should be able to answer the following questions.

1) The RAISE_APPLICATION_ERROR works with which of the following?
    a) _____Named user-defined exceptions only
    b) _____Unnamed user-defined exceptions only
    c) _____Built-in and unnamed user-defined exceptions

2) The RAISE_APPLICATION_ERROR procedure requires which of the following parameters?
    a) _____error_number, error_text, keep_error
    b) _____error_text, keep_error
    c) _____error_number, error_text

3) The error number used in the RAISE_APPLICATION_ERROR must be which of the following?
    a) _____A negative number between −20,000 and −20,999
    b) _____A positive number between 20,000 and 20,999

4) The RAISE_APLICATION_ERROR halts the execution of the program.
    a) _____True
    b) _____False

5) When the parameter keep_error is set to TRUE, which of the following occurs?
    a) _____An error message is displayed on the screen.
    b) _____An error number is displayed on the screen.
    c) _____A new error message is added to the list of raised error messages.

Quiz answers appear in Appendix A, Section 10.1.

LAB 10.2

EXCEPTION_INIT PRAGMA

LAB OBJECTIVES

After this lab, you will be able to:

✔ Use EXCEPTION_INIT Pragma

Often your programs need to handle an Oracle error having a particular number associated with it, but no name by which it can be referenced. As a result, you are unable to write a handler to trap this error. In a case like this, you can use a construct called a *pragma*. A pragma is a special instruction to the PL/SQL compiler. It is important to note pragmas are processed at the time of the compilation. The *EXCEPTION_INIT pragma* allows you to associate an Oracle error number with a name of a user-defined error. Once you associate an error name with an Oracle error number, you can reference the error and write a handler for it.

The EXCEPTION_INIT pragma appears in the declaration section of a block as shown below:

```
DECLARE
    exception_name EXCEPTION;
    PRAGMA EXCEPTION_INIT(exception_name, error_code);
```

Notice that the declaration of the user-defined exception appears before the EXCEPTION_INIT pragma where it is used. The EXCEPTION_INIT pragma has two parameters: `exception_name` and `error_code`. The `exception_name` is the name of your exception, and the `error_code` is the number of the Oracle error you want to associate with your exception. Consider the following:

■ FOR EXAMPLE

```
DECLARE
    v_zip ZIPCODE.ZIP%TYPE := '&sv_zip';
BEGIN
    DELETE FROM zipcode
    WHERE zip = v_zip;
    DBMS_OUTPUT.PUT_LINE
        ('Zip '||v_zip||' has been deleted');
    COMMIT;
END;
```

In this example, the record corresponding to the value of zipcode provided by a user is deleted from the ZIPCODE table. Next, the message that a specific zipcode has been deleted is displayed on the screen.

Compare the results running this example entering 06870 for the value of v_zip. As a result, the example produces the following output:

```
Enter value for sv_zip: 06870
old    2:    v_zip ZIPCODE.ZIP%TYPE := '&sv_zip';
new    2:    v_zip ZIPCODE.ZIP%TYPE := '06870';
DECLARE
*
ERROR at line 1:
ORA-02292: integrity constraint (STUDENT.STU_ZIP_FK)
violated - child record found
ORA-06512: at line 4
```

The error message generated by this example occurs because you are trying to delete a record from the ZIPCODE table while its child records exist in the STUDENT table, thus violating the referencial integrity constraint STU_ZIP_FK. In other words, there is a record with a foreign key (STU_ZIP_FK) in the STUDENT table (child table) that references a record in the ZIPCODE table (parent table).

Notice that this error has Oracle error number ORA-02292 assigned to it, but it does not have a name. As a result, you need to associate this error number with a user-defined exception, so you can handle this error in the script.

Contrast the example if you modify it as follows (all changes are shown in bold letters):

**LAB
10.2**

■ *FOR EXAMPLE*

```
DECLARE
    v_zip ZIPCODE.ZIP%TYPE := '&sv_zip';
    e_child_exists EXCEPTION;
    PRAGMA EXCEPTION_INIT(e_child_exists, -2292);
BEGIN
    DELETE FROM zipcode
    WHERE zip = v_zip;
    DBMS_OUTPUT.PUT_LINE
        ('Zip '||v_zip||' has been deleted');
    COMMIT;
EXCEPTION
    WHEN e_child_exists
    THEN
        DBMS_OUTPUT.PUT_LINE
            ('Delete students for this zipcode first');
END;
```

In the example shown above, you declare the exception e_child_exists. Then, you associate the exception with the error number –2292. It is important to note you do not use ORA-02292 in the EXCEPTION_INIT pragma. Next, you add the exception-handling section to the PL/SQL block, so you trap this error. Notice, even though the exception e_child_exists is user-defined, you do not use the RAISE statement as you saw in Chapter 9. Why do you think you don't use the RAISE statement?

When you run this example using the same value of zipcode, the following output is produced:

```
Enter value for sv_zip: 06870
old   2:     v_zip ZIPCODE.ZIP%TYPE := '&sv_zip';
new   2:     v_zip ZIPCODE.ZIP%TYPE := '06870';
Delete students for this zipcode first
PL/SQL procedure successfully completed.
```

Notice, this output contains a new error message displayed by the DBMS_OUTPUT.PUT_LINE statement. This version of the output is more descriptive than the previous version. Remember, the user of the program probably does not know about the referencial integrity constraints existing in the database. Therefore, the EXCEPTION_INIT pragma improves the readability of your error-handling interface. If the need arises, you can use multiple EXCEPTION_INIT pragmas in your program.

LAB 10.2 EXERCISES

10.2.1 USING EXCEPTION_INIT PRAGMA

In this exercise, you insert a record in the COURSE table. The original PL/SQL script does not contain any exception handlers. So, you are asked to define an exception and add the EXCEPTION_INIT pragma.

Create the following PL/SQL script:

```
-- ch10_2a.sql, version 1.0
SET SERVEROUTPUT ON
BEGIN
    INSERT INTO course (course_no, description,
                            created_by, created_date)
    VALUES (COURSE_NO_SEQ.NEXTVAL, 'TEST COURSE', USER,
           SYSDATE);
    COMMIT;
    DBMS_OUTPUT.PUT_LINE('One course has been added');
END;
```

Notice that the INSERT statement contains an Oracle pseudo-column called USER. At first glance, this pseudo-column looks like a variable that has not been declared. This pseudo-column returns the name of the current user. In other words, it returns the login name that you used when connecting to Oracle.

Execute the script, then answer the following questions:

a) What output is printed on the screen?

_____

_____

b) Explain why the script does not execute successfully.

_____

_____

c) Add a user-defined exception to the script, so the error generated by the INSERT statement is handled.

d) Run the new version of the script. Explain the output produced by the new version of the script.

LAB 10.2 EXERCISE ANSWERS

10.2.1 ANSWERS

a) What output is printed on the screen?

Answer: Your output should look like the following:

```
DECLARE
*
ERROR at line 1:
ORA-01400: cannot insert NULL into
("STUDENT"."COURSE"."MODIFIED_BY")
ORA-06512: at line 4
```

b) Explain why the script does not execute successfully?

Answer: The script does not execute successfully because a NULL is inserted for the MODIFIED_BY and MODIFIED_DATE columns.

When a DESCRIBE statement

```
DESCRIBE course;
```

is issued on the COURSE table, the following output is produced:

Name	Null?	Type
COURSE_NO	NOT NULL	NUMBER(38)
DESCRIPTION	NOT NULL	VARCHAR2(50)
COST		NUMBER(9,2)

PREREQUISITE		NUMBER(38)
CREATED_BY	NOT NULL	VARCHAR2(30)
CREATED_DATE	NOT NULL	DATE
MODIFIED_BY	NOT NULL	VARCHAR2(30)
MODIFIED_DATE	NOT NULL	DATE

Notice, there are six columns having a NOT NULL constraint. The IN-SERT statement

```
INSERT INTO course (course_no, description,
                    created_by, created_date)
   VALUES (COURSE_NO_SEQ.NEXTVAL, 'TEST COURSE',
           'ELENA', SYSDATE);
```

has only four columns having NOT NULL constraints. The columns MODIFIED_BY and MODIFIED_DATE are not included in the INSERT statement. Any column of a table not listed in the INSERT statement has NULL assigned to it when a new record is added to the table. If a column has a NOT NULL constraint and is not listed in the INSERT statement, the INSERT statement fails and causes an error.

c) Add a user-defined exception to the script, so the error generated by the INSERT statement is handled.

Answer: Your script should look similar to the script shown below. All changes are shown in bold letters.

```
-- ch10_2b.sql, version 2.0
SET SERVEROUTPUT ON
DECLARE
   e_missing_column EXCEPTION;
   PRAGMA EXCEPTION_INIT(e_missing_column, -1400);
BEGIN
   INSERT INTO course (course_no, description,
created_by,
                       created_date)
   VALUES (COURSE_NO_SEQ.NEXTVAL, 'TEST COURSE', USER,
           SYSDATE);
   COMMIT;
   DBMS_OUTPUT.PUT_LINE('One course has been added');
EXCEPTION
   WHEN e_missing_column
   THEN
      DBMS_OUTPUT.PUT_LINE
         ('INSERT statement is missing a column');
END;
```

In this script, you declared the e_missing_column exception. Then, using the EXCEPTION_INIT pragma to associate the exception with the Oracle error number ORA-01400, the handler is written for the new exception e_missing_column.

d) Run the new version of the script. Explain the output produced by the new version of the script.

Answer: Your output should look similar to the following:

```
INSERT statement is missing a column
PL/SQL procedure successfully completed.
```

Once you define an exception and associated the Oracle error number with it, you are able to write an exception handler for it. As a result, as soon as the INSERT statement causes an error, the control of the execution is transferred to the exception-handling section of the block. Then, the message "INSERT statement . . ." is displayed on the screen. Notice, once an exception is raised, the execution of the program does not halt. The script completes successfully.

LAB 10.2 SELF-REVIEW QUESTIONS

In order to test your progress, you should be able to answer the following questions.

1) A pragma is which of the following?
   a) _____A special procedure provided by Oracle
   b) _____A special instruction to the compiler

2) A pragma is processed during which time?
   a) _____Runtime
   b) _____Compile time

3) The EXCEPTION_INIT pragma does which of the following?
   a) _____Associates a built-in exception with a user-defined error number
   b) _____Associates a user-defined exception with a user-defined error number
   c) _____Associates a user-defined exception with an Oracle error number

4) The EXCEPTION_INIT pragma needs which of the following parameters?
   a) _____error_number only
   b) _____error_name only
   c) _____error_name and error_number

5) Which of the following is a valid `error_number` parameter?
   a) _____ORA-02292
   b) _____2292
   c) _____–2292

Quiz answers appear in Appendix A, Section 10.2.

L A B   1 0 . 3

SQLCODE AND SQLERRM

> ## LAB OBJECTIVES
>
> After this lab, you will be able to:
>
> ✔ Use SQLCODE and SQLERRM

In Chapter 6, you learned about the Oracle exception OTHERS. You will recall that all Oracle errors can be trapped with the help of the OTHERS exception handler. Consider the following example.

■ *FOR EXAMPLE*

```
DECLARE
    v_zip VARCHAR2(5) := '&sv_zip';
    v_city VARCHAR2(15);
    v_state CHAR(2);
BEGIN
    SELECT city, state
      INTO v_city, v_state
      FROM zipcode
     WHERE zip = v_zip;
    DBMS_OUTPUT.PUT_LINE(v_city||', '||v_state);
EXCEPTION
    WHEN OTHERS
    THEN
        DBMS_OUTPUT.PUT_LINE('An error has occurred');
END;
```

When "07458" is entered for the value of zip code, this example produces the following output:

```
Enter value for sv_zip: 07458
old    2:    v_zip VARCHAR2(5) := '&sv_zip';
new    2:    v_zip VARCHAR2(5) := '07458';
An error has occurred
PL/SQL procedure successfully completed.
```

This output informs you an error has occurred at runtime. However, you do not know what the error is and what caused it. Maybe there is no record in the ZIPCODE table corresponding to the value provided at runtime, or maybe there is a data type mismatch caused by the SELECT INTO statement. As you can see, even though this is a simple example, there are a number of possible runtime errors that can occur.

**LAB
10.3**

Of course, you cannot always know all possible runtime errors that may occur when a program is running. So, it is a good practice to have the OTHERS exception handler in your script. To improve the error-handling interface of your program, Oracle provides you with two built-in functions, *SQLCODE* and *SQLERRM,* used with the OTHERS exception handler. The SQLCODE function returns the Oracle error number, and the SQLERRM function returns the error message. The maximum length of a message returned by the SQLERRM function is 512 bytes.

Consider what happens if you modify the example shown above by adding the SQLCODE and SQLERRM functions as follows (all changes are shown in bold letters):

■ *FOR EXAMPLE*

```
DECLARE
    v_zip VARCHAR2(5) := '&sv_zip';
    v_city VARCHAR2(15);
    v_state CHAR(2);
    v_err_code NUMBER;
    v_err_msg VARCHAR2(200);
BEGIN
    SELECT city, state
      INTO v_city, v_state
      FROM zipcode
     WHERE zip = v_zip;
    DBMS_OUTPUT.PUT_LINE(v_city||', '||v_state);
EXCEPTION
    WHEN OTHERS
    THEN
        v_err_code := SQLCODE;
        v_err_msg := SUBSTR(SQLERRM, 1, 200);
```

```
DBMS_OUTPUT.PUT_LINE
    ('Error code: '||v_err_code);
DBMS_OUTPUT.PUT_LINE
    ('Error message: '||v_err_msg);
END;
```

When executed, this example produces the output shown below:

```
Enter value for sv_zip: 07458
old    2:    v_zip VARCHAR2(5) := '&sv_zip';
new    2:    v_zip VARCHAR2(5) := '07458';
Error code: -6502
Error message: ORA-06502: PL/SQL: numeric or value error
PL/SQL procedure successfully completed.
```

In this example, two variables are declared: v_err_code and v_err_msg. Then, in the exception-handling section of the block, SQLCODE is assigned to the variable v_err_code, and the SQLERRM is assigned to the variable v_err_msg. Next, the DBMS_OUTPUT.PUT_LINE statements display the error number and the error message on the screen.

Notice, this output is more informative than the output produced by the previous version of the example because it displays the error message. Once you know which runtime error has occurred in your program, you can take steps to prevent this error's recurrence.

Generally, the SQLCODE function returns a negative number for an error number. However, there are a few exceptions:

- When SQLCODE is referenced outside the exception section, it returns 0 for the error code. The value of 0 means successful completion.
- When SQLCODE is used with the user-defined exception, it returns +1 for the error code.
- SQLCODE returns a value of 100 when the NO_DATA_FOUND exception is raised.

The SQLERRM function accepts an error number as a parameter, and it returns an error message corresponding to the error number. Usually, it works with the value returned by SQLCODE. However, you can provide the error number yourself if such a need arises. Consider the following example:

■ *FOR EXAMPLE*

```
BEGIN
   DBMS_OUTPUT.PUT_LINE('Error code: '||SQLCODE);
   DBMS_OUTPUT.PUT_LINE('Error message1: '||SQLERRM);
   DBMS_OUTPUT.PUT_LINE
      ('Error message2: '||SQLERRM(100));
   DBMS_OUTPUT.PUT_LINE
      ('Error message3: '||SQLERRM(200));
   DBMS_OUTPUT.PUT_LINE
      ('Error message4: '||SQLERRM(-20000));
END;
```

**LAB
10.3**

In this example, SQLCODE and SQLERRM are used in the executable section of the PL/SQL block. The SQLERRM function accepts the value of the SQLCODE in the first DBMS_OUTPUT.PUT_LINE statement. In the following DBMS_OUPUT.PUT_LINE statements, the SQLERRM accepts the values of 100, 200, and –20,000 respectively. When executed, this example produces the output shown below:

```
Error code: 0
Error message1: ORA-0000: normal, successful completion
Error message2: ORA-01403: no data found
Error message3:   -200: non-ORACLE exception
Error message4: ORA-20000:
PL/SQL procedure successfully completed.
```

The first DBMS_OUTPUT.PUT_LINE statement displays the value of the SQLCODE function. Since there is no exception raised, it returns 0. Next, the value returned by the SQLCODE function is accepted as a parameter by SQLERRM. This function returns the message "ORA-0000: normal, ..." Next, SQLERRM accepts 100 as its parameter and returns "ORA-01402: no data . . . ." Notice that when the SQLERRM accepts 200 as its parameter, it is not able to find an Oracle exception that corresponds to the error number 200. Finally, when the SQLERRM accepts –20,000 as its parameter, no error message is returned. Remember, –20,000 is an error number that can be associated with a named user-defined exception.

LAB 10.3 EXERCISES

10.3.1 USING SQLCODE AND SQLERRM

In this exercise, you add a new record to the ZIPCODE table. The original PL/SQL script does not contain any exception handlers. So, you are asked to add an exception-handling section to this script.

Create the following PL/SQL script:

```
-- ch10_3a.sql, version 1.0
SET SERVEROUTPUT ON
BEGIN
    INSERT INTO ZIPCODE(zip, city, state, created_by,
                        created_date, modified_by,
                        modified_date)
    VALUES('10027', 'NEW YORK', 'NY', USER, SYSDATE,
           USER, SYSDATE);
    COMMIT;
END;
```

Execute the script and answer the following questions:

a) What output is printed on the screen?

_____

_____

b) Modify the script so that the script completes successfully, and the error number and message are displayed on the screen.

_____

_____

c) Run the new version of the script. Explain the output produced by the new version of the script.

_____

_____

LAB 10.3 EXERCISE ANSWERS

10.3.1 ANSWERS

a) What output is printed on the screen?

Answer: Your output should look like the following:

```
BEGIN
*
ERROR at line 1:
ORA-00001: unique constraint (STUDENT.ZIP_PK) violated
ORA-06512: at line 2
```

The INSERT statement

```
INSERT INTO ZIPCODE(zip, city, state, created_by,
                    created_date, modified_by,
                    modified_date)
VALUES('10027', 'NEW YORK', 'NY', USER, SYSDATE,
       USER, SYSDATE);
```

causes an error because a record with zip code 10027 already exists in the ZIPCODE table. Column ZIP of the ZIPCODE table has a primary key constraint defined on it. Therefore, when you try to insert another record with the value of ZIP already existing in the ZIPCODE table, the error message "ORA-00001: unique constraint . . ." is generated.

b) Modify the script so that the script completes successfully, and the error number and message are displayed on the screen.

Answer: Your script should resemble the script shown below. All changes are shown in bold letters.

```
-- ch10_3b.sql, version 2.0
SET SERVEROUTPUT ON
BEGIN
   INSERT INTO ZIPCODE(zip, city, state, created_by,
                       created_date, modified_by,
                       modified_date)
   VALUES('10027', 'NEW YORK', 'NY', USER, SYSDATE,
          USER, SYSDATE);
   COMMIT;
EXCEPTION
   WHEN OTHERS
```

```
    THEN
        DECLARE
            v_err_code NUMBER := SQLCODE;
            v_err_msg VARCHAR2(100) :=
                SUBSTR(SQLERRM, 1, 100);
        BEGIN
            DBMS_OUTPUT.PUT_LINE
                ('Error code: '||v_err_code);
            DBMS_OUTPUT.PUT_LINE
                ('Error message: '||v_err_msg);
        END;
END;
```

In this script, you add an exception-handling section with the OTHERS exception handler. Notice, two variables are declared, v_err_code and v_err_msg, in the exception-handling section of the block, adding an inner PL/SQL block.

c) Run the new version of the script. Explain the output produced by the new version of the script.

Answer: Your output should look similar to the following:

```
Error code: -1
Error message: ORA-00001: unique constraint
(STUDENT.ZIP_PK) violated
PL/SQL procedure successfully completed.
```

Because the INSERT statement causes an error, control is transferred to the OTHERS exception handler. The SQLCODE function returns –1, and the SQLERRM function returns the text of the error corresponding to the error code –1. Once the exception-handling section completes its execution, control is passed to the host environment.

LAB 10.3 SELF-REVIEW QUESTIONS

In order to test your progress, you should be able to answer the following questions.

1) The SQLCODE function returns an Oracle error number.
   a) _____True
   b) _____False

2) The SQLERRM function returns the error text corresponding to a specific error number.
   a) _____True
   b) _____False

3) When the SQLERRM function cannot return an error message corresponding to a particular error number, which of the following occurs?
a) _____SQLERRM causes an error.
b) _____SQLERRM does not return anything.
c) _____SQLERRM returns "non-ORACLE exception" message.

4) What is the maximum length of the error text returned by the SQLERRM function?
a) _____450 bytes
b) _____550 bytes
c) _____512 bytes

5) The SQLCODE function always returns a negative number.
a) _____True
b) _____False

Quiz answers appear in Appendix A, Section 10.3.

LAB
10.3

CHAPTER 10

TEST YOUR THINKING

In this chapter you learned about built-in exceptions. Here are some projects that will help you test the depth of your understanding.

1) Create the following script. Modify the script created in this section in Chapter 9. Raise a user-defined exception with the RAISE_APPLICATION_ERROR statement. Otherwise, display how many students there are in a section. Make sure your program is able to process all sections.

2) Create the following script. Try to add a record to the Instructor table without providing values for the columns MODIFIED_BY and MODIFIED_DATE. Define an exception and associate it with the Oracle error number so the error generated by the INSERT statement is handled.

3) Modify the script created in the previous exercise. Instead of declaring a user-defined exception, add the OTHERS exception handler to the exception-handling section of the block. Then, display the error number and the error message on the screen.

CHAPTER 11

PROCEDURES

PL/SQL STORED CODE

All the PL/SQL that you have written up to this point has been anonymous blocks that were run as scripts and compiled by the database server at runtime. Now you will begin to use modular code. *Modular code* is a methodology to build a program from distinct parts (modules), each of which performs a specific function or task toward the final objective of the program. Once modular code is stored on the database server, it becomes a database object, or subprogram, that is available to other program units for repeated execution. In order to save code into the database, the source code needs to be sent to the server so that it can be compiled into p-code and stored in the database. In the first lab, you will learn more about stored code and how to write one type of stored code known as *procedures*. In the second lab, you will learn about passing parameters into and out of procedures.

L A B   1 1 . 1

CREATING
PROCEDURES

LAB OBJECTIVES

After this lab, you will be able to:

✔ Create Procedures
✔ Query the Data Dictionary for Information on Procedures

BENEFITS OF MODULAR CODE

A PL/SQL module is any complete logical unit of work. There are four types of PL/SQL modules: (1) anonymous blocks that are run with a text script (this is the type you have used until now), (2) procedures, (3) functions, and (4) packages.

There are two main benefits to using modular code: (1) It is more reusable and (2) it is more manageable.

You create a procedure either in SQL*Plus or in one of the many tools for creating and debugging stored PL/SQL code. If you are using SQL*Plus, you will need to write your code in a text editor and then run it at the SQL*Plus prompt.

BLOCK STRUCTURE

The block structure is common for all the module types. The block begins with a Header (for named blocks only), which consists of (1) the name of the module, and (2) a parameter list (if used).

The Declaration section consists of variable, cursors, and subblocks that will be needed in the next section.

The main part of the module is the Execution section, where all the calculations and processing is performed. This will contain executable code such as IF – THEN – ELSE, LOOPS, calls to other PL/SQL modules, and so on.

The last section of the module is an optional exception handler, which is where the code to handle exceptions is placed.

ANONYMOUS BLOCK

Until this chapter, you have only been writing anonymous blocks. Anonymous blocks are very much the same as modules, which were just introduced (except anonymous blocks do not have headers). There are important distinctions, though. As the name implies, anonymous blocks have no name and thus cannot be called by another block. They are not stored in the database and must be compiled and then run each time the script is loaded.

PROCEDURES

A procedure is a module performing one or more actions; it does not need to return any values. The syntax for creating a procedure is as follows:

```
CREATE OR REPLACE PROCEDURE name
    [(parameter[, parameter, ...])]
AS
    [local declarations]
BEGIN
    executable statements
[EXCEPTION
    exception handlers]
END [name];
```

A procedure may have 0 to many parameters. This will be covered in the next lab. Every procedure has two parts: (1) the header portion, which comes before AS (sometimes you will see IS—they are interchangeable), keyword (this contains the procedure name and the parameter list), (2) the bodys, which is everything after the IS keyword. The word REPLACE is optional. When the word REPLACE is not used in the header of the procedure, in order to change the code in the procedure, it must be dropped first and then re-created. Since it is very common to change the code of the procedure, especially, when it is under the development, it is strongly recommended to use the OR REPLACE option.

LAB 11.1 EXERCISES

11.1.1 CREATING PROCEDURES

In this exercise, you will run a script that creates a procedure.
Using a text editor such as Notepad, create a file with the following script.

```
-- ch11_01a.sql
CREATE OR REPLACE PROCEDURE Discount
AS
  CURSOR c_group_discount
  IS
    SELECT distinct s.course_no, c.description
      FROM section s, enrollment e, course c
     WHERE s.section_id = e.section_id
       AND c.course_no = s.course_no
     GROUP BY s.course_no, c.description,
              e.section_id, s.section_id
    HAVING COUNT(*) >=8;
BEGIN
   FOR r_group_discount IN c_group_discount
   LOOP
      UPDATE course
         SET cost = cost * .95
       WHERE course_no = r_group_discount.course_no;
      DBMS_OUTPUT.PUT_LINE
         ('A 5% discount has been given to'||
          r_group_discount.course_no||' '||
          r_group_discount.description
         );
   END LOOP;
END;
```

At the SQL*Plus session, run the script.

a) What did you see on your screen? Explain what happened.

_____

_____

In order to execute in SQL*Plus use the following syntax:

```
EXECUTE Procedure_name
```

b) Execute the Discount Procedure. How did you accomplish this? What are the results that you see in your SQL*Plus screen?

_____

_____

c) The script did not contain a COMMIT. Discuss the issues involved with placing a COMMIT in the procedure and indicate where the COMMIT could be placed.

_____

_____

11.1.2 QUERYING THE DATA DICTIONARY FOR INFORMATION ON PROCEDURES

There are two main views in the data dictionary that provide information on stored code. They are the USER_OBJECTS view, to give information about the objects, and the USER_SOURCE, to give the text of the source code. Remember, the data dictionary also has an ALL_ and DBA_ version of these views.

a) Write the select statement to get pertinent information from the USER_OBJECTS view about the discount procedure you just wrote. Run the query and describe the results.

_____

_____

b) Write the SELECT statement to display the source code from the USER_SOURCE view for the discount procedure.

_____

_____

LAB 11.1 EXERCISE ANSWERS

11.1.1 ANSWERS

a) What did you see on your screen? Explain what happened.

Answer: `Procedure created.` *The procedure named Discount was compiled into p-code and stored in the database for later execution. Note if you saw an error— this is due to a typing mistake. Recheck the code against the example in the book and recompile.*

b) Execute the Discount procedure. How did you accomplish this? What are the results that you see in your SQL*Plus screen?

Answer: `SQL> EXECUTE Discount`

`5% discount has been given to 25   Adv. Word Perfect`

. . . . (through each course with an enrollment over 8)

`PL/SQL procedure successfully completed.`

c) The script did not contain a COMMIT. Discuss the issues involved with placing a COMMIT in the procedure and indicate where the COMMIT could be placed.

Answer: There is no COMMIT in this procedure, which means the procedure will not update the database. A COMMIT needs to be issued after the procedure is run, if you want the changes to be made. Alternatively, you can enter a COMMIT either before or after the END LOOP. If you put the COMMIT before the END LOOP, then you are committing changes after every loop. If you put the COMMIT after the END LOOP, then the changes will not be committed until after the procedure is near completion. It is wiser to take the second option. This way you are better prepared for handling errors.

If you receive an error, then type the command:

`Show error`
`You can also add to the command:`
`L start_line_number end_line_number`
`  to see a portion of the code in order to isolate errors`

11.1.2 ANSWERS

a) Write the SELECT statement to get pertinent information from the USER_OBJECTS view about the discount procedure you just wrote. Run the query and describe the results.

Answer

```
SELECT object_name, object_type, status
  FROM user_objects
 WHERE object_name = 'DISCOUNT';
```

Result is:

OBJECT_NAME	OBJECT_TYPE	STATUS
DISCOUNT	PROCEDURE	VALID

The status indicates where the procedure was complied successfully. An invalid procedure cannot be executed.

b) Write the select statement to display the source code from the USER_SOURCE view for the discount procedure.

Answer:

```
SQL> column text format a70
     SELECT TO_CHAR(line, 99)||'>', text
       FROM user_source
     WHERE name = 'DISCOUNT'
```

A procedure can become invalid if the table it is based on is deleted or changed. You can recompile an invalid procedure with the command

alter procedure procedure_name compile;

LAB 11.2

PASSING PARAMETERS IN AND OUT OF PROCEDURES

LAB OBJECTIVES

After this lab, you will be able to:

✔ Use IN and OUT Parameters with Procedures

PARAMETERS

Parameters are the means to pass values to and from the calling environment to the server. These are the values that will be processed or returned via the execution of the procedure. There are three types of parameters: IN, OUT, and IN OUT.

MODES

Modes specify whether the parameter passed is read in or a receptacle for what comes out.

Figure 11.1 illustrates the relationship between the parameters when they are in the procedure header versus when the procedure is executed.

FORMAL AND ACTUAL PARAMETERS

Formal parameters are the names specified within parentheses as part of the header of a module. *Actual parameters* are the values—expressions specified within parentheses as a parameter list—when a call is made to the module. The formal parameter and the related actual parameter must be of the same or compatible datatypes.

Mode	Description	Usage
IN	Passes a value into the program	Read only value
		Constants, literals, expressions
		Cannot be changed within program
		Default mode
OUT	Passes a value back from the program	Write only value
		Cannot assign default values
		Has to be a variable
		Value assigned only if the program is successful
IN OUT	Passes values in and also send values back	Has to be a variable
		Value will be read and then written

PASSING OF CONSTRAINTS (DATATYPE) WITH PARAMETER VALUES

Formal parameters do not require constraints in datatype—for example, instead of specifying a constraint such as VARCHAR2(60), you just say VARCHAR2 against the parameter name in the formal parameter list. The constraint is passed with the value when a call is made.

MATCHING ACTUAL AND FORMAL PARAMETERS

Two methods can be used to match actual and formal parameters: positional notation and named notation. *Positional notation* is simply association by position: The order of the parameters used when executing the procedure matches the order in the procedure's header exactly. *Named notation* is explicit association using the symbol =>

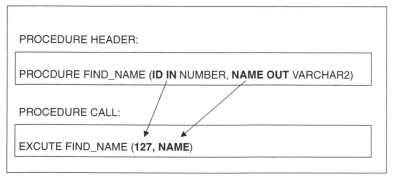

PROCEDURE HEADER:

PROCDURE FIND_NAME (**ID IN** NUMBER, **NAME OUT** VARCHAR2)

PROCEDURE CALL:

EXCUTE FIND_NAME (**127, NAME**)

Figure 11.1 ■ Matching Procedure Call to Procedure Header

Syntax: `formal_parameter_name => argument_value`

In named notation, the order does not matter. If you mix notation, list positional notation before named notation.

Default values can be used if a call to the program does not include a value in the parameter list. Note that it makes no difference which style is used; they will both function similarly.

LAB 11.2 EXERCISES

11.2.1 USING IN AND OUT PARAMETERS WITH PROCEDURES

Create the following text file in a text editor. Run the script at a SQL*Plus session.

```
-- ch11_02a.sql
CREATE OR REPLACE PROCEDURE find_sname
  (i_student_id IN NUMBER,
   o_first_name OUT VARCHAR2,
   o_last_name OUT VARCHAR2
   )
AS
BEGIN
  SELECT first_name, last_name
    INTO o_first_name, o_last_name
    FROM student
   WHERE student_id = i_student_id;
EXCEPTION
  WHEN OTHERS
  THEN
    DBMS_OUTPUT.PUT_LINE('Error in finding student_id:
      '||i_student_id);
END find_sname;
```

a) Explain what is happening in the find_sname procedure. What parameters are being passed into and out of the procedure? How would you call the procedure?

_____

_____

Call the find_sname script with the following anonymous block:

```
-- ch11_03a.sql
DECLARE
   v_local_first_name student.first_name%TYPE;
   v_local_last_name student.last_name%TYPE;
BEGIN
   find_sname
      (145, v_local_first_name, v_local_last_name);
   DBMS_OUTPUT.PUT_LINE
      ('Student 145 is: '||v_local_first_name||
      ' '|| v_local_last_name||'.'
      );
END;
```

b) Explain the relationship between the parameters that are in the procedures header definition versus the parameters that are passed IN and OUT of the procedure.

_____

_____

LAB 11.2 EXERCISE ANSWERS

11.2.1 ANSWERS

a) Explain what is happening in the find_sname procedure. What parameters are being passed into and out of the procedure? How would you call the procedure?

Answer: The procedure takes in a `student_id` *via the parameter named* `p_student_id`*. It passes out the parameters* `p_first_name` *and* `p_last_name`*. The procedure is a simple SELECT statement retrieving the* `first_name` *and* `last_name` *from the Student table where the* `student_id` *matches the value of the* `p_student_id`*, which is the only in parameter that exists in the procedure. To call the procedure, a value must be passed in for the* `p_student_id` *parameter.*

b) Explain the relationship between the parameters that are in the procedures header definition versus the parameters that are passed out and in of the procedure.

Answer: When calling the procedure find_sname, a valid `student_id` *should be passed in for the* `p_student_id`*. If it is not a valid* `student_id`*, the exception will* be raised. Two variables must also be listed when calling the procedure. These variables, `v_local_first_name` and `v_local_last_name`, are used to hold the values of the parameters that are being passed out. After the procedure has been executed, the local variables will have value and can then be displayed with a DBMS_OUTPUT.PUT_LINE.

LAB 11 SELF-REVIEW QUESTIONS

1) The benefits of module code are that
   a) _____ it takes IN and OUT parameters.
   b) _____ it can be called by many types of calling environments.
   c) _____ it is stored in the database.
   d) _____ it is always valid.

2) All module code contains the following components:
   a) _____ Header
   b) _____ Footer
   c) _____ Declaration
   d) _____ Exception
   e) _____ Execution

3) If a procedure has an IN parameter, then it must have an OUT parameter.
   a) _____ True
   b) _____ False

4) Which are valid parameter definitions in the header of a parameter?
   a) _____ P_LAST_NAME IN OUT VARCHAR2(20)
   b) _____ P_STUDID OUT IN NUMBER
   c) _____ P_ZIPCODE NUMBER
   d) _____ P_COURSE_COST IN NUMBER := 1095

5) The view USER_SOURCE only contains the code of valid procedures.
   a) _____ True
   b) _____ False

C H A P T E R   1 1

TEST YOUR THINKING

In this chapter, we have learned about creating procedures, with and without the use of parameters. Additionally, you learned about where information and source code for these procedures can be found.

1) Write a procedure with no parameters. The procedure will let you know if the current day is a weekend or a weekday. Additionally, it will let you know the user name and current time. It will also let you know how many valid and invalid procedures are in the database.

2) Write a procedure that takes in a zipcode, city, and state and inserts the values into the zipcode table. There should be a check to see if the zipcode is already in the database. If it is, an exception will be raised and an error message will be displayed. Write an anonymous block that uses the procedure and inserts your zipcode.

C H A P T E R 1 2

FUNCTIONS

A function that is stored in the database is much like a procedure in that it is a named PL/SQL block that can take parameters and be invoked. There are key differences both in the way it is created and how it is used. In this chapter, you will cover the basics of how to create, make use of, and drop a function.

L A B   1 2 . 1

CREATING AND USING FUNCTIONS

LAB OBJECTIVES

After this lab, you will be able to:

✔ Create Stored Functions
✔ Make Use of Functions
✔ Invoke Functions in SQL Statements
✔ Write Complex Functions

FUNCTION BASICS

Functions are another type of stored code and are very similar to procedures. The significant difference is that a function is a PL/SQL block that *returns* a single value. Functions can accept one, many, or no parameters, but a function must have a return clause in the executable section of the function. The datatype of the return value must be declared in the header of the function. A function is not a stand-alone executable in the way that a procedure is: It must be used in some context. You can think of it as a sentence fragment. A function has output that needs to be assigned to a variable, or it can be used in a SELECT statement.

FUNCTION SYNTAX

The syntax for creating a function is as follows:

```
CREATE [OR REPLACE] FUNCTION function_name
    (parameter list)
    RETURN datatype
```

```
IS
BEGIN
   <body>
   RETURN (return_value);
END;
```

The function does not necessarily have any parameters, but it must have a RETURN value declared in the header, and it must return values for all the varying possible execution streams. The RETURN statement does not have to appear as the last line of the main execution section, and there may be more than one RETURN statement (there should be a RETURN statement for each exception). A function may have IN, OUT, or IN OUT parameters, but you rarely see anything except IN parameters since it is bad programming practice to do otherwise.

■ FOR EXAMPLE

```
-- ch12_01a.sql ver 1.0
CREATE OR REPLACE FUNCTION show_description
   (i_course_no number)
RETURN varchar2
AS
   v_description varchar2(50);
BEGIN
   SELECT description
     INTO v_description
     FROM course
    WHERE course_no = i_course_no;
   RETURN v_description;
EXCEPTION
   WHEN NO_DATA_FOUND
   THEN
     RETURN('The Course is not in the database');
   WHEN OTHERS
   THEN
     RETURN('Error in running show_description');
END;
```

LAB 12.1 EXERCISES

12.1.1 CREATING STORED FUNCTIONS

a) Put the create script for the function in the above example into a text file. Open SQL*Plus, log into the student schema, and run the script from above. What do you expect to see? Explain the function line by line.

---

b) Create another function using the following script. Explain what is happening in this function. Pay close attention to the method of creating the Boolean return.

```
-- ch12_01b.sql, version 1.0
CREATE OR REPLACE FUNCTION id_is_good
  (i_student_id IN NUMBER)
  RETURN BOOLEAN
AS
  v_id_cnt NUMBER;
BEGIN
  SELECT COUNT(*)
    INTO v_id_cnt
    FROM student
   WHERE student_id = i_student_id;
  RETURN 1 = v_id_cnt;
EXCEPTION
  WHEN OTHERS
  THEN
    RETURN FALSE;
END id_is_good;
```

12.1.2 MAKING USE OF FUNCTIONS

In this exercise, you will learn how to make use of the stored functions that you created in Lab 12.1.1.

a) Use the following anonymous block to run the function. When prompted, enter 350. Then try other numbers. What is produced?

```
SET SERVEROUTPUT ON
DECLARE
  v_description VARCHAR2(50);
BEGIN
  v_description := show_description(&sv_cnumber);
  DBMS_OUTPUT.PUT_LINE(v_description);
 END;
```

b) Now create a similar anonymous block to make use of the function id_is_good. Try running it for a number of different ids.

12.1.3 INVOKING FUNCTIONS IN SQL STATEMENTS

a) Now you will try another method of using a stored function. Before you type the following SELECT statement, think about what the function show_description is doing. Will this statement produce an error? If not, then what will be displayed?

```
SELECT course_no, show_description(course_no)
  FROM course;
```

12.1.4 WRITING COMPLEX FUNCTIONS

a) Create the function with the following script. Before you execute the function, analyze this script and explain line by line what the function will perform. When could you use this function?

```
-- ch12_01c.sql, version 1.0
CREATE OR REPLACE FUNCTION new_instructor_id
   RETURN instructor.instructor_id%TYPE
AS
   v_new_instid instructor.instructor_id%TYPE;
BEGIN
   SELECT INSTRUCTOR_ID_SEQ.NEXTVAL
     INTO v_new_instid
     FROM dual;
   RETURN v_new_instid;
EXCEPTION
   WHEN OTHERS
   THEN
      DECLARE
         v_sqlerrm VARCHAR2(250)
            := SUBSTR(SQLERRM,1,250);
      BEGIN
         RAISE_APPLICATION_ERROR(-20003,
            'Error in    instructor_id: '||v_sqlerrm);
      END;
END new_instructor_id;
```

LAB 12.1 EXERCISE ANSWERS

12.1.1 ANSWERS

a) Put the create script for the function in the above example into a text file. Open SQL*Plus, log into the student schema, and run the script from above. What do you expect to see? Explain the function line by line.

*Answer: When a function has been compiled without errors, the SQL*Plus session will return*

```
 Function created.
```

which indicates that the function was successfully compiled. The script is for the function show_description. *The function heading indicates that the function takes in a parameter of the number datatype and returns a VARCHAR2. The function makes use of a VARCHAR2(5) variable called* v_description. *The function gives the variable the value of the description of the course, whose number is passed into the function. The return value is then the variable. There are two exceptions, the first is the WHEN NO_DATA_FOUND exception, the one most likely to occur. The second exception is the WHEN OTHERS exception, which is being used as a catchall for any other error that may occur. It is important for you to note that the RETURN clause is* one of the last statements in the function. The reason is that the program focus will return to the calling environment once the RETURN clause is issued.

b) Create another function using the following script. Explain what is happening in this function. Pay close attention to the method of creating the Boolean return.

Answer: The function id_is_good *is a check to see if the ID passed in exists in the database. The function takes in a number (which is assumed to be a student ID) and returns a BOOLEAN value. The function uses the variable* v_id_cnt *as a means to process the data. The SELECT statement determines a count of the number of students with the numeric value that was passed in. If the student is in the database, because the* student_id *is the primary key, the value of* v_id_cnt *will be 1. If the student is not in the database, the SELECT statement will throw the focus down to the exception section where the function returns a value of FALSE. The function makes use of a very interesting method to return TRUE. If the student is in the database, then* v_id_cnt *will equal 1, thus the code* RETURN 1 = v_id_cnt *will actually return a value of TRUE when* v_id_cnt *equals 1.*

12.1.2 ANSWERS

a) Use the following anonymous block to run the function. When prompted, enter 350. Then try other numbers. What is produced?

Answer: Since there is a lexical parameter of &cnumber in the PL/SQL block, the user will be prompted as follows:

```
Enter value for cnumber:
```

If you enter "350," you will see the following:

```
old   4:   v_descript := show_description(&sv_cnumber);
new   4:   v_descript := show_description(350);
Intro to SQL
PL/SQL procedure successfully completed.
```

This means that the value for &sv_cnumber *has been replaced with 350. The function* show_description *returns a VARCHAR2 value, which is the course description for the course number that is passed in. The PL/SQL block initializes the* v_description *value with the return from the* show_description *function. This value is then displayed with the* DBMS_OUTPUT *package.*

b) Now create a similar anonymous block to make use of the function id_is_good. Try running it for a number of different ids.

Answer: The following is one method of testing the id_is_good *function:*

```
DECLARE
    V_id number;
BEGIN
    V_id := &id
    IF id_is_good(v_id);
    THEN
        DBMS_OUTPUT.PUT_LINE
            ('Student ID: '||v_id||' is good.');
    ELSE
        DBMS_OUTPUT.PUT_LINE
            ('Student ID: '||v_id|| 'is not good.');
    END IF;
  END;
```

This PL/SQL block evaluates the return from the function and then determines which output to project.

12.1.3 ANSWERS

a) Now try another method of using a stored function. Before you type the following SELECT statement, think about what the function show_description is doing. Will this statement produce an error? If not, then what will be displayed?

```
SELECT course_no, show_description(course_no)
    FROM course;
```

Answer: This SELECT statement will be identical to the SELECT statement that follows:

```
SELECT course_no, description
    FROM course.
```

Functions can be used in a SQL statement. In fact, you have been using them all along and may not have realized it. As a simple example, imagine how UPPER('bill'), where BILL is a function that returns the upper case value of the parameter that was passed in, could be very helpful for complex calculations.

Note that for a user-defined function to be called in a SQL expression it must be a ROW function, not a GROUP function, and the datatypes must be SQL datatypes. The datatypes cannot be PL/SQL datatypes like Boolean, table, or record. Additionally, the function is not allowed to have any DML (insert, update, delete).

Note that in order to use a function in an SQL select statement, it must have a certain level of purity. This is accomplished with the PRAGMA RESTRICT_REFERENCES clause. This will be discussed in detail in the next chapter in the context of functions within packages.

LAB 12.1 REVIEW QUESTIONS

1) What is the distinguishing characteristic that makes functions different from procedures? (check all that apply)

   a) _____ Functions require a PRAGMA RESTRICT clause.

   b) _____ Functions only take IN parameters.

   c) _____ Functions are stored in the database.

   d) _____ Functions require a return value.

   e) _____ None of the above.

2) The parameters of a function must be labeled IN or the function will not compile successfully.

   a) _____True

   b) _____False

3) What statement(s) will cause control to return to the calling environment in a function?

   a) _____ The raising of an exception.

   b) _____ The initialization of an OUT parameter.

   c) _____ Writing to a database table.

   d) _____ The RETURN statement.

   e) _____ None of the above.

4) IN OUT parameters are permissible in functions.

   a) _____ True

   b) _____ False

   c) _____ The function will compile with an IN OUT parameter, but it is not advisable to use them.

5) If a function declares a user-defined exception but never explicitly raises the exception, which of the following will be true?

   a) _____ The function will not be able to compile.

   b) _____ The function will fail a purity level check.

   c) _____ The exception will never be raised.

   d) _____ As long as the exception has a RETURN clause, there is no error in having a user-defined exception and not calling it.

C H A P T E R   1 2

TEST YOUR THINKING

In this chapter, you have learned about functions.

1) Write a stored function called `new_student_id` that takes in no parameters and returns a `student.student_id%TYPE`. The value returned will be used when inserting a new student into the CTA application. It will be derived by using the formula: `student_id_seq.NEXTVAL`.

2) Write a stored function called `zip_does_not_exist` that takes in a `zipcode.zip%TYPE` and returns a *Boolean*. The function will return TRUE if the zipcode passed into it *does not* exist. It will return a FALSE if the zipcode *exists*. Hint: An example of how it might be used is:

```
DECLARE
    cons_zip CONSTANT zipcode.zip%TYPE := '&sv_zipcode';
    e_zipcode_is_not_valid EXCEPTION;
BEGIN
    IF zipcode_does_not_exist(cons_zip);
    THEN
        RAISE e_zipcode_is_not_valid;
    ELSE
     -- An insert of an instructor's record which
     --    makes use of the checked zipcode might go here.
        NULL;
    END IF;
EXCEPTION
    WHEN e_zipcode_is_not_valid
    THEN
        RAISE_APPLICATION_ERROR
            (-20003, 'Could not find zipcode '||
            cons_zip||'.'
            );
END;
```

3) Create a new function. For a given instructor, determine how many sections he or she is teaching. If the number is greater or equal to 3, return a message saying the instructor needs a vacation. Otherwise, return a message saying how many sections this instructor is teaching.

CHAPTER 13

PACKAGES

A package is a collection of PL/SQL objects grouped together under one package name. Packages include procedures, functions, cursors, declarations, types, and variables. There are numerous benefits in collecting objects into a package. In this chapter, you learn what these benefits are, and how to use them.

L A B   1 3 . 1

THE BENEFITS OF UTILIZING PACKAGES

LAB OBJECTIVES

After this lab, you will be able to:

✔ Create Package Specifications
✔ Create Package Bodies
✔ Call Stored Packages
✔ Create Private Objects
✔ Create Package Variables and Cursors

THE BENEFITS OF USING PACKAGES

There are numerous benefits of using packages as a method to bundle your functions and procedures, the first being that a well-designed package is a logical grouping of objects—such as functions, procedures, global variables, and cursors. All of the code (parse tree and pseudocode [p-code]) is loaded on the first call of the package. This means that the first call to the package is very expensive, but all subsequent calls will result in an improved performance. Packages are therefore often used in applications where procedures and functions are used repeatedly.

There is also an additional level of security using packages. When a user executes a procedure in a package (or stored procedures and functions), the procedure operates with the same permissions as its owner. Packages also allow the creation of private functions and procedures, which can only be called from other functions and procedures in the package. This enforces information hiding. The structure of the package also encourages top-down design.

THE PACKAGE SPECIFICATION

The package specification contains information about the contents of the package, but not the code for the procedures and functions. It also contains declarations of global/public variables. Anything placed in the declarative section of a PL/SQL block may be coded in a package specification. All objects placed in the package specification are called *public objects*. Any function or procedure not in the package specification but coded in a package body is called a *private function* or *procedure*.

THE PACKAGE BODY

The package body contains the actual executable code for the objects described in the package specification. The package body contains code for all procedures and functions described in the specification and may additionally contain code for objects not declared in the specification; the latter type of packaged object is invisible outside the package and is referred as being hidden. When creating stored packages, the package specification and body can be compiled separately.

RULES FOR THE PACKAGE BODY

There are a number of rules that must be followed in package body code: (1) There must be an exact match between the cursor and module headers and their definitions in package specification. (2) Do not repeat declaration of variables, exceptions, type, or constants in the specification again in the body. (3) Any element *declared* in the specification can be *referenced* in the body.

REFERENCING PACKAGE ELEMENTS

Use the following notation when calling packaged elements from outside of the package: `package_name.element`.

You do not need to qualify elements when declared and referenced inside the body of the package or when declared in a specification and referenced inside the body of the same package.

LAB 13.1 EXERCISES

13.1.1 CREATING THE PACKAGE SPECIFICATION

■ FOR EXAMPLE

```
-- ch13_1a.sql
 1   CREATE OR REPLACE PACKAGE manage_students
 2   AS
 3     PROCEDURE find_sname
 4        (i_student_id IN student.student_id%TYPE,
 5         o_first_name OUT student.first_name%TYPE,
 6         o_last_name OUT student.last_name%TYPE
 7        );
 8     FUNCTION id_is_good
 9        (i_student_id IN student.student_id%TYPE)
10        RETURN BOOLEAN;
11   END manage_students;
```

Answer the following questions:

a) Type the above code into a text file. Then run the script in a SQL*Plus session. Explain what happened.

_____

_____

b) If the following script was run from a SQL*PLUS session, what would the result be and why?

```
-- ch13_2a.sql
SET SERVEROUTPUT ON
DECLARE
   v_first_name student.first_name%TYPE;
   v_last_name student.last_name%TYPE;
BEGIN
   manage_students.find_sname
      (125, v_first_name, v_last_name);
   DBMS_OUTPUT.PUT_LINE(v_first_name||' '||v_last_name);
END;
```

c) Create a package specification for a package named `student_ta_api`. The package contains the procedure discount from Chapter 11 and the function `new_instructor_id` from Chapter 12.

13.1.2 CREATING THE PACKAGE BODY

Now we will create the body of the `manage_students` package, which was specified in the previous section.

■ *FOR EXAMPLE*

```
-- ch13_3a.sql
 1   CREATE OR REPLACE PACKAGE BODY manage_students
 2   AS
 3     PROCEDURE find_sname
 4       (i_student_id IN student.student_id%TYPE,
 5        o_first_name OUT student.first_name%TYPE,
 6        o_last_name OUT student.last_name%TYPE
 7        )
 8     IS
 9      BEGIN
10        SELECT first_name, last_name
11          INTO o_first_name, o_last_name
12          FROM student
13         WHERE student_id = i_student_id;
14      EXCEPTION
15        WHEN OTHERS
16        THEN
17          DBMS_OUTPUT.PUT_LINE
18      ('Error in finding student_id: '||v_student_id);
19      END find_sname;
20      FUNCTION id_is_good
21        (i_student_id IN student.student_id%TYPE)
22        RETURN BOOLEAN
23        IS
```

```
24          v_id_cnt number;
25       BEGIN
26         SELECT COUNT(*)
27           INTO v_id_cnt
28           FROM student
29          WHERE student_id = i_student_id;
30          RETURN 1 = v_id_cnt;
31       EXCEPTION
32       WHEN OTHERS
33       THEN
34          RETURN FALSE;
35       END id_is_good;
36    END manage_students;
```

a) Type the above code into a text file. Then run the script in a SQL*Plus session. Explain what happens.

_____

_____

b) Create a package body for the package named `cta_api` that you just created.

_____

_____

13.1.3 CALLING STORED PACKAGES

Now we will use elements of the `manage_student` package in another code block.

■ FOR EXAMPLE

```
-- ch13_4a.sql
DECLARE
  v_first_name student.first_name%TYPE;
  v_last_name student.last_name%TYPE;
BEGIN
  IF manage_students.id_is_good(&v_id)
  THEN
    manage_students.find_sname(&&v_id, v_first_name,
      v_last_name);
```

```
    DBMS_OUTPUT.PUT_LINE('Student No. '||&&v_id||' is '
        ||v_last_name||', '||v_first_name);
ELSE
    DBMS_OUTPUT.PUT_LINE
    ('Student ID: '||&&v_id||' is not in the database.');
END IF;
END;
```

a) The previous example displays how a procedure within a package is executed. What results do you expect if you run this PL/SQL block?

_____

_____

b) Run the script and see the results. How does this compare with what you expected? Explain what the script is accomplishing line by line.

_____

_____

c) Create a script testing the `cta_api` package.

_____

_____

13.1.4 CREATING PRIVATE OBJECTS

PUBLIC AND PRIVATE PACKAGE ELEMENTS

Public elements are elements defined in the package specification. If an object is defined only in the package body, then it is private.

Private elements cannot be accessed directly by any programs outside of the package.

You can think of the package specification as being a "menu" of packaged items that are available to users; there may be other objects working behind the scenes but they aren't accessible.

a) Replace the last lines of the `manage_students` package specification with the following and recompile the package specification:

```
11          PROCEDURE display_student_count;
12       END manage_students;
```

Replace the end of the body with the following and recompile the package body:

```
36          FUNCTION student_count_priv
37            RETURN NUMBER
38           IS
39            v_count NUMBER;
40           BEGIN
41            select count(*)
42            into v_count
43            from student;
44            return v_count;
45           EXCEPTION
46            WHEN OTHERS
47              THEN
48              return(0);
49           END student_count_priv;
50           PROCEDURE display_student_count
51            is
52            v_count NUMBER;
53           BEGIN
54            v_count := student_count_priv;
55            DBMS_OUTPUT.PUT_LINE
                  ('There are '||v_count||' students.');
56           END display_student_count;
57        END manage_students;
```

What have you added to the `manage_student` package?

_____

_____

b) If you run the following from your SQL*PLUS session, what are the results?

```
DECLARE
   V_count NUMBER;
BEGIN
```

```
    V_count := Manage_students.student_count_priv;
    DBMS_OUTPUT.PUT_LINE(v_count);
END;
```

---

c) If you were to run the following, what do you expect to see?

```
SET SERVEROUTPUT ON
Execute manage_students.display_student_count;
```

d) Add a private function to the `school_api` called `get_course_descript_private`. It accepts a `course.course_no%TYPE` and returns a `course.description%TYPE`. It searches for and returns the course description for the course number passed to it. If the course does not exist or if an error occurs, it returns a NULL.

13.1.5 CREATING PACKAGE VARIABLES AND CURSORS

The first time a package is called within a user session, the code in the initialization section of the package will be executed if it exists. This is only done once and not repeated if other procedures or functions for that package are called by the user.

Variables, cursors, and user-defined datatypes used by numerous procedures and functions can be declared once at the beginning of the package and can then be used by the functions and procedures within the package without having to declare them again.

a) Add a package wide variable called `v_current_date` to `cta_api`; additionally, add an initialization section that assigns the current sysdate to the variable `v_current_date`.

LAB 13.1 EXERCISE ANSWERS

13.1.1 ANSWERS

a) Type the code above into a text file. Then run the script in a SQL*Plus session. Explain what happens.

Answer: The specification for the package `manage_students` *has been compiled into the database. The specification for the package now indicates there is one procedure and one function. The procedure* `find_sname` *requires one IN parameter, which is the student ID, and it returns two OUT parameters, one being the student's first name, and the other being the student's last name. The function* `id_is_good` *takes in a single parameter of a student ID and returns a Boolean (true or false). Although the body has not yet been entered into the database, the package is still available for other applications. For example, if you included a call to one of these procedures in another stored procedure, that procedure would compile (but would not execute).*

b) If the following script is run from a SQL*PLUS session, what are the results and why?

*Answer: The procedure cannot run because only the specification for the procedure exists in the database, not the body. The SQL*Plus session returns the following:*

```
ERROR at line 1:
ORA-04068: existing state of packages has been dis-
carded
ORA-04067: not executed, package body
"STUDENT.MANAGE_STUDENTS" does not exist
ORA-06508: PL/SQL: could not find program unit being
called
ORA-06512: at line 5
```

c) Create a package specification named `school_api`. The package contains the procedure named discount from Chapter 11, and the function named `new_instructor_id` from Chapter 12.

Answer:

```
1    CREATE OR REPLACE PACKAGE  school_api as
2        PROCEDURE discount_cost;
3        FUNCTION new_instructor_id
4            RETURN instructor.instructor_id%TYPE;
5    End school_api;
```

13.1.2 ANSWERS

a) Type the code above into a text file. Then run the script in a SQL*Plus session. Explain what happens.

Answer: The package body `manage_students` *is compiled into the database. The package contains the procedure* `manage_students.find_sname`, *which accepts the parameter* `student_id` *and returns the student's* `last_name` *and* `first_name` *from the Student table.*

b) Create a package body for the package named `cta_api` that you just created.

Answer:

```
-- ch13_5a.sql
 1  CREATE OR REPLACE PACKAGE BODY school_api AS
 2     PROCEDURE discount_cost
 3     IS
 4        CURSOR c_group_discount
 5        IS
 6        SELECT distinct s.course_no, c.description
 7          FROM section s, enrollment e, course c
 8         WHERE s.section_id = e.section_id
 9         GROUP BY s.course_no, c.description,
10                  e.section_id, s.section_id
11         HAVING COUNT(*) >=8;
12     BEGIN
13        FOR r_group_discount IN c_group_discount
14        LOOP
15        UPDATE course
16           SET cost = cost * .95
17         WHERE course_no = r_group_discount.course_no;
18         DBMS_OUTPUT.PUT_LINE
19            ('A 5% discount has been given to'
20            ||r_group_discount.course_no||'
21         '||r_group_discount.description);
22      END LOOP;
23     END discount_cost;
24     FUNCTION new_instructor_id
25        RETURN instructor.instructor_id%TYPE
26     IS
27        v_new_instid instructor.instructor_id%TYPE;
28     BEGIN
29        SELECT INSTRUCTOR_ID_SEQ.NEXTVAL
30          INTO v_new_instid
```

```
31            FROM dual;
32         RETURN v_new_instid;
33      EXCEPTION
34         WHEN OTHERS
35         THEN
36           DECLARE
37             v_sqlerrm VARCHAR2(250) :=
                    SUBSTR(SQLERRM,1,250);
38           BEGIN
39             RAISE_APPLICATION_ERROR(-20003,
40           'Error in    instructor_id: '||v_sqlerrm);
41           END;
42      END new_instructor_id;
43   End school_api;
```

13.1.3 ANSWERS

a) The previous example displays how a procedure within a package is executed. What results do you expect to see when you run this PL/SQL block?

Answer: This is a correct PL/SQL block for running the function and the procedure in the package manage_students. *If an existing* student_id *is entered, then the name of the student is displayed. If the id is not valid, then the error message is displayed.*

b) Run the script and observe the results. How does this compare with what you expected? Explain what the script is accomplishing line by line.

Answer: Initially the following appears:

```
Enter value for v_id:
```

If you enter "145," then you see:

```
old 5: IF manage_students.id_is_good(&v_id)
new 5: IF manage_students.id_is_good(145)
old 7:    manage_students.find_sname(&&v_id,
v_first_name,
new 7: manage_students.find_sname(145, v_first_name,
old 9: DBMS_OUTPUT.PUT_LINE('Student No. '||&&v_id||
       ' is '
new 9: DBMS_OUTPUT.PUT_LINE('Student No. '||145||' is '
old 13: ('Student ID: '||&&v_id||' is not in the
        database.');
```

```
new 13: ('Student ID: '||145||' is not in the
        database.');
Student No. 145 is Lefkowitz, Paul
PL/SQL procedure successfully completed.
```

The function id_is_good *returns TRUE for an existing* student_id *such as 145. The control then flows to the first part of the IF statement and the procedure* manage_students.find_sname *finds the first and last name for* student_id *145, which happens to be Lefkowitz, Paul.*

C) Create a script that tests the cta_api *package.*

```
SET SERVEROUTPUT ON
DECLARE
   V_instructor_id instructor.instructor_id%TYPE;
BEGIN
   cta_api.Discount;
   v_instructor_id := cta_api.new_instructor_id;
   DBMS_OUTPUT.PUT_LINE
       ('The new id is: '||v_instructor_id);
END;
```

13.1.4 ANSWERS

a) What have you added to the manage_student package?

Answer: A private function, student_count_privs, *and a public procedure,* display_student_count, *calling the private function.*

b) If you run the following from your SQL*PLUS session, what are the results?

Answer: Since the private function, student_count_privs, *cannot be called from outside the package, you receive an error message as follows:*

```
ERROR at line 1:
ORA-06550: line 4, column 31:
PLS-00302: component 'STUDENT_COUNT_PRIV' must be
declared
ORA-06550: line 4, column 3:
PL/SQL: Statement ignored
```

It appears as if the private function does not exist. This is important to keep in mind. You can see this can be useful when you are writing PL/SQL packages used by other developers. In order to simplify the package for them, they only need to see the package specification. This way they know what is being passed into the procedures and functions and what is being returned. They do not need to see the inner workings. If a number of procedures make use of the same logic, it may make more sense to put them into a private function called by the procedures.

c) If you run the following, what do you expect to see?

Answer: This is a valid method of running a procedure. A line is displayed indicating the number of students in the database. Note that the procedure in the package manage_students *is using the private function* student_count_priv *to retrieve the student count.*

Note, that if you forget to include a procedure or function in a package specification, it becomes private. On the other hand, if you declare a procedure or function in the package specification, and then you do not define it when you create the body, you receive the following error message:

PLS-00323: subprogram or cursor 'procedure_name' is declared in a package specification and must be defined in the package body

d) Add a private function to the school_api called get_course_descript_private. It accepts a course.course_no%TYPE and returns a course.description%TYPE. It searches for and returns the course description for the course number passed to it. If the course does not exist, or if an error occurs, it returns a NULL.

Answer: Add the following lines to the package body: There is nothing that needs to be added to the package specification, since you are only adding a private object.

```
44     FUNCTION get_course_descript_private
45       (i_course_no   course.course_no%TYPE)
46       RETURN course.description%TYPE
47     IS
48       v_course_descript course.description%TYPE;
49     BEGIN
50       SELECT description
51         INTO v_course_descript
52         FROM course
53        WHERE course_no = i_course_no;
54       RETURN v_course_descript;
55     EXCEPTION
56       WHEN OTHERS
57       THEN
58         RETURN NULL;
59     END get_course_descript_private;
60   End school_api;
```

a) Add a package-wide variable called `v_current_date` to `school_api`. Additionally, add an initialization section that assigns the current sysdate to the variable `v_current_date`.

Answer: Add the following line to the beginning of the package specification:

```
1   CREATE OR REPLACE PACKAGE  school_api as
2      v_current_date DATE;
3      PROCEDURE Discount;
4      FUNCTION new_instructor_id
5         RETURN instructor.instructor_id%TYPE;
6   End school_api;
```

Add the following to the end of the package body:

```
59   BEGIN
60     SELECT trunc(sysdate, 'DD')
61       INTO v_current_date
62       FROM dual;
63   End school_api;
```

LAB 13.1 SELF-REVIEW QUESTIONS

In order to test your progress, you should be able to answer the following questions.

1) The main advantages to grouping procedures and functions into packages are as follows (check all that apply):
   a) _____ It follows the trendy object method of programming.
   b) _____ It is a more efficient way of utilizing the processor memory.
   c) _____ It makes greater use of the security privileges of various users.
   d) _____ It is a more efficient method to maximize tablespace storage.
   e) _____ It keeps you on good terms with the DBA.

2) If user Tashi has SELECT privilege on the student table and user Sonam does not, then Sonam can make use of a procedure created by Tashi to get access to the student table if he has execute privileges on Tashi's procedure.
   a) _____ True
   b) _____ False

3) All procedures and functions in a package body must be declared in the package specification.

   a) _____ True

   b) _____ False

4) Th initialization section of a package refers to

   a) _____ another term for the package header.

   b) _____ the first part of the package.

   c) _____ the executable code at the end of the package.

   d) _____ the evolutionary rudiments in code that are left over from programming methods of cavemen.

5) The package specification is merely a formality for other programmers to let them know what parameters are being passed in and out of the procedures and functions. It hides the program logic but in actuality it is not necessary and is incorporated into the package body.

   a) _____ True

   b) _____ False

Quiz answers appear in Appendix A, Section 13.1.

CHAPTER 13

TEST YOUR THINKING

In this chapter, you have learned about packages. Here are some projects that will help you test the depth of your understanding.

1) Add a procedure to the `student_api` package called `remove_student`. This procedure accepts a `student_id` and returns nothing. Based on the student id passed in, it removes the student from the database. If the student does not exist or there is a problem removing the student (such as a foreign key constraint violation), then let the calling program handle it.

2) Alter `remove_student` in the `student_api` package body to accept an additional parameter. This new parameter is a VARCHAR2 and is called `p_ri`. Make `p_ri` default to "R." The new parameter may contain a value of "R" or "C." If "R" is received, it represents DELETE RESTRICT and the procedure acts as it does now. If there are enrollments for the student, the delete is disallowed. If a "C" is received, it represents DELETE CASCADE. This functionally means that the `remove_student` procedure locates all records for the student in all of the CTA tables and removes them from the database before attempting to remove the student from the student table. Decide how to handle the situation where the user passes in a code other than "C" or "R."

CHAPTER 14

STORED CODE

In Chapter 11 you learned about procedures, in Chapter 12 you learned about functions, and in Chapter 13 you learned about the process of grouping functions and procedures into a package. Now, you will learn more about what it means to have code bundled into a package. There are numerous Data Dictionary views that can be accessed to gather information about the objects in a package.

Functions in packages are also required to meet additional restrictions in order to be used in a SELECT statement. In this chapter, you learn what they are and how to enforce them. You will also learn an advanced technique to overload a function or procedure so that it executes different code, depending on the type of the parameter passed in.

L A B   1 4 . 1

ADVANCED FEATURES
OF STORED CODE

LAB OBJECTIVES

After this lab, you will be able to:

✔ Get Stored Code Information from the Data
Dictionary
✔ Enforce Purity Level with RESTRICT_REFERENCES
Pragma
✔ Overload Modules

GATHERING STORED CODE INFORMATION

Stored programs are stored in compiled form in the database. Information about the stored programs is accessible through various data dictionary views. In Chapter 11 you learned about the two data dictionary views USER_OBJECTS and USER_SOURCE. Additionally, you learned about the USER_TRIGGERS view in Chapter 8. There are a few more data dictionary views that are useful for obtaining information about stored code. In this lab, you will learn how to take advantage of these.

LAB 14.1 EXERCISES

14.1.1 GETTING STORED CODE INFORMATION
FROM THE DATA DICTIONARY

Answer the following questions:

a) Query the data dictionary to determine all the stored procedures, functions, and packages in the current schema of the database. Also include the current status of the stored code. Write the select statement below.

_____

_____

b) Type the following script into a text file and run the script in SQL*Plus. It creates the function scode_at_line. Explain what the purpose of this function is. What is accomplished by running it? When does a developer find it useful?

■ *FOR EXAMPLE*

```
-- ch14_1a.sql
CREATE OR REPLACE FUNCTION scode_at_line
    (i_name_in IN VARCHAR2,
     i_line_in IN INTEGER := 1,
     i_type_in IN VARCHAR2 := NULL)
RETURN VARCHAR2
IS
   CURSOR scode_cur IS
      SELECT text
        FROM user_source
       WHERE name = UPPER (i_name_in)
         AND (type = UPPER (i_type_in)
          OR i_type_in IS NULL)
         AND line = i_line_in;
   scode_rec scode_cur%ROWTYPE;
BEGIN
   OPEN scode_cur;
   FETCH scode_cur INTO scode_rec;
   IF scode_cur%NOTFOUND
      THEN
         CLOSE scode_cur;
         RETURN NULL;
   ELSE
      CLOSE scode_cur;
      RETURN scode_rec.text;
   END IF;
END;
```

_____

_____

c) Type DESC USER_ERRORS. What do you see? In what way do you think this view is useful for you?

_____

_____

d) Type the following script to force an error.

```
CREATE OR REPLACE PROCEDURE FORCE_ERROR
as
BEGIN
    SELECT course_no
    INTO v_temp
    FROM course;
END;
```

Now type:

```
SHO ERR
```

What do you see?

_____

_____

e) How can you get this information from the USER_ERRORS view?

_____

_____

f) Type DESC USER_DEPENDENCIES. What do you see? How can you make use of this view?

_____

_____

g) Type the following:

```
SELECT referenced_name
FROM user_dependencies
WHERE name = 'SCHOOL_API';
```

Analyze what you see and explain how it is useful.

h) Type DESC `school_api`. What do you see?

---

i) Explain what you are seeing. How is this different from the USER_DEPENDENCEIS view?

14.1.2 ENFORCING PURITY LEVEL WITH RESTRICT_REFERENCES PRAGMA

Answer the following questions:

a) Add the following function to the `school_api` package specification:

```
6          FUNCTION total_cost_for_student
7             (i_student_id IN student.student_id%TYPE)
8          RETURN course.cost%TYPE;
9       End school_api;
```

Append to the body:

```
60    FUNCTION total_cost_for_student
61       (i_student_id IN student.student_id%TYPE)
62        RETURN course.cost%TYPE
63    IS
64      v_cost course.cost%TYPE;
65    BEGIN
66       SELECT sum(cost)
67         INTO v_cost
68         FROM course c, section s, enrollment e
69        WHERE c.course_no = s.course_no
70          AND e.section_id = s.section_id
71          AND e.student_id = i_student_id;
72       RETURN v_cost;
73    EXCEPTION
```

```
74          WHEN OTHERS THEN
75              RETURN NULL;
76      END total_cost_for_student;
77      BEGIN
78        SELECT trunc(sysdate, 'DD')
79          INTO v_current_date
80          FROM dual;
81      END school_api;
```

If you performed the following SELECT statement, what would you expect to see?

```
SELECT school_api.total_cost_for_student(student_id),
       student_id
FROM student;
```

A pragma is a special directive to the PL/SQL compiler. You use the RESTRICT_REFERENCES pragma to tell the compiler about the purity level of a packaged function.

To assert the purity level use the syntax:

```
PRAGMA RESTRICT_REFERENCES
       (function_name, WNDS [,WNPS], [,RNDS] [,RNPS])
```

b) Alter the package specification for school_api as follows:

```
6       FUNCTION total_cost_for_student
7           (i_student_id IN student.student_id%TYPE)
8           RETURN course.cost%TYPE;
9           PRAGMA RESTRICT_REFERENCES
10              (total_cost_for_student, WNDS, WNPS, RNPS);
11  End school_api;
```

Now run the SELECT statement from the question above. What do you expect to see?

c) What is the "purity level" of the function `school_api.total_cost_for_student`?

_____

_____

d) If you add the following three lines, will the package compile without error?

```
81       UPDATE STUDENT
82          SET employer = 'Prenctice Hall'
83        WHERE employer is null;
84    END school_api;
```

14.1.3 OVERLOADING MODULES

When you overload modules, you give two or more modules the same name. The parameter lists of the modules must differ in a manner significant enough for the compiler (and runtime engine) to distinguish between the different versions.

You can overload modules in three contexts:

1. In a local module in the same PL/SQL block.
2. In a package specification.
3. In a package body.

a) Add the following lines to the package specification of `school_api`. Then recompile the package specification. Explain what you have created.

```
11       PROCEDURE get_student_info
12          (i_student_id   IN  student.student_id%TYPE,
13           o_last_name    OUT student.last_name%TYPE,
14           o_first_name   OUT student.first_name%TYPE,
15           o_zip          OUT student.zip%TYPE,
16           o_return_code  OUT NUMBER);
17       PROCEDURE get_student_info
18          (i_last_name    IN student.last_name%TYPE,
19           i_first_name   IN student.first_name%TYPE,
20           o_student_id   OUT student.student_id%TYPE,
21           o_zip          OUT student.zip%TYPE,
```

```
22              o_return_code OUT NUMBER);
23   End school_api;
```

b) Add the following code to the body of the package `school_api`. Explain what has been accomplished.

```
77   PROCEDURE get_student_info
78   (i_student_id    IN  student.student_id%TYPE,
79    o_last_name     OUT student.last_name%TYPE,
80    o_first_name    OUT student.first_name%TYPE,
81    o_zip           OUT student.zip%TYPE,
82    o_return_code   OUT NUMBER)
83   IS
84   BEGIN
85     SELECT last_name, first_name, zip
86       INTO o_last_name, o_first_name, o_zip
87       FROM student
88      WHERE student.student_id = i_student_id;
89     o_return_code := 0;
90   EXCEPTION
91     WHEN NO_DATA_FOUND
92     THEN
93       DBMS_OUTPUT.PUT_LINE
                ('Student ID is not valid.');
94       o_return_code := -100;
95       o_last_name := NULL;
96       o_first_name := NULL;
97       o_zip    := NULL;
98     WHEN OTHERS
99       THEN
100       DBMS_OUTPUT.PUT_LINE
                ('Error in procedure get_student_info');
101  END get_student_info;
102  PROCEDURE get_student_info
103    (i_last_name    IN student.last_name%TYPE,
104     i_first_name   IN student.first_name%TYPE,
105     o_student_id   OUT student.student_id%TYPE,
106     o_zip          OUT student.zip%TYPE,
107     o_return_code  OUT NUMBER)
108  IS
109  BEGIN
110    SELECT student_id, zip
111      INTO o_student_id, o_zip
112      FROM student
113     WHERE UPPER(last_name)  = UPPER(i_last_name)
```

```
114        AND UPPER(first_name) = UPPER(i_first_name);
115     o_return_code := 0;
116   EXCEPTION
117     WHEN NO_DATA_FOUND
118       THEN
119         DBMS_OUTPUT.PUT_LINE
                ('Student name is not valid.');
120         o_return_code := -100;
121         o_student_id := NULL;
122         o_zip     := NULL;
123     WHEN OTHERS
124       THEN
125         DBMS_OUTPUT.PUT_LINE
                ('Error in procedure get_student_info');
126   END get_student_info;
127    BEGIN
128      SELECT TRUNC(sysdate, 'DD')
129        INTO v_current_date
130        FROM dual;
131   END school_api;
```

c) Write a PL/SQL block using the overloaded function you just created.

LAB 14.1 EXERCISE ANSWERS

14.1.1 ANSWERS

a) Query the data dictionary to determine all the stored procedures, functions, and packages in the current schema of the database. Also include the current status of the stored code.

Answer: You can use the USER_OBJECTS view you learned about in Chapter 11. This view has information about all database objects in the schema of the current user. Remember, if you want to see all the objects in other schemas that the current user has access to, then use the ALL_OBJECTS view. There is also a DBA_OBJECTS view for a list of all objects in the database regardless of privilege. The STATUS will either be VALID or INVALID. An object can change status from VALID to INVALID if an underlying table is altered or privileges on an referenced object have been revoked from the creator of the function, procedure, or package. The following SELECT statement produces the answer you are looking for.

```
SELECT  OBJECT_TYPE, OBJECT_NAME, STATUS
FROM    USER_OBJECTS
WHERE   OBJECT_TYPE IN
          ('FUNCTION', 'PROCEDURE', 'PACKAGE',
           'PACKAGE_BODY')
ORDER BY OBJECT_TYPE;
```

b) Type the following script into a text file and run the script in SQL*Plus. It creates the function `scode_at_line`. Explain the purpose of this function. What is accomplished by running it? When does a developer find it useful?

Answer: The `scode_at_line` *function provides an easy mechanism for retrieving the text from a stored program for a specified line number. This is useful if a developer receives a compilation error message referring to a particular line number in an object. The developer can then make use of this function to find out the text that is in error.*

The procedure uses three parameters:

`name_in`   *The name of the stored object.*

`line_in`   *The line number of the line you wish to retrieve. The default value is 1.*

`type_in`   *The type of object you want to view. The default for type_in is NULL.*

The default values are designed to make this function as easy as possible to use.

*The output from a call to SHOW ERRORS in SQL*Plus displays the line number in which an error occurred, but the line number doesn't correspond to the line in your text file. Instead, it relates directly to the line number stored with the source code in the USER_SOURCE view.*

c) Type DESC USER_ERRORS. What do you see? In what way do you think this view is useful for you?

Answer: The view stores current errors on the user's stored objects. The text file contains the text of the error. This is useful in determining the details of a compilation error. The next exercise walks you through using this view.

Name	Null?	Type
NAME	NOT NULL	VARCHAR2(30)
TYPE		VARCHAR2(12)
SEQUENCE	NOT NULL	NUMBER
LINE	NOT NULL	NUMBER
POSITION	NOT NULL	NUMBER
TEXT	NOT NULL	VARCHAR2(2000) ---

d) Type the following script to force an error. Now type: SHO ERR. What do you see?

```
Errors for PROCEDURE FORCE_ERROR:
LINE/COL ERROR
-------- ---------------------------------------------
4/4      PL/SQL: SQL Statement ignored
5/9      PLS-00201: identifier 'V_TEMP' must be declared
```

e) How can you retrieve information from the USER_ERORS view?

```
SELECT line||'/'||position "LINE/COL", TEXT "ERROR"
FROM user_errors
WHERE name = 'FORCE_ERROR'
```

It is important for you to know how to retrieve this information from the USER_ ERRORS view since the SHO ERR command only shows you the most recent errors. If you run a script creating a number of objects, then you have to rely on the USER_ ERRORS view.

f) Type DESC USER_DEPENDENCIES. What do you see?

Answer: The DEPENDENCIES view is useful for analyzing the impact that may occur from table changes or changes to other stored procedures. If tables are about to be redesigned, an impact assessment can be made from the information in USER_DEPENDENCIES. ALL_DEPENDENCIES and DBA_DEPENDENCIES show all dependencies for procedures, functions, package specifications, and package bodies.

Name	Null?	Type
NAME	NOT NULL	VARCHAR2(30)
TYPE		VARCHAR2(12)
REFERENCED_OWNER		VARCHAR2(30)
REFERENCED_NAME	NOT NULL	VARCHAR2(30)
REFERENCED_TYPE		VARCHAR2(12)
REFERENCED_LINK_NAME		VARCHAR2(30)
TIP		

g) Type the following:

```
SELECT referenced_name
FROM user_dependencies
WHERE name = 'SCHOOL_API';
```

Analyze what you see and explain how it is useful.

```
REFERENCED_NAME
-------------------------------
DUAL
DUAL
STANDARD
STANDARD
DBMS_STANDARD
DBMS_OUTPUT
DBMS_OUTPUT
INSTRUCTOR_ID_SEQ
COURSE
COURSE
ENROLLMENT
INSTRUCTOR
INSTRUCTOR
SECTION
STUDENT
STUDENT
DBMS_OUTPUT
DUAL
SCHOOL_API
```

This list of dependencies for the school_api package lists all objects referenced in the package. This includes tables, sequences, and procedures (even Oracle-supplied packages). This information is very useful when you are planning a change to the database structure. You can easily pinpoint what the ramifications are for any database changes.

h) Type DESC school_api, what do you see?

Answer:

```
PROCEDURE DISCOUNT
FUNCTION NEW_INSTRUCTOR_ID RETURNS NUMBER(8)
FUNCTION TOTAL_COST_FOR_STUDENT RETURNS NUMBER(9,2)
Argument Name     Type                  In/Out Default?
------------------------------- ----------------------
I_STUDENT_ID      NUMBER(8)                  IN
```

DEPTREE

There is also an Oracle-supplied utility called DEPTREE that shows you, for a given object, which other objects are dependent upon it. There are three pieces to this utility. You need to have DBA access to the database in order to use this utility.

utldtree.sql script

DEPTREE_FILL(type, schema, object_name) procedure

ideptree view

First, run *utldtree.sql* in your schema. This creates the necessary objects to map the dependencies. The location of *utldtree.sql* is dependent upon your particular installation, so ask your DBA. (`c:\orant\rdbms80\admin\utldtree.sql`)

(`$ORACLE_HOME/rdbms/admin/utldtree.sql`)

Second, fill the deptree e_temptab table by running DEPTREE_FILL

Example: `SQL> exec DEPTREE_FILL('TABLE', USER, 'MESSAGE_LOG')`

Third, look at the deptree information in the ideptree view.

Example: `SQL> SELECT * FROM ideptree;`

The result contains the kind of information you see below.

DEPENDENCIES

TABLE CTA.MESSAGE_LOG

PACKAGE BODY CTA.API

TRIGGER CTA.COURSE_AFTER_I

PACKAGE CTA.API

PACKAGE BODY CTA.API

i) Explain what you are seeing. How is this different from the USER_DEPEND-ENCIES view?

Answer: The DESC command you have been using to describe the columns in a table is also used for procedures, packages, and functions. The DESC command shows all the parameters with their default values and an indication of whether they are IN or

OUT. If the object is a function, then the return datatype is displayed. This is very different from the USER_DEPENDENCIES view, which has information on all the objects that are referenced in a package, function, or procedure.

14.1.2 ANSWERS

a) If you perform the following SELECT statement, what do you expect to see?

Answer: At first glance you may have thought you would see a list of student_ids with the total cost for the courses they took. But instead you see the following error:

```
ERROR at line 1:
ORA-06571: Function TOTAL_COST_FOR_STUDENT does not
guarantee not to update database
```

Although functions can be used in a SELECT statement, if a function is in a package, it requires some additional definitions to enforce its purity.

Requirements for Stored Functions in SQL

1) The function must be stored in the database (Not in the library of an Oracle tool).

2) The function must be a row-specific function and not a column or group function.

3) As for all functions (whether to be used in SQL statements or not), parameters must be the IN mode.

4) Datatypes of the function parameters and the function RETURN clause must be recognized within the Oracle Server. (Not, as of yet, BOOLEAN, BINARY_INTEGER, PL/SQL tables, PL/SQL records, and programmer-defined subtypes. Maybe in the future—keep your fingers crossed).

There are numerous function side effects that must be considered. Modification of database tables in stored functions may have ripple effects on queries using the function. Modification of package variables can have an impact on other stored functions or procedures, or in turn the SQL statement using the stored function. Stored functions in the WHERE clause may subvert the query optimization process. A SQL statement may use a stand-alone function or package function as an operator on one or more columns, provided the function returns a valid Oracle database type.

A user-defined function may select from database tables or call other procedures or functions, whether stand alone or packaged. When a function is used in a SELECT statement, it may not modify data in any database table with an INSERT, UPDATE, or DELETE statement, or read or write package variables across user sessions.

The Oracle Server automatically enforces the rules for stand-alone functions, but not with a stored function in a package. The purity level (the extent to which the function is free of side effects) of a function in a package must be stated explicitly. This is done via a pragma.

The reason the error message was received above is because the pragma was not used. You will now learn how to make use of a pragma.

b) Alter the package specification for `school_api` as follows: Run the SELECT statement from the question above. What do you expect to see?

Answer: The pragma restriction is added to the package specification and insures that the function `total_cost_for_student` *has met the required purity restriction for a function to be in a SELECT statement. The SELECT statement now functions properly and projects a list of the total cost for each student and the student's ID.*

Rules for Using Pragma Restrictions

Only the WNDS level is mandatory.

You need a separate pragma statement for each packaged function used in a SQL statement.

The pragma must come after the function declaration in the *package specification.*

---

c) What is the "purity level" of the function `school_api. total_cost_for_student`?

Answer: The extent to which a function is free of side effects is called the purity level *of the function. The function is now very pure. It has the following levels of purity: (1) WNDS means write no database state; that is, it does not make any changes to database tables. (2) WNPS means the function writes no package state; that is, the function does not alter the values of any package variables. (3) RNPS means it reads no package state; that is, no package variables are read in order to calculate the return for the function. There is also a RNDS pragma, which means no database tables are read. If this is added, the function is too pure for the needs here and cannot be used in a SELECT statement.*

Here is a summary of the codes and their meanings.

Purity Level	Code Description	Assertion
WNDS	Writes No Database State	No modification of any database table.
WNPS	Writes No Package State	No modification of any packaged variable.
RNDS	Reads No Database State	No reading of any database table.
RNPS	Reads No Package State	No reading of any package variables.

d) If you add the following three lines, does the package compile without any errors?

Answer: No. You added an update statement and violated the purity level of the pragma restriction WNDS—writes no database state. You receive the following error message when you try to compile the new package:

```
Errors for PACKAGE BODY SCHOOL_API:
LINE/COL ERROR
-------- ---------------------------------------------
0/0      PL/SQL: Compilation unit analysis terminated
60/2     PLS-00452: Subprogram 'TOTAL_COST_FOR_STUDENT'
                     violates its  associated pragma
```

14.1.3 ANSWERS

a) Add the following lines to the package specification `school_api`. Then compile the package specification. Explain what you created.

Answer: No, you have not created Frankenstein, it's just an overloaded procedure. The specification has two procedures with the same name and different IN parameters both in number and in datatype. The OUT parameters are also different in number and datatype. This overloaded function accepts either of the two sets of IN parameters and performs the version of the function corresponding to the datatype passed in.

b) Add the following code to the package body `school_api`. Explain what you accomplished.

Answer: A single function name, `get_student_info`, accepts either a single IN parameter of `student_id` or two parameters consisting of a student's `last_name` and `first_name`. If a number is passed in, then the procedure looks for the name and zipcode of the student. If it finds them, they are returned as well as a return code of 0. If they cannot be found, then null values are returned and a return code of −100. If two VARCHAR2 parameters are passed in, then the procedure searches for the `student_id` corresponding to the names passed in. As with the other version of this procedure, if a match is found the procedure returns a `student_id`, the student's zipcode, and a return code of 0. If a match is not found, then the values returned are null as well as an exit code of −100.

PL/SQL uses overloading in many common functions and built-in packages. For example, TO_CHAR converts both numbers and dates to strings. Overloading makes it easy for other programmers to use your code in an API.

The main benefits of overloading are as follows: (1) Overloading simplifies the call interface of packages and reduces many program names to one. (2) Modules are easier to use and hence more likely to be used. The software determines the context. (3) The volume of code is reduced because code required for different datatypes is often the same.

The rules for overloading are as follows: (1)The compiler must be able distinguish between the two calls at runtime. Distinguishing between the uses of the overloaded module is what is important and not solely the spec or header. (2) The formal parameters must differ in number, order, or datatype family. (3) You cannot overload the names of stand-alone modules. (4) Functions differing only in RETURN datatypes cannot be overloaded.

c) Write a PL/SQL block using the overloaded function you just created.

Answer: A suitable bride for Frankenstein is as follows:

```
SET SERVEROUTPUT ON
PROMPT ENTER A student_id
ACCEPT p_id
PROMPT ENTER a differnt student's first name surrounded
PROMPT by quotes
ACCEPT p_first_name
PROMPT Now enter the last name surrounded by quotes
ACCEPT p_last_name
DECLARE
    v_student_ID   student.student_id%TYPE;
    v_last_name    student.last_name%TYPE;
    v_first_name   student.first_name%TYPE;
    v_zip          student.zip%TYPE;
    v_return_code NUMBER;
BEGIN
    school_api.get_student_info
```

```
        (&&p_id, v_last_name, v_first_name,
        v_zip,v_return_code);
   IF v_return_code = 0
   THEN
      DBMS_OUTPUT.PUT_LINE
        ('Student with ID '||&&p_id||' is '||v_first_name
        ||' '||v_last_name
        );
   ELSE
   DBMS_OUTPUT.PUT_LINE
        ('The ID '||&&p_id||'is not in the database'
        );
   END IF;
   school_api.get_student_info
        (&&p_last_name , &&p_first_name, v_student_id,
        v_zip , v_return_code);
   IF v_return_code = 0
   THEN
      DBMS_OUTPUT.PUT_LINE
        (&&p_first_name||' '|| &&p_last_name||
        ' has an ID of '||v_student_id
        );
   ELSE
   DBMS_OUTPUT.PUT_LINE
        (&&p_first_name||' '|| &&p_last_name||
        'is not in the database'
        );
   END IF;
END;
```

It is important for you to realize the benefits of using a && variable. The value for the variable need only be entered once, but if you run the code a second time, you will not be prompted to enter the value again since it is now in memory.

Here are a few things to keep in mind when you overload functions or procedures.

These two procedures cannot be overloaded:

```
PROCEDURE calc_total (reg_in IN CHAR);
PROCEDURE calc_total (reg_in IN VARCHAR2).
```

In these two versions of calc_total *the two different IN variables cannot be distinguished from each other.*

In the example below, an anchored type (%TYPE) is relied upon to establish the datatype of the second calc's parameter.

```
DECLARE
PROCEDURE calc (comp_id_IN IN NUMBER)
   IS
BEGIN ... END;
PROCEDURE calc
(comp_id_IN IN company.comp_id%TYPE)
   IS
BEGIN ... END;
```

PL/SQL does not find a conflict at compile time with overloading even though `comp_id` *is a numeric column. Instead, you get the following message at runtime:*

```
PLS-00307: too many declarations of '<program>'
match this call
```

LAB 14.1 SELF-REVIEW QUESTIONS

In order to test your progress, you should be able to answer the following questions.

1) What is the purpose of the USER_ERRORS view?
   a) _____ It prevents you from having to make use of the SHO ERR command.
   b) _____ It has the details on database objects in an invalid state.
   c) _____ It is a record of all compilation errors you have ever made.
   d) _____ It has no purpose but to take up database space.

2) The DESC command behaves like an overloaded procedure.
   a) _____ True
   b) _____ False

3) All functions require a pragma restriction to be used in an SQL statement.
   a) _____ True
   b) _____ False

4) What does the purity level of a pragma restriction mean?
   a) _____ It refers to whether it is kosher or not.
   b) _____ It tells you if the function can be used in a SELECT statement.
   c) _____ It shows the effect executing the function will have on other objects in the database or the package.
   d) _____ It tells you if the function is overloaded.

5)   What is the principal benefit of an overloaded function?

    a) _____ An overloaded function is able to bypass any pragma restriction.

    b) _____ An overloaded function behaves differently depending on the type of data passed in when it is called.

    c) _____ It is just a lot of hype—overloaded functions have no benefit.

    d) _____ An overloaded function is like a ghost function.

Quiz answers appear in Appendix A, Section 14.1.

CHAPTER 14

TEST YOUR THINKING

In this chapter you learned about stored code. Here are some projects to help you test the depth of your understanding. Add the following to the `school_api`.

1) Add a function in `school_api` package specification called `get_course_descript`. The caller takes a `course.cnumber%TYPE` parameter and it returns a `course.description%TYPE`.

2) Create a function in the `school_api` package body called `get_course_description`. A caller passes in a course number and it returns the course description. Instead of searching for the description itself, it makes a call to `get_course_descript_private`. It passes its course number to `get_course_descript_private`. It passes back to the caller the description it gets back from `get_course_descript_private`.

3) Add a PRAGMA RESTRICT_REFERENCES for `get_course_description` specifying: writes no database state, writes no package state, and reads no package state.

C H A P T E R   1 5

TRIGGERS

In Chapters 11 through 14, you explored the concepts of stored code and different types of named PL/SQL blocks such as procedures, functions, and packages. In this chapter, you will learn about another type of named PL/SQL block called a database *trigger*. You will also learn about different characteristics of triggers and their usage in the database.

L A B   1 5 . 1

WHAT TRIGGERS ARE

LAB OBJECTIVES

After this lab, you will be able to:

✔ Understand What a Trigger Is
✔ Use BEFORE and AFTER Triggers

A database trigger is a named PL/SQL block stored in a database and executed implicitly when a *triggering event* occurs. An act of executing a trigger is referred to as *firing a trigger*. A triggering event is a DML (INSERT, UPDATE, or DELETE) statement executed against a database table. A trigger can fire before or after a triggering event. For example, if you have defined a trigger to fire before an INSERT statement on the STUDENt table, this trigger fires each time before you insert a row in the STUDENT table.

The general syntax for creating a trigger is as follows (the reserved words and phrases surrounded by brackets are optional):

```
CREATE [OR REPLACE] TRIGGER trigger_name
{BEFORE|AFTER} triggering_event ON table_name
[FOR EACH ROW]
[WHEN condition]
DECLARE
    Declaration statements
BEGIN
    Executable statements
EXCEPTION
    Exception-handling statements
END;
```

The reserved word CREATE specifies that you are creating a new trigger. The reserved word REPLACE specifies that you are modifying an existing trigger. REPLACE is optional. However, notice that, most of the time, both CREATE and REPLACE are present. Consider the following situation. You create a trigger as follows:

```
CREATE TRIGGER trigger_name
...
```

In a few days you decide to modify this trigger. If you do not include the reserved word REPLACE in the CREATE clause of the trigger, this generates an error message when you compile the trigger. The error message states the name of your trigger is already used by another object. Once REPLACE is included in the CREATE clause of the trigger, there is less of a chance for an error because, if it is a new trigger, it is created, and if it is an old trigger, it is replaced.

The *trigger_name* references the name of the trigger. BEFORE or AFTER specify when the trigger fires (before or after the triggering event). The *triggering_event* references a DML statement issued against the table. The *table_name* is the name of the table associated with the trigger. The clause, FOR EACH ROW, specifies a trigger is a row trigger and fires once for each row either inserted, updated, or deleted. You will encounter row and statement triggers in the next lab of this chapter. A WHEN clause specifies a *condition* that must evaluate to TRUE for the trigger to fire. For example, this condition may specify a certain restriction on the column of a table. Next, the trigger body is defined. It is important for you to realize if you drop a table, the table's database triggers are dropped as well.

However, you should be careful when using the reserved word REPLACE for a number of reasons. First, if you happen to use REPLACE and a name of an existing stored function, procedure, or package, it will be replaced by the trigger. Second, when you use the reserved word REPLACE and decide to associate a different table with your trigger an error message is generated. For example, assume you created a trigger STUDENT_BI on the STUDENT table. Next, you decided to modify this trigger and associate it with the Enrollment table. As a result, the following error message is generated:

```
ERROR at line 1:
ORA-04095: trigger 'STUDENT_BI' already exists on an-
other table, cannot replace it
```

Triggers are used for different purposes. Some uses for triggers are:

- Enforcing complex business rules that cannot be defined by using integrity constraints.
- Maintaining complex security rules.

- Automatically generating values for derived columns.
- Collecting statistical information on table accesses.
- Preventing invalid transactions.
- Providing value auditing.

The body of a trigger is a PL/SQL block. However, there are several restrictions that you need to know to create a trigger. These restrictions are:

- A trigger may not issue a transactional control statement such as COMMIT, SAVEPOINT, or ROLLBACK. When the trigger fires, all operations performed become part of a transaction. When this transaction is committed or rolled back, the operations performed by the trigger are committed or rolled back as well.
- Any function or a procedure called by a trigger may not issue a transactional control statement.
- It is not permissible to declare LONG or LONG RAW variables in the body of a trigger.

BEFORE TRIGGERS

Consider the following example of a trigger on the Student table mentioned earlier in the chapter. This trigger fires before the INSERT statement on the Student table and populates STUDENT_ID, CREATED_DATE, MODIFIED_DATE, CREATED_BY, and MODIFIED_BY columns. Column STUDENT_ID is populated with the number generated by the STUDENT_ID_SEQ sequence, and columns CREATED_DATE, MODIFIED_DATE, CREATED_USER, and MODIFIED_USER are populated with current date and current user name information respectively.

■ FOR EXAMPLE

```
CREATE OR REPLACE TRIGGER student_bi
BEFORE INSERT ON student
FOR EACH ROW
DECLARE
   v_student_id STUDENT.STUDENT_ID%TYPE;
BEGIN
   SELECT STUDENT_ID_SEQ.NEXTVAL
     INTO v_student_id
     FROM dual;
   :NEW.student_id := v_student_id;
   :NEW.created_by := USER;
```

```
        :NEW.created_date := SYSDATE;
        :NEW.modified_by := USER;
        :NEW.modified_date := SYSDATE;
   END;
```

This trigger fires before each INSERT statement on the Student table. Notice, the name of the trigger is STUDENT_BI, where STUDENT references the name of the table the trigger is defined, and the letters BI mean BEFORE INSERT. There is no specific requirement for naming triggers; however, this approach to naming a trigger is descriptive because the name of the trigger contains the name of the table affected by the triggering event, the time of the triggering event (before or after), and the triggering event itself.

In the body of the trigger, there is a pseudo-record, :NEW, allowing you to access a row currently being processed. In other words, a row is being inserted into the Student table. The :NEW pseudo-record is of a type TRIGGERING_TABLE%TYPE, so, in this case, it is of the STUDENT%TYPE type. In order to access individual members of the pseudo-record :NEW, *dot notation* is used. In other words, :NEW.CREATED_BY refers to the member, CREATED_BY, of the :NEW pseudo-record, and the name of the record is separated by the dot from the name of its member.

Before you create this trigger, consider the following INSERT statement on the Student table:

```
INSERT INTO student (student_id, first_name,
        last_name,
    zip, registration_date, created_by, created_date,
    modified_by, modified_date)
VALUES (STUDENT_ID_SEQ.NEXTVAL, 'John', 'Smith',
'00914',
    SYSDATE, USER, SYSDATE, USER, SYSDATE);
```

This INSERT statement contains values for the columns STUDENT_ID, CREATED_BY, CREATED_DATE, MODIFIED_BY, and MODIFIED_DATE. It is important to note for every row you insert into the STUDENT table, the values for these columns must be provided, and they are always derived in the same fashion. Why do you think the values for these columns must be provided when inserting a record into the STUDENT table?

Once the trigger shown earlier is created, there is no need to include these columns in the INSERT statement because the trigger will populate them with the required information. Therefore, the INSERT statement can be modified as follows:

```
INSERT INTO student (first_name, last_name, zip,
    registration_date)
VALUES ('John', 'Smith', '00914', SYSDATE);
```

Notice, this version of the INSERT statement looks significantly shorter than the previous version. The columns STUDENT_ID, CREATED_BY, CREATED_DATE, MODIFIED_BY, and MODIFIED_DATE are not present. However, their values are provided by the trigger. As a result, there is no need to include them in the INSERT statement, and there is less of a chance for a transaction error.

You should use BEFORE triggers in the following situations:

- When a trigger provides values for derived columns before an INSERT or UPDATE statement is completed. For example, the column FINAL_GRADE in the Enrollment table holds the value of the student's final grade for a specific course. This value is calculated based on the student performance for the duration of the course.

- When a trigger determines whether an INSERT, UPDATE, or DELETE statement should be allowed to complete. For example, when you insert a record into the Instructor table, a trigger can verify if the value provided for the column ZIP is valid. In other words, if there is a record in the ZIPCODE table corresponding to the value of zip that you provided.

AFTER TRIGGERS

Assume there is a table called Statistics having the following structure:

```
Name                                  Null?     Type
------------------------------------- --------- ----
TABLE_NAME                                      VARCHAR2(30)
TRANSACTION_NAME                                VARCHAR2(10)
TRANSACTION_USER                                VARCHAR2(30)
TRANSACTION_DATE                                DATE
```

This table is used to collect statistical information on different tables of the database. For example, you can record who deleted records from the Instructor table and when they were deleted.

Consider the following example of a trigger on the Instructor table. This trigger fires after an UPDATE or DELETE statement is issued on the IN-STRUCTOR table.

■ *FOR EXAMPLE*

```
CREATE OR REPLACE TRIGGER instructor_aud
BEFORE UPDATE OR DELETE ON INSTRUCTOR
DECLARE
   v_type VARCHAR2(10);
BEGIN
   IF UPDATING
   THEN
      v_type := 'UPDATE';
   ELSIF DELETING
   THEN
      v_type := 'DELETE';
   END IF;
   UPDATE statistics
      SET transaction_user = USER,
          transaction_date = SYSDATE
    WHERE table_name = 'INSTRUCTOR'
      AND transaction_name = v_type;
   IF SQL%NOTFOUND
   THEN
      INSERT INTO statistics
      VALUES ('INSTRUCTOR', v_type, USER, SYSDATE);
   END IF;
END;
```

This trigger fires after an UPDATE or DELETE statement on the Instructor table. In the body of the trigger, there are two Boolean functions, UPDAT-ING and DELETING. The function UPDATING evaluates to TRUE if an UPDATE statement is issued on the table, and the function DELETING evaluates to TRUE if a DELETE statement is issued on the table. There is another Boolean function called INSERTING. As you have probably guessed, this function evaluates to TRUE when an INSERT statement is issued against the table.

This trigger updates a record or inserts a new record into the Statistics table when an UPDATE or DELETE operation is issued against the Instructor table. First, the trigger determines the type of the DML statement issued against the Instructor table. The type of the DML statement is determined with the help of UPDATING and DELETING functions.

Next, the trigger tries to update a record in the Statistics table where `table_name` is equal to INSTRUCTOR and `transaction_name` is equal to the current transaction (UPDATE or DELETE). Then, the status of the UPDATE statement is checked with the help of SQL%NOTFOUND constructor. The SQL%NOTFOUND constructor evaluates to TRUE if the update statement does not update any rows and FALSE otherwise. So, if SQL%FOUND evaluates to TRUE, a new record is added to the Statistics table.

Once this trigger is created on the Instructor table, any UPDATE or DELETE operation causes modification of old records or creation of new records in the Statistics table. Furthermore, you can enhance this trigger by calculating how many rows are updated or deleted from the Instructor table.

You should use AFTER triggers in the following situations:

- When a trigger should fire after a DML statement is executed.
- When a trigger performs actions not specified in a BEFORE trigger.

LAB 15.1 EXERCISES

15.1.1 UNDERSTANDING WHAT A TRIGGER IS

In this exercise, you need to determine the trigger firing event, its type, and so on based on the CREATE clause of the trigger.

Consider the following CREATE clause:

```
CREATE TRIGGER student_au
BEFORE UPDATE ON STUDENT
FOR EACH ROW
WHEN (NVL(NEW.ZIP, ' ') <> OLD.ZIP)
    Trigger Body...
```

In the WHEN statement of the CREATE clause, there is a pseudo-record, :OLD, allowing you to access a row currently being processed. It is important for you to note that neither :NEW nor :OLD are prefixed by the colon (:) when they are used in the condition of the WHEN statement.

You are already familiar with the pseudo-record :NEW. The :OLD pseudo-record allows you to access current information of the record being updated. In other words, it is information currently present in the Student table for a specified record. The :NEW pseudo-record allows you to access the new information for the current record. In other words, :NEW indicates the updated values. For example, consider the following UPDATE statement:

```
UPDATE student
   SET zip = '01247'
 WHERE zip = '02189';
```

The value "01247" of the ZIP column is a new value, and the trigger references it as :NEW.ZIP. The value "02189" in the ZIP column is the previous value and is referenced as :OLD.ZIP.

It is important for you to note that :OLD is undefined for INSERT statements and :NEW is undefined for DELETE statements. However, the PL/SQL compiler does not generate syntax errors when :OLD or :NEW is used in triggers where the triggering event is an INSERT or DELETE operation. In this case, the field values are set to NULL for :OLD and :NEW pseudo-records.

Answer the following questions:

a) Assume a trigger named STUDENT_AU already exists in the database. If you use the CREATE clause to modify the existing trigger, what error message is generated? Explain your answer.

_____

_____

b) If an update statement is issued on the STUDENT table, how many times does this trigger fire?

_____

_____

c) How many times does this trigger fire if an update statement is issued against the STUDENT table, but the ZIP column is not changed?

_____

_____

d) Why do you think there is a NVL function present in the WHEN statement of the CREATE clause?

_____

_____

15.1.2 USING *BEFORE* AND *AFTER* TRIGGERS

In this exercise, you create a trigger on the Instructor table firing before an INSERT statement is issued against the table. The trigger determines the values for the columns CREATED_BY, MODIFIED_BY, CREATED_DATE, and MODIFIED_DATE. In addition, it determines if the value of zip provided by an INSERT statement is valid.

Create the following trigger:

```
-- ch15_1a.sql, version 1.0
CREATE OR REPLACE TRIGGER instructor_bi
BEFORE INSERT ON INSTRUCTOR
FOR EACH ROW
DECLARE
   v_work_zip CHAR(1);
BEGIN
   :NEW.CREATED_BY := USER;
   :NEW.CREATED_DATE := SYSDATE;
   :NEW.MODIFIED_BY := USER;
   :NEW.MODIFIED_DATE := SYSDATE;
   SELECT 'Y'
     INTO v_work_zip
     FROM zipcode
    WHERE zip = :NEW.ZIP;
EXCEPTION
   WHEN NO_DATA_FOUND
   THEN
       RAISE_APPLICATION_ERROR
          (-20001, 'Zip code is not valid!');
END;
```

Answer the following questions:

a) If an INSERT statement issued against the Instructor table is missing a value for the column ZIP, does the trigger raise an exception? Explain your answer.

_____

_____

b) Modify this trigger so another error message is displayed when an INSERT statement is missing a value for the column ZIP.

_____

_____

c) Modify this trigger so there is no need to supply the value for the instructor's ID at the time of the INSERT statement.

_____

_____

LAB 15.1 EXERCISE ANSWERS

15.1.1 ANSWERS

a) Assume a trigger named STUDENT_AU already exists in the database. If you use this CREATE clause to modify the existing trigger, what error message is generated? Explain your answer.

_Answer: An error message stating STUDENT_AU name is already used by another object is displayed on the screen. The CREATE clause has the ability to create new objects in the database, and it is unable to handle modifications. In order to modify the existing trigger, the REPLACE statement must be added to the CREATE clause. In this case, the old version of the trigger is dropped without warning, and the new version of the trigger is created._

b) If an update statement is issued on the STUDENT table, how many times does this trigger fire?

Answer: The trigger fires as many times as there are rows affected by the triggering event because the FOR EACH ROW statement is present in the CREATE trigger clause.

When the FOR EACH ROW statement is not present in the CREATE trigger clause, the trigger fires once for the triggering event. In this case, if the following UPDATE statement

```
UPDATE student
   SET zip = '01247'
 WHERE zip = '02189';
```

is issued against the STUDENT table. The trigger updates 10 records, and fires only once instead of 10 times.

c) How many times does this trigger fire if an update statement is issued against the Student table, but the ZIP column is not changed?

Answer: The trigger does not fire because the condition of the WHEN statement evaluates to FALSE.

The condition

```
(NVL(NEW.ZIP, ' ') <> OLD.ZIP)
```

of the WHEN statement compares the new value of zipcode to the old value of zipcode. If the value of the zipcode is not changed, this condition evaluates to FALSE. As a result, this trigger does not fire if an UPDATE statement does not modify the value of zipcode for a specified record.

d) Why do you think there is a NVL function present in the WHEN statement of the CREATE clause?

Answer: If an UPDATE statement does not modify the column ZIP, the value of the field NEW.ZIP is undefined. In other words, it is NULL. A NULL value of ZIP cannot be compared with a non-NULL value of ZIP. Therefore, the NVL function is present in the WHEN condition.

Because the column ZIP has a NOT NULL constraint defined, there is no need to use the NVL function for the OLD.ZIP field. For an UPDATE statement issued against the Student table, there is always a value of ZIP currently present in the table.

15.1.2 ANSWERS

a) If an INSERT statement is issued against the Instructor table is missing the value for the column ZIP, does the trigger raise an exception? Explain your answer.

Answer: Yes, the trigger raises an exception. When an INSERT statement does not provide a value for the column ZIP, the value of the :NEW.ZIP is NULL. This value is used in the WHERE clause of the SELECT INTO statement. As a result, the SELECT INTO statement is unable to return data. Therefore, the exception NO_DATA_ FOUND is raised by the trigger.

b) Modify this trigger so another error message is displayed when an INSERT statement is missing a value for the column ZIP.

Answer: Your script should look similar to the script shown below. All changes are shown in bold letters.

```
-- ch15_1b.sql, version 2.0
CREATE OR REPLACE TRIGGER instructor_bi
BEFORE INSERT ON INSTRUCTOR
FOR EACH ROW
DECLARE
   v_work_zip CHAR(1);
BEGIN
   :NEW.CREATED_BY := USER;
   :NEW.CREATED_DATE := SYSDATE;
   :NEW.MODIFIED_BY := USER;
   :NEW.MODIFIED_DATE := SYSDATE;
   IF :NEW.ZIP IS NULL
   THEN
      RAISE_APPLICATION_ERROR
         (-20002, 'Zip code is missing!');
   ELSE
      SELECT 'Y'
        INTO v_work_zip
        FROM zipcode
       WHERE zip = :NEW.ZIP;
   END IF;
EXCEPTION
   WHEN NO_DATA_FOUND
   THEN
      RAISE_APPLICATION_ERROR
         (-20001, 'Zip code is not valid!');
END;
```

Notice that an IF-ELSE statement is added to the body of the trigger. This IF-ELSE statement evaluates the value of :NEW.ZIP. If the value of :NEW.ZIP is NULL, the IF-ELSE statement evaluates to TRUE, and another error message is displayed stating the value of ZIP is missing. If the IF-ELSE statement evaluates to FALSE, the control is passed to the ELSE part of the statement, and the SELECT INTO statement is executed.

c) Modify this trigger so there is no need to supply the value for the instructor's ID at the time of the INSERT statement.

Answer: This answer contains only a portion of the code helping to illustrate the changes. All changes are shown in bold letters.

```
-- ch15_1c.sql, version 3.0
CREATE OR REPLACE TRIGGER instructor_bi
BEFORE INSERT ON INSTRUCTOR
FOR EACH ROW
DECLARE
    v_work_zip CHAR(1);
    v_instructor_id INSTRUCTOR.INSTRUCTOR_ID%TYPE;
BEGIN
    SELECT INSTRUCTOR_ID_SEQ.NEXTVAL
      INTO v_instructor_id
      FROM dual;
    :NEW.INSTRUCTOR_ID := v_instructor_id;
    :NEW.CREATED_BY := USER;
    ...
END;
```

The original version of this trigger does not derive a value for the instructor's ID. There-fore, an INSERT statement issued against the INSTRUCTOR table has to populate the instructor_id *column as well. The new version of the trigger populates the value of the* instructor_id *column, so the INSERT statement does not have to do it.*

Generally, it is a good idea to populate columns holding IDs in the trigger because when a user issues an INSERT statement, he or she might not know an ID that must be populated at the time of the insert. Furthermore, a user may not know—and more than likely does not know—how to operate sequences to populate the ID.

LAB 15.1 SELF-REVIEW QUESTIONS

In order to test your progress, you should be able to answer the following questions.

1) A trigger can fire for which of the following?
   a) _____ Before a triggering event.
   b) _____ After a triggering event.
   c) _____ Before or after a triggering event.

2) How is a trigger executed?
   a) _____ Explicitly when a triggering event occurs.
   b) _____ Implicitly when a triggering event occurs.

3) In order for a trigger to fire, the WHEN condition must evaluate to which of the following?
   a) _____ True
   b) _____ False

4) A BEFORE INSERT trigger fires for which of the following?
    a) _____ Before an UPDATE is issued against the triggering table.
    b) _____ After an INSERT is issued against the triggering table.
    c) _____ Before an INSERT is issued against the triggering table.

5) When a SELECT statement is issued against the triggering table, which of the following triggers fire?
    a) _____ BEFORE trigger.
    b) _____ AFTER trigger.
    c) _____ BEFORE trigger and AFTER trigger.
    d) _____ Triggers are not fired at all.

Quiz answers appear in Appendix A, Section 15.1.

TYPES OF TRIGGERS

LAB OBJECTIVES

After this lab, you will be able to:

✔ Use Row and Statement Triggers

In the previous lab of this chapter, you encountered the term *row trigger*. A row trigger is fired as many times as there are rows affected by the triggering statement. When the statement FOR EACH ROW is present in the CREATE TRIGGER clause, the trigger is a row trigger. Consider the following code:

■ FOR EXAMPLE

```
CREATE OR REPLACE TRIGGER course_au
AFTER UPDATE ON COURSE
FOR EACH ROW
...
```

In this code fragment, the statement FOR EACH ROW is present in the CREATE TRIGGER clause. Therefore, this trigger is a row trigger. If an UPDATE statement causes 20 records in the COURSE table to be modified, this trigger fires 20 times.

A *statement trigger* is fired once for the triggering statement. In other words, a statement trigger fires once, regardless of the number of rows affected by the triggering statement. To create a statement trigger, you omit the FOR EACH ROW in the CREATE TRIGGER clause. Consider the following code fragment:

■ FOR EXAMPLE

```
CREATE OR REPLACE TRIGGER enrollment_ad
AFTER DELETE ON ENROLLMENT
...
```

This trigger fires once after a DELETE statement is issued against the Enrollment table. Whether the DELETE statement removes one row or five rows from the Enrollment table, this trigger fires only once.

Statement triggers should be used when the operations performed by the trigger do not depend on the data in the individual records. For example, if you want to limit access to a table to business hours only, a statement trigger is used. Consider the following example:

■ FOR EXAMPLE

```
CREATE OR REPLACE TRIGGER instructor_biud
BEFORE INSERT OR UPDATE OR DELETE ON INSTRUCTOR
DECLARE
    v_day VARCHAR2(10);
BEGIN
    v_day := RTRIM(TO_CHAR(SYSDATE, 'DAY'));
    IF v_day LIKE ('S%')
    THEN
        RAISE_APPLICATION_ERROR
            (-20000, 'A table cannot be modified during
off'||
            ' hours');
    END IF;
END;
```

This is a statement trigger on the INSTRUCTOR table, and it fires before an INSERT, UPDATE, or DELETE statement is issued. First, the trigger determines the day of the week. If the day happens to be Saturday or Sunday, an error message is generated. When the following UPDATE statement on the Instructor table is issued on Saturday or Sunday

```
update INSTRUCTOR
   SET zip = 10025
 WHERE zip = 10015;
```

the trigger generates the error message shown below

```
update instructor
       *
ERROR at line 1:
ORA-20000: A table cannot be modified during off hours
ORA-06512: at "STUDENT.INSTRUCTOR_BIUD", line 7
ORA-04088: error during execution of trigger
'STUDENT.INSTRUCTOR_BIUD'
```

Notice, this trigger checks for a specific day of the week. However, it does not check time of the day. You can create a more sophisticated trigger that checks what day of the week it is and if the current time is between 9:00 AM and 5:00 PM. If the day falls on the business week and the time of the day is not between 9:00 AM and 5:00 PM, the error is generated.

**LAB
15.2**

So far you have seen triggers that are defined on the database tables. PL/SQL provides another kind of triggers. These triggers are called *INSTEAD OF triggers*, and they are defined on the database views. An INSTEAD OF trigger fires instead of the DML statement that has been issued against a view, and they are always defined as row triggers.

You can find more information on the INSTEAD OF triggers on the accompanying WEB site.

`http://www.phptr.com/Rosenzweig`

LAB 15.2 EXERCISES

15.2.1 USING ROW AND STATEMENT TRIGGERS

In this exercise, you create a trigger on the Course table. This trigger fires before an INSERT statement is issued against the Course table.

Create the following trigger:

```
-- ch15_2a.sql, version 1.0
CREATE OR REPLACE TRIGGER course_bi
BEFORE INSERT ON COURSE
FOR EACH ROW
DECLARE
   v_course_no COURSE.COURSE_NO%TYPE;
BEGIN
   SELECT COURSE_NO_SEQ.NEXTVAL
     INTO v_course_no
     FROM DUAL;
   :NEW.COURSE_NO := v_course_no;
   :NEW.CREATED_BY := USER;
   :NEW.CREATED_DATE := SYSDATE;
   :NEW.MODIFIED_BY := USER;
   :NEW.MODIFIED_DATE := SYSDATE;
END;
```

Create this trigger, then answer the following questions:

a) What type of trigger is created on the COURSE table (row or statement)? Explain your answer.

_____

_____

b) Based on the answer you provided for the question above, explain why this particular type is chosen for the trigger.

_____

_____

c) When an INSERT statement is issued against the COURSE table, which actions are performed by the trigger?

_____

_____

LAB 15.2 EXERCISE ANSWERS

15.2.1 ANSWERS

a) What type of trigger is created on the COURSE table (row or statement)? Explain your answer.

Answer: The trigger created on the COURSE table is a row trigger because the CREATE TRIGGER clause contains the statement FOR EACH ROW. It means this trigger fires every time a record is added to the COURSE table.

b) Based on the answer you provided for the question above, explain why this particular type is chosen for the trigger.

Answer: This trigger is a row trigger because its operations depend on the data in the individual records. For example, for every record inserted into the COURSE table, the trigger calculates the value for the column COURSE_NO. All values in this column must be unique, because it is defined as a primary key. A row trigger guarantees every record added to the COURSE table has a unique number assigned to the COURSE_NO column.

c) When an INSERT statement is issued against the COURSE table, which actions are performed by the trigger?

Answer: First, the trigger assigns a number derived from the sequence COURSE_ NO_SEQ to the variable v_course_no *via the SELECT INTO statement. Second, the variable* v_course_no *is assigned to the field COURSE_NO of the :NEW pseudo-record. Finally, the values containing the current user's name and date are assigned to the fields CREATED_BY, MODIFIED_BY, CREATED_DATE, and MODIFIED_DATE of the :NEW pseudo-record.*

LAB 15.2 SELF-REVIEW QUESTIONS

In order to test your progress, you should be able to answer the following questions.

1) How many times does a row trigger fire if a DML (INSERT, UPDATE, or DELETE) operation is issued against a table?
   a) _____ As many times as there are rows affected by the DML operation.
   b) _____ Once per DML operation.

2) How many times does a statement trigger fire if a DML (INSERT, UPDATE, or DELETE) operation is issued against a table?
   a) _____ As many times as there are rows affected by the DML operation.
   b) _____ Once per DML operation.

3) What does the statement FOR EACH ROW mean?
   a) _____ A trigger is a statement trigger.
   b) _____ A trigger is a row trigger.

4) INSTEAD OF triggers are defined on which of the following?
   a) _____ Table
   b) _____ View
   c) _____ None of the above

5) INSTEAD OF triggers must always be which of the following?
   a) _____ Statement trigger
   b) _____ Row trigger

Quiz answers appear in Appendix A, Section 15.2.

L A B 1 5 . 3

MUTATING TABLE ISSUES

LAB OBJECTIVES

After this lab, you will be able to:

✔ Understand Mutating Tables

There are some restrictions on the SQL statements you may issue in the body of a trigger. In order to understand these restrictions, it is necessary to define mutating and constraining tables. A table having a DML statement issued against it is called *mutating table*. For a trigger, it is the table on which this trigger is defined. A table read from for a referential integrity constraint is called a *constraining table*.

The restrictions on the SQL statement issued in the body of a trigger are:

- An SQL statement may not read or modify a mutating table.
- An SQL statement may not modify the columns of the constraining table having primary, foreign, or unique constraints defined on them.

Consider the following example of a trigger causing a mutating table error. It is important for you to note that mutating table error is a run-time error.

■ FOR EXAMPLE

```
CREATE OR REPLACE TRIGGER section_biu
BEFORE INSERT OR UPDATE ON section
FOR EACH ROW
DECLARE
```

```
         v_total NUMBER;
         v_name  varchar2(30);
BEGIN
   SELECT COUNT(*)
     INTO v_total
     FROM section  - SECTION is MUTATING
    WHERE instructor_id = :NEW.INSTRUCTOR_ID;
   -- check if the current instructor is overbooked
   IF v_total >= 10
   THEN
      SELECT first_name||' '||last_name
        INTO v_name
        FROM instructor
       WHERE instructor_id = :NEW.instructor_id;
      RAISE_APPLICATION_ERROR
          (-20000, 'Instructor, '||v_name||
           ', is overbooked');
   END IF;
      EXCEPTION
         WHEN NO_DATA_FOUND
         THEN
          RAISE_APPLICATION_ERROR
             (-20001, 'This is not a valid instructor');
END;
```

This trigger fires before an INSERT or UPDATE statement is issued on the SECTION table. The trigger checks if the specified instructor is teaching too many sections. If the number of sections taught by an instructor is equal to or greater than 10, the trigger issues an error message stating this instructor teaches too much.

Now, consider the following UPDATE statement issued against the Section table.

```
UPDATE section
   SET instructor_id = 101
 WHERE section_id = 80
   AND course_no = 10;
```

When this UPDATE statement is issued against the Section table, the following error message is displayed:

UPDATE section
       *
ERROR at line 1:

```
ORA-04091: table STUDENT.SECTION is mutating,
trigger/function may not see it
ORA-06512: at "STUDENT.SECTION_BIU", line 5
ORA-04088: error during execution of trigger
'STUDENT.SECTION_BIU'
```

Notice that the error message is stating that the Section table is mutating and the trigger may not see it. This error message is generated because there is a SELECT INTO statement,

```
SELECT COUNT(*)
   INTO v_total
   FROM section
  WHERE instructor_id = :NEW.INSTRUCTOR_ID;
```

issued against the Section table that is being modified and is therefore mutating.

In order to correct this problem, an additional trigger must be created on the Section table. The trigger used in the example above is a row trigger. This trigger can record the instructor's ID, and it should query the Section table. A new trigger should be created as a statement trigger. This trigger can query the Section table and use the recorded instructor ID. In order to record the value for the INSTRUCTOR_ID, a global variable for the current schema must be declared with the help of a package.

You can find more information on mutating table issues on the accompanying WEB site. http://www.phptr.com/Rosenzweig

LAB 15.3 EXERCISES

15.3.1 UNDERSTANDING MUTATING TABLES

In this exercise, you delete a record from the Zipcode table. You create a trigger firing before a DELETE operation is issued against the Zipcode table.

Issue the following DELETE statement:

```
DELETE FROM ZIPCODE
WHERE zip = '06830';
```

Answer the following questions:

a) What is printed on the screen?

_____

_____

b) Explain why this DELETE statement does not succeed?

_____

_____

Create the following trigger:

```
CREATE OR REPLACE TRIGGER zipcode_bd
BEFORE DELETE ON ZIPCODE
FOR EACH ROW
BEGIN
   DELETE FROM student
   WHERE zip = :OLD.ZIP;
   DELETE FROM instructor
   WHERE zip = :OLD.ZIP;
END;
```

c) Try to issue the DELETE statement again. Explain what happens.

_____

_____

LAB 15.3 EXERCISE ANSWERS

15.3.1 ANSWERS

a) What is printed on the screen?

Answer: Your output should look as follows:

```
DELETE FROM ZIPCODE
          *
ERROR at line 1:
ORA-02292: integrity constraint (STUDENT.STU_ZIP_FK)
violated - child record found
```

b) Explain why this DELETE statement does not succeed?

Answer: This DELETE statement does not succeed because there are records in the STUDENT table having a value of 06830 in the ZIP column. The ZIP column in the Student table has a foreign key constraint defined on it. Therefore, the Student table is a child of the ZIPCODE table. In order to delete records from the parent table (Zipcode), records from the child table (Student) must be deleted first. It is also important to remember that the INSTRUCTOR table is a child of the ZIPCODE table as well.

c) Try to issue the DELETE statement again. Explain what happens.

Answer: Your output should look similar to the following:

```
DELETE FROM ZIPCODE
         *
ERROR at line 1:
ORA-04094: table STUDENT.STUDENT is constraining,
trigger may not modify it
ORA-06512: at "STUDENT.ZIPCODE_BD", line 2
ORA-04088: error during execution of trigger
'STUDENT.ZIPCODE_BD'
```

In the trigger created on the ZIPCODE table, you are trying to delete records from the Student and Instructor tables with corresponding values in the ZIP columns. However, this trigger causes an error because both Student and Instructor are constraining tables for the ZIPCODE table. Therefore, the trigger cannot modify them.

LAB 15.3 SELF-REVIEW QUESTIONS

In order to test your progress, you should be able to answer the following questions.

1) You are allowed to issue any SQL statement in the body of a trigger.
   a) _____ True
   b) _____ False

2) It is always permissible to issue a SELECT statement in the body of a trigger. However, it is not always permissible to issue an INSERT, UPDATE, or DELETE statement.
   a) _____True
   b) _____ False

3) Which of the following is a SQL statement restriction?
   a) _____ No SQL statement may be issued against any table in the body of a trigger.
   b) _____ No SQL statement may be issued against the mutating table in the body of a trigger.
   c) _____ A SQL statement can be issued only against the mutating table in the body of a trigger.

4) Which of the following is a mutating table?
   a) _____ A table having a SELECT statement issued against it.
   b) _____ A table having a trigger defined on it.
   c) _____ A table being modified by a DML statement.

5) Which of the following is a constraining table?
   a) _____ A table having a SELECT statement issued against it.
   b) _____ A table having a trigger defined on it.
   c) _____ A table needing to be read from for referential integrity constraint.

Quiz answers appear in Appendix A, Section 15.3.

CHAPTER 15

TEST YOUR THINKING

In this chapter you learned about triggers. Here are some projects that will help you test the depth of your understanding.

1) Create the following trigger. Create or modify a trigger on the Enrollment table. This trigger fires before an INSERT statement is issued against the Enrollment table. Make sure all columns that have NOT NULL and foreign key constraints defined on them are populated with their proper values.

2) Create the following trigger. Create or modify a trigger on the Section table. This trigger fires before an UPDATE statement is issued against the Section table. Which columns do you think must be populated with their proper values?

CHAPTER 16

PL/SQL TABLES

PL/SQL tables are Oracle's version of an array. For those of you who are new to programming, you can think of an array as being a list. A list similar to an Excel worksheet with only two columns. In the same way you refer to a cell in the Excel worksheet by its column letter and row number, the elements of a PL/SQL table are referenced by referring to its index number. In this chapter, you will learn how to make use of PL/SQL tables.

L A B   1 6 . 1

MAKING USE OF PL/SQL TABLES

> ## LAB OBJECTIVES
>
> After this lab, you will be able to:
>
> ✔ Declare and Reference a PL/SQL Table
> ✔ Make Use of PL/SQL Table Attributes

PL/SQL TABLE BASICS

PL/SQL tables are PL/SQL's way of providing arrays. Arrays are like temporary tables in memory and thus are processed very quickly. It is important for you to realize that they are not database tables, and DML statements cannot be issued against them. This type of table is indexed by a binary integer counter (it cannot be indexed by another type of number) whose value can be referenced using the number of the index. Remember that PL/SQL tables exist in memory only, and therefore don't exist in any persistent way, disappearing after the session ends.

A PL/SQL TABLE DECLARATION

There are two steps in the declaration of a PL/SQL table. First, you must define the table structure using the TYPE statement. Second, once a table type is created, you then declare the actual table.

■ FOR EXAMPLE

```
DECLARE
    TYPE LnameType IS TABLE OF
    -- Table structure definition
    student.last_name%TYPE
    INDEX BY BINARY_INTEGER;
-- Create the actual table
    SlnameTab LnameType;
    IlnameTab LnameType;
BEGIN
    NULL; -- ...
END;
```

REFERENCING AND MODIFYING PL/SQL TABLE ROWS

In order to specify a particular row in a PL/SQL table, you must name the table and the index.

```
Syntax:          <table_name> (<index_value>)
```

The datatype of the index value must be compatible with the BINARY_INTEGER datatype. You assign values to a row using the standard assignment operator.

Referencing a nonexistent row raises the NO_DATA_FOUND exception.

LAB 16.1 EXERCISES

16.1.1 DECLARING AND REFERENCING A PL/SQL TABLE

■ FOR EXAMPLE

```
-- ch16_1a.sql
SET SERVEROUTPUT ON
DECLARE
    CURSOR c_slname IS
        SELECT last_name, student_id, ROWNUM
          FROM student
```

```
            WHERE student_id < 110
         ORDER BY last_name;
      TYPE type_lname_tab IS TABLE OF
         student.last_name%TYPE
         INDEX BY BINARY_INTEGER;
      tab_slname type_lname_tab;
      v_slname_counter NUMBER := 0;
   BEGIN
      FOR r_slname IN c_slname
      LOOP
         v_slname_counter := v_slname_counter + 1;
         tab_slname(v_slname_counter):=
   r_slname.last_name;
      END LOOP;
      FOR i_slname IN 1 .. v_slname_counter
      LOOP
         DBMS_OUTPUT.PUT_LINE('Here is a last name: '||
            Tab_slname(i_slname));
      END LOOP;
   END;
```

Answer the following questions:

a) Explain the code in `ch16_1a.sql` above. How is this block making using use of a PL/SQL table?

_____

_____

b) What would you expect the output to be if this was run? Try it and explain any differences you see.

_____

_____

■ FOR EXAMPLE

```
-- ch16_2a.sql
SET SERVEROUTPUT ON
DECLARE
   CURSOR c_student IS
      SELECT last_name || ' ' || first_name sname,
            student_id, ROWNUM
```

```
        FROM student
       WHERE student_id < 110
      ORDER BY last_name;
    TYPE type_student_tab IS TABLE OF
       c_student%ROWTYPE
       INDEX BY BINARY_INTEGER;
    tab_student type_student_tab;
    v_max_rownum NUMBER;
BEGIN
    FOR r_student IN c_student
    LOOP
       Tab_student(r_student.ROWNUM):= r_student;
       v_max_rownum := r_student.ROWNUM;
    END LOOP;
    DBMS_OUTPUT.PUT_LINE('Student ID  Student Name ');

DBMS_OUTPUT.PUT_LINE('==============================');
    FOR i_student IN 1 .. v_max_rownum
    LOOP
       DBMS_OUTPUT.PUT_LINE
          (Tab_student(i_student).student_id||
          '            ' ||
          Tab_student(i_student).sname);
    END LOOP;
END;
```

c) Explain the code in `ch16_2a.sql` above. How is this block using a PL/SQL table?

_____

_____

d) What would you expect the output to be if this was run? Try it, and explain any differences you see.

_____

_____

16.1.2 MAKING USE OF PL/SQL TABLE ATTRIBUTES

PL/SQL TABLE ATTRIBUTES

Here are seven PL/SQL table attributes you can use to gain information about a PL/SQL table or to modify a row in a PL/SQL table:

- **DELETE**—Deletes rows in a table.
- **EXISTS**—Return TRUE if the specified entry exists in the table.
- **COUNT**—Returns the number of rows in the table.
- **FIRST**—Returns the index of the first row in the table.
- **LAST**—Returns the index of the last row in the table.
- **NEXT**—Returns the index of the next row in the table after the specified row.
- **PRIOR**—Returns the index of the previous row in the table before the specified row.

PL/SQL table attributes are used with the following syntax:

```
<table_name>.<attribute>
tab_student.COUNT
```

If you declare a PL/SQL table named t_student then you get a rowcount for the table as follows:

```
v_count := t_student.count;
```

The DELETE and EXISTS attributes function differently than the other attributes. These two generally operate on one row at a time, so you must add the following syntax:

```
<TableName>.<attribute>(<IndexNumber>
[,<IndexNumber>])
```

t.student.delete deletes all rows from the t_student table, whereas t_student.delete(15) deletes the fifteenth row of the t_student table. Likewise, t_student.exists(100) returns a value of true if there is a one-hundredth row and a value of false if there is not.

The EXISTS attribute can be used to determine if a particular index value exists in the PL/SQL table or not.

Answer the following questions:

> **a)** How would you modify `ch16_2a.sql` so that, instead of calcu-
> lating the number of rows in the PL/SQL table, the PL/SQL table at-
> tribute LAST is used?

_____

_____

■ FOR EXAMPLE

```
-- ch16_4a.sql
DECLARE
   TYPE t_szip_type IS TABLE OF
   zipcode.city%TYPE
      INDEX BY BINARY_INTEGER;
   t_szip t_szip_type;
   v_szip_index BINARY_INTEGER;
BEGIN
   t_szip(10010) := 'Manhattan';
   t_szip(12345) := 'Brooklyn';
   t_szip(99999) := 'Los Angeles';
BEGIN
   v_szip_index := t_szip.first;
   LOOP
      DBMS_OUTPUT.PUT_LINE(t_szip(v_szip_index));
      EXIT WHEN v_szip_index = t_szip.LAST;
      v_szip_index := t_szip.NEXT(v_szip_index);
   END LOOP;
   RAISE NO_DATA_FOUND;
EXCEPTION
   WHEN NO_DATA_FOUND
   THEN
      DBMS_OUTPUT.PUT_LINE
         ('The last zipcode has been reached.'
         );
   END;
END;
```

b) In the example above (`ch16_4a.sql`), a number of PL/SQL table attributes are used. Go through each line of code and explain what is happening in the code with particular emphasis to how the PL/SQL attributes are being used.

LAB 16.1 EXERCISE ANSWERS

16.1.1 ANSWERS

a) Explain the code in `ch16_1a.sql` above. How is this block making use of a PL/SQL table?

Answer: The declaration section declares a cursor named `c_slname`*, which has a student last name and ID, as well as rownum for each row in the cursor. There is a type named* `type_lname_tab`*, which is a PL/SQL table of a student last name indexed by a binary integer. A PL/SQL table, named* `tab_slname`*, is declared to be of the type* `type_lname_tab`*. There is also a variable named* `v_slname`*, of number datatype.*

In the executable section of the block, the cursor `c_slname` *is opened with a FOR LOOP. For each iteration of the loop, the variable* `v_slname_counter` *is incremented by 1 and a row in the table* `tab_slname` *is given the value of the student last name for the current row in the cursor. Once the FOR LOOP has completed, the variable* `v_slname_counter` *has the value of the total number of rows in the table. (In the next section of this chapter you will learn a more efficient method to determine this value.) Another loop is then processed. This uses the previously determined value for* `v_slname_counter` *as the number of iterations of the second loop. The DBMS_OUTPUT displays the value of the table for each index number corresponding to the* `v_slname_counter`*.*

b) What do you expect the output to be if this is run? Try it and explain any differences you see.

Answer: You will see the following output when you run this script (Note that this is the state of the data at initial import. Your data may be in a different state.):

```
Here is a last name: Crocitto
Here is a last name: Enison
Here is a last name: Landry
Here is a last name: Mierzwa
Here is a last name: Moskowitz
```

```
Here is a last name: Olvsade
Here is a last name: Sethi
Here is a last name: Walter
PL/SQL procedure successfully completed.
```

c) Explain the code in `ch16_2a.sql` above. How is this block using a PL/SQL table?

Answer: This is a more complex use of a PL/SQL table. In this example, the table is a rowtype indexed by binary integer. The declaration block declares a cursor `c_student`, *which has a concatenation of a student last and first name, a* `student_id` *and a row number. The type* `type_student_tab` *is declared as a PL/SQL table, with a row of the* `c_student` *indexed by a binary integer. There is also a variable* `v_max_rownum` *of NUMBER datatype.*

When a table is declared of this type, the elements of each row will be referenced as follows:

```
table_name(index_number.row_item)
```

As the cursor FOR LOOP is processed, each row of the `tab_student` *PL/SQL table is initialized to have the value of the current row of the* `c_student` *cursor. The variable* `v_max_rownum` *is initialized to be the rownum of the current row in the cursor. When the cursor FOR LOOP exits, the variable has the value of the total number of rows in the PL/SQL table. A second loop is used to display the values in the table. The value of the* `v_max_rownum` *is used to determine now many iterations are required to complete the cycle of the* `tab_student` *table.*

d) What do you expect the output to be if this is run? Try it and explain any differences you see.

Answer: The output from this script will be as follows:

```
Student ID     Student Name
============================
102            Crocitto Fred
103            Landry J.
104            Enison Laetia
105            Moskowitz Angel
106            Olvsade Judith
107            Mierzwa Catherine
108            Sethi Judy
109            Walter Larry
PL/SQL procedure successfully completed.
```

16.1.2 ANSWERS

a) How would you modify `ch16_2a,sql` so that instead of calculating the number of rows in the PL/SQL table, the PL/SQL table attribute LAST is used?

Answer: This is one method of accomplishing the task:

```
-- ch16_3a.sql
DECLARE
   CURSOR c_student IS
      SELECT last_name || ' ' || first_name sname,
             student_id, ROWNUM
        FROM student
       WHERE student_id < 110
       ORDER BY last_name;
   TYPE type_student_tab IS TABLE OF
      c_student%ROWTYPE
      INDEX BY BINARY_INTEGER;
   tab_student type_student_tab;
BEGIN
   FOR r_student IN c_student
   LOOP
      tab_student(NVL(tab_student.last,0)+ 1)
         := r_student;
   END LOOP;
      DBMS_OUTPUT.PUT_LINE
         ('Student ID      Student Name ');
      DBMS_OUTPUT.PUT_LINE
         ('================================');
   FOR i_student IN tab_student.first ..
tab_student.last
   LOOP
      DBMS_OUTPUT.PUT_LINE
         (Tab_student(i_student).student_id||
          '            ' ||
          Tab_student(i_student).sname
         );
   END LOOP;
END;
```

The LAST PL/SQL table attribute returns the index number for the last row in the `tab_student` *table. The first loop is used to initialize the table. For each iteration of the loop, the value of the LAST attribute increases as the table simultaneously increases.*

b) In the example above (ch16_4a.sql), a number of PL/SQL table attributes are being used. Go through each line of code and explain what is happening in the code with particular emphasis on how the PL/SQL attributes are being used.

Answer: The declarative section declares a table type t_szip_type, *which is a PL/SQL table of the type of the city item in the Zipcode table indexed by binary integer. A PL/SQL table named* t_szip *is then declared to be of the type* t_szip_type. *There is also a variable* v_szip_index, *which is a binary integer. The executable section populates the PL/SQL table* t_szip *with three noncontiguous zipcode numbers and their values (cities).*

Another BEGIN statement opens the loop. The second BEGIN is there so the exception can be trapped. The value of the variable v_szip_index *is set to be the first value of the table* t_szip *using the PL/SQL attribute FIRST. The loop is then started with a DBMS_OUTPUT of the value for the current row in the PL/SQL table. The loop exits when the variable* v_szip_index *equals the last value of the PL/SQL table* t_szip. *This prevents a value error from occurring by using the PL/SQL table attribute LAST. The value of the variable is incremented to be the value of the next index using the PL/SQL table attribute NEXT. The end of the loop causes the exception NO_DATA_FOUND to be raised. This will output the last DBMS_OUTPUT line.*

If you have not gone to the companion web site for this book, located at http://www.phptr.com/Rosenzweig *then you are missing out on a great resource. Go there now! This is your last chapter, so take advantage of the additional review questions on PL/SQL tables available on the site.*

LAB 16.1 SELF-REVIEW QUESTIONS

In order to test your progress, you should be able to answer the following questions.

1) The primary difference between a PL/SQL table and a database table is that the database table is stored in a data table and remains there when the database is shut down, whereas a PL/SQL table does not remain once the database is shutdown.
   a) _____ True
   b) _____ False

2) You can reference rows in a PL/SQL table by:
   a) _____ calling them on the telephone.
   b) _____ referencing the index number.
   c) _____ matching the value with a defined variable.
   d) _____ referencing the table type and index number.

3) A PL/SQL table can be indexed by which of the following datatypes? Choose all that apply.

a) _____ DATE

b) _____ CHAR

c) _____ NUMBER

d) _____ INTEGER

e) _____ LOB

4) What is the benefit of the EXISTS PL/SQL table attribute? Choose all that apply.

a) _____ It has no real benefit.

b) _____ It is useful to avoid an ORA-1403 error.

c) _____ You can determine if a row with that index number exists or not and then you can assign it a value.

d) _____ It helps you to prevent referencing a nonexistent row in the table.

5) The PL/SQL table attribute COUNT can be used in a SELECT statement in the same way as with a database table.

a) _____ True

b) _____ False

Quiz answers appear in Appendix A, Section 16.1.

CHAPTER 16

TEST YOUR THINKING

In this chapter, you have learned about PL/SQL tables. Here are some projects that will help you test the depth of your understanding.

I) Add the following definition to the `student_api` package header you developed in the previous chapters: a type called `t_zip_type`. `t_zip_type` will be a table of `zipcode.zip%TYPE`.

2) Add a function called `get_city_zips` to the `student_api` package specification. The function will accept a `zipcode.city%TYPE` and return a PL/SQL table of `standard_cta.t_zip_type`.

3) Add a function called `get_city_zips` to the `student_api` package body. The function will accept a `zipcode.city%TYPE` and return a PL/SQL table of `standard_cta.t_zip_type`.

The function will accept a city and will return in the PL/SQL table all the zipcodes that exist in the zipcode table for that city. If there are no zipcodes for the city, or if there is an error, a null PL/SQL table will be returned.

4) Add a function to `student_api` package specification called `median_grade` that takes in a course number (`p_cnumber`), a section number (`p_snumber`), and a grade type (`p_grade_type`) and returns a `work_grade.grade%TYPE`.

5) Add a function to `student_api` package specification called `median_grade` that takes in a course number (`p_cnumber`), a section number (`p_snumber`), and a grade type (`p_grade_type`). The function will return the median grade (`work_grade.grade%TYPE datatype`) based on those three components. For example, one might use this function to answer the question, "What is the median grade of homework assignments in QC2203 section 2?" A true median can contain two values. Since this function can return only one value, if the median is made of two values, then return the average of the two. You will need to make use of a PL/SQL table in order to make this calculation.

You have now completed the entire `student_api` *package. Go to the companion web site to see the code for the entire package.*
`http://www.phptr.com/Rosenzweig`

APPENDIX A

ANSWERS TO SELF-REVIEW QUESTIONS

CHAPTER 1

Lab 1.1 ■ Self-Review Answers

Questions	Answers	Comments
1)	A	
2)	B	
3)	B	
4)	B	
5)	A	

Lab 1.2 ■ Self-Review Answers

Questions	Answers	Comments
1)	C	
2)	B	
3)	B	Linear execution of code assumes that statements are executed in the order they appear.
4)	A	
5)	B	A SELECT statement may be formatted perfectly and still produce incorrect results.

CHAPTER 2

Lab 2.1 ■ Self-Review Answers

Questions	Answers	Comments
1)	B	
2)	B	
3)	B	
4)	A	A PL/SQL compiler cannot detect any runtime errors because they occur during the execution of the program. Compilation of the program occurs before it can be run.
5)	B	

Lab 2.2 ■ Self-Review Answers

Questions	Answers	Comments
1)	B	
2)	A	
3)	A	
4)	A	
5)	C	

CHAPTER 3

Lab 3.1 ■ Self-Review Answers

Questions	Answers	Comments
1)	A	
2)	B	
3)	A, B, C, E	
4)	D	
5)	A	

CHAPTER 4

Lab 4.1 ■ Self-Review Answers

Questions	Answers	Comments
1)	B, D	
2)	A, D	You cannot create a table or sequence within a PL/SQL block.

CHAPTER 4

Lab 4.1 ■ Self-Review Answers (Continued)

Questions	Answers	Comments
3)	C	
4)	A, B, D	A sequence will generate unique numbers but you cannot count it as a method to generate contiguous number.

Lab 4.2 ■ Self-Review Answers

Questions	Answers	Comments
1)	B	When you issue a ROLLBACK, it only applies to the current session of the user you are logged in as. It has no effect on other sessions.
2)	A, C	
3)	D	
4)	B	

CHAPTER 5

Lab 5.1 ■ Self-Review Answers

Questions	Answers	Comments
1)	C	
2)	A	
3)	A	
4)	D	
5)	B	

Lab 5.2 ■ Self-Review Answers

Questions	Answers	Comments
1)	B	
2)	B	
3)	C	
4)	C	As soon as the first condition evaluates to TRUE, statements associated with it are executed. The rest of the statement is ignored.
5)	B	

Lab 5.3 ■ Self-Review Answers

Questions	Answers	Comments
1)	C	
2)	C	
3)	B	
4)	A	
5)	C	

CHAPTER 6

Lab 6.1 ■ Self-Review Answers

Questions	Answers	Comments
1)	B	
2)	B	
3)	B	
4)	B	
5)	B, C	Both options are correct. However, you should remember that the value of number 1 is not important. It is number 2 that causes an exception to be raised when its value is equal to 0.

Lab 6.2 ■ Self-Review Answers

Questions	Answers	Comments
1)	A	
2)	B	
3)	B	When a group function is used in the SELECT INTO statement, at least one row is returned.
4)	B	
5)	B	An exception-handling section may contain multiple exception handlers. For example, NO_DATA_FOUND and OTHERS.

CHAPTER 7

Lab 7.1 ■ Self-Review Answers

Questions	Answers	Comments
1)	C	

Lab 7.1 ■ Self-Review Answers (Continued)

Questions	Answers	Comments
2)	B	As soon as the EXIT statement is encountered, the loop is terminated.
3)	A	
4)	C	
5)	B	An EXIT condition of a simple loop is located inside the body of the loop. Therefore, the loop will execute at least partly before the EXIT condition is evaluated.

Lab 7.2 ■ Self-Review Answers

Questions	Answers	Comments
1)	A	
2)	C	
3)	B, C	
4)	A	
5)	A	

Lab 7.3 ■ Self-Review Answers

Questions	Answers	Comments
1)	B	
2)	A	
3)	C	
4)	C	
5)	B	

Lab 7.4 ■ Self-Review Answers

Questions	Answers	Comments
1)	C	
2)	B	
3)	B	
4)	B	
5)	B	

CHAPTER 8

Lab 8.1 ■ Self-Review Answers

Questions	Answers	Comments
1)	B	
2)	None	Cursor attributes are used for getting information about cursors. They cannot be used to control or close cursors.
3)	1-B Declare, 2-E Open, 3-A Fetch, 4-C Close	
4)	D	Cursor attributes can be used with both implicit and explicit cursors.
5)	D	

Lab 8.2 ■ Self-Review Answers

Questions	Answers	Comments
1)	A	
2)	B	
3)	B	
4)	B	A child cursor in a nested cursor loop will open, loop, and then close for each iteration of the parent loop.
5)	C	

Lab 8.3 ■ Self-Review Answers

Questions	Answers	Comments
1)	A	
2)	A, B, E	
3)	C	
4)	C	
5)	A	A WHERE CURRENT clause in a FOR UPDATE cursor allows you to update a row without having to match the row in the WHERE clause.

CHAPTER 9

Lab 9.1 ■ Self-Review Answers

Questions	Answers	Comments
1)	C	
2)	B	

Lab 9.1 ■ Self-Review Answers (Continued)

Questions	Answers	Comments
3)	B	
4)	B	
5)	B	

Lab 9.2 ■ Self-Review Answers

Questions	Answers	Comments
1)	B	
2)	B	
3)	B	A user-defined exception cannot be raised in the outer block because once control is transferred from the inner block to the outer block, the user-defined exception ceases to exist.
4)	B	
5)	A	

Lab 9.3 ■ Self-Review Answers

Questions	Answers	Comments
1)	B	
2)	B	
3)	A	
4)	B	
5)	B	

CHAPTER 10

Lab 10.1 ■ Self-Review Answers

Questions	Answers	Comments
1)	C	
2)	C	
3)	A	
4)	A	
5)	C	

Lab 10.2 ■ Self-Review Answers

Questions	Answers	Comments
1)	B	

Lab 10.2 ■ Self-Review Answers (Continued)

Questions	Answers	Comments
2)	B	
3)	C	
4)	C	
5)	C	

Lab 10.3 ■ Self-Review Answers

Questions	Answers	Comments
1)	A	
2)	A	
3)	C	
4)	C	
5)	B	When there is no exception raised, the SQLCODE function returns 0.

CHAPTER 11

Lab 11.1 ■ Self-Review Answers

Questions	Answers	Comments
1)	C	
2)	A, C, D, E	There is no foot section in stored code. The specification can be called the header but the body is never called the footer.
3)	B	An OUT parameter is not a required component of a procedure.
4)	A, B, D	C is a valid definition for the declarative section. All header definitions refer to IN, OUT or IN/OUT parameters.
5)	B	The USER_SOURCE view shows the text for code in valid and invalid objects.

CHAPTER 12

Lab 12.1 ■ Self-Review Answers

Questions	Answers	Comments
1)	D	
2)	B	A function can have IN, OUT, and IN OUT parameters, but it is considered bad style to have anything but IN parameters in a function.

Lab 12.1 ■ Self-Review Answers (Continued)

Questions	Answers	Comments
3)	D	
4)	C	
5)	C, D	

CHAPTER 13

Lab 13.1 ■ Self-Review Answers

Questions	Answers	Comments
1)	B	When a package is first called, all the procedures and functions in that package are brought into memory and will run quickly when they are used in the same session.
2)	A	
3)	B	Procedures and functions that are not declared in the package specification will be private.
4)	C	
5)	B	A package specification is a database object and must be compiled prior to compiling the package body. This can be done in one or two scripts.

CHAPTER 14

Lab 14.1 ■ Self-Review Answers

Questions	Answers	Comments
1)	B	The USER_ERRORS view only has details on code that is currently in an invalid state. Once the code become valid, it will no longer be present in the USER_ERRORS view.
2)	A	The DESC command can be used on tables and packages. It will give different results for tables and packages.
3)	B	Only functions within packages require pragma restrictions used in SQL statements.
4)	C	
5)	B	

CHAPTER 15

Lab 15.1 ■ Self-Review Answers

Questions	Answers	Comments
1)	C	
2)	B	
3)	A	
4)	C	
5)	D	

Lab 15.2 ■ Self-Review Answers

Questions	Answers	Comments
1)	A	
2)	B	
3)	B	
4)	B	
5)	B	

Lab 15.3 ■ Self-Review Answers

Questions	Answers	Comments
1)	B	
2)	B	
3)	B	
4)	C	
5)	C	

CHAPTER 16

Lab 16.1 ■ Self-Review Answers

Questions	Answers	Comments
1)	A	
2)	B	
3)	C, D	
4)	C, D	
5)	B	

APPENDIX B

PL/SQL FORMATTING GUIDE

PL/SQL CODE NAMING CONVENTIONS AND FORMATTING GUIDELINES

CASE

PL/SQL, like SQL is case-insensitive. The guideline here is:

- Use upper case for key words (BEGIN, EXCEPTION, END, IF THEN ELSE, LOOP, END LOOP, etc.), datatypes (VARCHAR2, NUMBER), functions (LEAST, SUBSTR, etc.), and user-defined procedures.
- Use lower case for variable names (as well as column and tables names in SQL).

WHITE SPACE

White space (extra lines and spaces) is as important here as well as it is in SQL. It provides the main readability factor. Put spaces on both sides of an equality sign or comparison operator. Suggestion: Line up structure words on the left (DECLARE BEGIN EXCEPTION END; IF THEN ELSE, LOOP END LOOP; etc.). Indent three spaces (use the spacebar, not the tab key) for structures within structures. Put blank lines between major sections—always use a comment mark in a blank line to make sure that debugging line numbers always match the error message. Put each part of the structure on a new line (e.g., IF THEN on one line, ELSE on another, END IF on another) even if the expression is short.

NAMING CONVENTIONS

To ensure against conflicts with keywords and column/table names, it is best to use the following prefixes:

```
v_variable_name
con_constant_name
i_in_parameter_
o_out_parameter_
io_in_out_parameter
c_cursor_name
rc_reference_cursor_name
r_record_name
        example: FOR r_stud IN c_stud LOOP...
rec_record_name (for record variables)
t_table (for PL/SQL tables)
TYPE rec_student_section_type IS RECORD
        (student_id student.studid%TYPE,
        description course.descript%TYPE,
        section_id section.section_id%TYPE,
        instructor_id section.instid%TYPE
        );
e exception_name
```

The name of a package should be the name of the larger context of the actions performed by procedures and functions contained within the package. The name of procedures should be the action description that is performed by the procedure. The name of a function should be the description of the return variable.

■ *FOR EXAMPLE*

```
PACKAGE student_admin
-- admin suffix may be used for administration.
PROCEDURE remove_student
        (i_student_id IN student.studid%TYPE);
FUNCTION student_enroll_count
        (i_student_id student.studid%TYPE)
        RETURN INTEGER;
```

COMMENTS

Comments are equally as important as in SQL. Comments should explain the main sections of the program and any major logic that is involved or nontrivial.

Suggestion: Use the "--" comments instead of the "/*" comments. PL/SQL treats them the same, but it is easier to comment out a set of code for debugging using the "/*" comments if the code has only "--" comments. This is because you cannot embed "/*" comments within "/*" comments.

OTHER

1. Since SQL is embedded in PL/SQL, use the same formatting guidelines for SQL to determine how it should appear.

2. Provide a comment header that explains the intent of the block, lists the creation date and author, and has a line for each revision with the author, date, and the description of the revision.

■ FOR EXAMPLE

The following example incorporates the suggestions above. Notice that it also uses a monospaced font (Courier) which makes the formatting easier. Proportional spaced fonts can hide spaces and make lining up clauses difficult. Most text and programming editors by default use monospaced fonts.

```
REM
******************************************************
REM * filename: coursediscount01.sql    version: 1
REM * purpose: To give discounts to courses
REM *          that have at least one section
REM *          with an enrollment of more than
REM *          10 students.
REM * args: none
REM * created: by: s.tashi    date: January 1, 2000
REM * modified: by y.sonam   date: February 1, 2000
REM * description: Fixed cursor,
REM *              comments and indentation
REM
******************************************************
DECLARE
    -- c_discount_cursor finds a
    -- list of courses that have
    -- at least one section
    -- with an enrollment
    -- of at least 10 students.
    CURSOR c_discount_course
    IS
```

```
      SELECT DISTINCT course_no
        FROM section sect
       WHERE 10 <=
             (SELECT COUNT(*)
                FROM enrollment enr
               WHERE enr.section_id = sect.section_id
             );
   con_discount_2000 CONSTANT NUMBER := .90;
   -- con_discount_2000 is the discount rate for
   -- courses that cost more than $2000.00
   con_discount_other CONSTANT NUMBER := .95;
    -- con_discount_other is the discount
    --rate for courses that cost
   -- between $1001.00 and $2000.00
   v_current_course_cost course.cost%TYPE;
   v_discount_all NUMBER;
   e_update_is_problematic EXCEPTION;
BEGIN
-- For courses to be discounted, determine
--    the current and new costs
   FOR r_discount_course in c_discount_course
   LOOP
      SELECT cost
        INTO v_current_course_cost
        FROM course
       WHERE course_no = r_discount_course.course_no;
      --
      IF v_current_course_cost > 2000
      THEN
        v_discount_all := con_discount_2000;
      ELSE
        IF v_current_course_cost > 1000
        THEN
          v_discount_all :=  con_discount_other;
        ELSE
          v_discount_all := 1;
        END IF;
      END IF;
      --
      BEGIN
         UPDATE course
            SET cost = cost * v_discount_all
          WHERE course_no =
                   r_discount_course.course_no;
      EXCEPTION
```

```
        WHEN OTHERS
        THEN
            RAISE e_update_is_problematic;
    END;    -- end of sub-block to update record
  END LOOP; -- end of main LOOP
  COMMIT;
EXCEPTION
  WHEN e_update_is_problematic
  THEN
  -- undo all transactions in this run of the program
    ROLLBACK;
    DBMS_OUTPUT.PUT_LINE
        ('There was a problem updating a'||
        ' course.cost.'
        );
  WHEN OTHERS
  THEN
    NULL;
END;
/
```

APPENDIX C

STUDENT DATABASE SCEMA

TABLE AND COLUMN DESCRIPTIONS

COURSE

Information for one course.

Column Name	Null	Type	Comments
COURSE_NO	NOT NULL	NUMBER(8, 0)	The identifying number for this course.
DESCRIPTION	NULL	VARCHAR2(50)	The full name of this course.
COST	NULL	NUMBER(9,2)	The dollar amount that is charged for enrollment in this course.
PREREQUISITE	NULL	NUMBER(8, 0)	The course number that must be taken as a prerequisite to this one.
CREATED_BY	NOT NULL	VARCHAR2(30)	Audit column—indicates user who inserted data
CREATED_DATE	NOT NULL	DATE	Audit column—indicates date of insert
MODIFIED_BY	NOT NULL	VARCHAR2(30)	Audit column—indicates who last made update
MODIFIED_DATE	NOT NULL	DATE	Audit column—date of last update

SECTION

Represents an individual class of a particular course.

Column Name	Null	Type	Comments
SECTION_ID	NOT NULL	NUMBER(8)	The unique ID for section.
COURSE_NO	NOT NULL	NUMBER(8,0)	The course number for which this is a section.
SECTION_NO	NOT NULL	NUMBER(3)	The individual section number within this course.
START_DATE_TIME	NULL	DATE	The date and time on which this course meets.
LOCATION	NULL	VARCHAR2(50)	The meeting room of the class.
INSTRUCTOR_ID	NOT NULL	NUMBER(8,0)	The ID number of instructor who teaches this section.
CAPACITY	NULL	NUMBER(3,0)	The maximum number of students allowed in this class.
CREATED_BY	NOT NULL	VARCHAR2(30)	Audit column—indicates user who inserted data
CREATED_DATE	NOT NULL	DATE	Audit column—indicates date of insert
MODIFIED_BY	NOT NULL	VARCHAR2(30)	Audit column—indicates who made last update
MODIFIED_DATE	NOT NULL	DATE	Audit column—date of last update

STUDENT

Profile information about a student.

Column Name	Null	Type	Comments
STUDENT_ID	NOT NULL	NUMBER(8,0)	The ID number of the student.
SALUTATON	NULL	VARCHAR2(5)	The student's title (Ms, Mr, Dr, etc.).
FIRST_NAME	NULL	VARCHAR2(25)	The student's first name.
LAST_NAME	NOT NULL	VARCHAR2(25)	The student's last name.
STREET_ADDRESS	NULL	VARCHAR2(50)	The student's street address.
ZIP	NOT NULL	VARCHAR2(5)	The postal zipcode of the student.
PHONE	NULL	VARCHAR2(15)	The phone number of the student, including area code.
EMPLOYER	NULL	VARCHAR2(50)	The name of the company where the student is employed.
REGISTRATION_DATE	NOT NULL	DATE	The date this student registered in the program.
CREATED_BY	NOT NULL	VARCHAR2(30)	Audit column—indicates user who inserted data
CREATED_DATE	NOT NULL	DATE	Audit column—indicates date of insert
MODIFIED_BY	NOT NULL	VARCHAR2(30)	Audit column—indicates who made last update
MODIFIED_DATE	NOT NULL	DATE	Audit column—date of last update

ENROLLMENT

Shows information about one student registered to a particular section (class).

Column Name	Null	Type	Comments
SECTION_ID	NOT NULL	NUMBER(8,0)	The unique ID for the section.
STUDENT_ID	NOT NULL	NUMBER(8,0)	The ID number that uniquely identifies the student.
FINAL_GRADE	NULL	NUMBER(3,0)	The final grade given to the student for all work in this section (class).
ENROLL_DATE	NOT NULL	DATE	The date the student registered for this section.
CREATED_BY	NOT NULL	VARCHAR2(30)	Audit column—indicates user who inserted data
CREATED_DATE	NOT NULL	DATE	Audit column—indicates date of insert
MODIFIED_BY	NOT NULL	VARCHAR2(30)	Audit column—indicates who last made update
MODIFIED_DATE	NOT NULL	DATE	Audit column—date of last update

INSTRUCTOR

Profile information about an instructor in the program.

Column Name	Null	Type	Comments
INSTRUCTOR_ID	NOT NULL	NUMBER(8)	The ID number of the instructor.
SALUTATION	NULL	VARCHAR2(5)	The title of the instructor (Mr, Ms, Dr, Rev, etc.).
FIRST_NAME	NULL	VARCHAR2(25)	The instructor's first name
LAST_NAME	NULL	VARCHAR2(25)	The instructor's last name.

(continued)

Column Name	Null	Type	Comments
STREET_ADDRESS	NULL	VARCHAR2(50)	The instructor's street address.
ZIP	NULL	VARCHAR2(5)	The postal zipcode of the instructor's address.
PHONE	NULL	VARCHAR2(15)	The instructor's phone number including area code.
CREATED_BY	NOT NULL	VARCHAR2(30)	Audit column—indicates user who inserted data
CREATED_DATE	NOT NULL	DATE	Audit column—indicates date of insert
MODIFIED_BY	NOT NULL	VARCHAR2(30)	Audit column—indicates who made last update
MODIFIED_DATE	NOT NULL	DATE	Audit column—date of last update

ZIPCODE

Postal zipcodes for cities and states.

Column Name	Null	Type	Comments
ZIP	NOT NULL	VARCHAR2(5)	The zipcode number, considered unique for this city and state.
CITY	NULL	VARCHAR2(25)	The city name for this zipcode.
STATE	NULL	VARCHAR2(2)	The postal abbreviation for the state of the US.
CREATED_BY	NOT NULL	VARCHAR2(30)	Audit column—indicates user who inserted data
CREATED_DATE	NOT NULL	DATE	Audit column—indicates date of insert
MODIFIED_BY	NOT NULL	VARCHAR2(30)	Audit column—indicates who made last update
MODIFIED_DATE	NOT NULL	DATE	Audit column—date of last update

GRADE_TYPE

Look-up table of grade types (codes) and descriptions.

Column Name	Null	Type	Comments
GRADE_TYPE_CODE	NOT NULL	CHAR(2)	The code that identifies a category of grade, i.e., MT, HW.
DESCRIPTION	NOT NULL	VARCHAR2(50)	The description for this code, i.e., Midterm, Homework
CREATED_BY	NOT NULL	VARCHAR2(30)	Audit column—indicates user who inserted data
CREATED_DATE	NOT NULL	DATE	Audit column—indicates date of insert
MODIFIED_BY	NOT NULL	VARCHAR2(30)	Audit column—indicates who last made update
MODIFIED_DATE	NOT NULL	DATE	Audit column—date of last update

GRADE_TYPE_WEIGHT

Information on how the final grade for a particular section is computed. For example, for a particular section, the midterm constitutes 50%, the quizzes 10%, and the final examination 40% of the final grade.

Column Name	Null	Type	Comments
SECTION_ID	NOT NULL	NUMBER(8)	The unique ID for section.
GRADE_TYPE_CODE	NOT NULL	CHAR(2)	The code that identifies a category of grade.
NUMBER_PER_SECTION	NOT NULL	NUMBER(3)	How many of these grade types will be used in

(continued)

Column Name	Null	Type	Comments
			this section; that is, there may be three quizzes.
PERCENT_OF_FINAL_GRADE	NOT NULL	NUMBER(3)	How much this category of grade contributes to the final grade.
DROP_LOWEST	NOT NULL	CHAR(1)	Is the lowest grade in this type removed when determining the final grade? (Y/N)
CREATED_BY	NOT NULL	VARCHAR2(30)	Audit column – indicates user who inserted data
CREATED_DATE	NOT NULL	DATE	Audit column – indicates date of insert
MODIFIED_BY	NOT NULL	VARCHAR2(30)	Audit column – indicates who last made update
MODIFIED_DATE	NOT NULL	DATE	Audit column – date of last update

GRADE

The individual grades a student received for a particular section (class).

Column Name	Null	Type	Comments
STUDENT_ID	NOT NULL	NUMBER(8)	The unique ID for the student
SECTION_ID	NOT NULL	NUMBER(8)	The unique ID for section.
GRADE_TYPE_CODE	NOT NULL	CHAR(2)	The code that identifies a category of grade.

(continued)

Column Name	Null	Type	Comments
GRADE_CODE_OCCURRENCE	NOT NULL	NUMBER(38)	The sequence number of one grade type for one section. For example, there could be multiple assignments numbered 1, 2, 3, etc.
GRADE_NUMERIC	NOT NULL	NUMBER(3)	Grade as number, i.e., 70, 75.
COMMENTS	NULL	VARCHAR2(2000)	Instructor's comments on this grade.
CREATED_BY	NOT NULL	VARCHAR2(30)	Audit column—indicates user who inserted data
CREATED_DATE	NOT NULL	DATE	Audit column—indicates date of insert
MODIFIED_BY	NOT NULL	VARCHAR2(30)	Audit column—indicates who last made update
MODIFIED_DATE	NOT NULL	DATE	Audit column—date of last update

GRADE_CONVERSION

Used to convert number to letter grades.

Column Name	Null	Type	Comments
LETTER_GRADE	NOT NULL	VARCHAR(2)	The grade as a letter (A, A–, B, B+, etc.).
GRADE_POINT	NOT NULL	NUMBER(3,2)	The number grade on a scale from 0 (F) to 4 (A).
MIN_GRADE	NOT NULL	NUMBER(3)	The lowest grade number that makes this letter grade.
MAX_GRADE	NOT NULL	NUMBER(3)	The highest grade number that makes this letter grade.

Column Name	Null	Type	Comments
CREATED_BY	NOT NULL	VARCHAR2(30)	Audit column—indicates user who inserted data
CREATED_DATE	NOT NULL	DATE	Audit column—indicates date of insert
MODIFIED_BY	NOT NULL	VARCHAR2(30)	Audit column—indicates who last made update
MODIFIED_DATE	NOT NULL	DATE	Audit column—date of last update

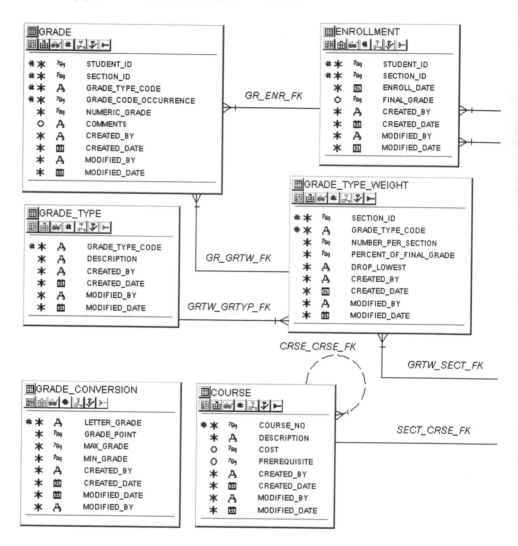

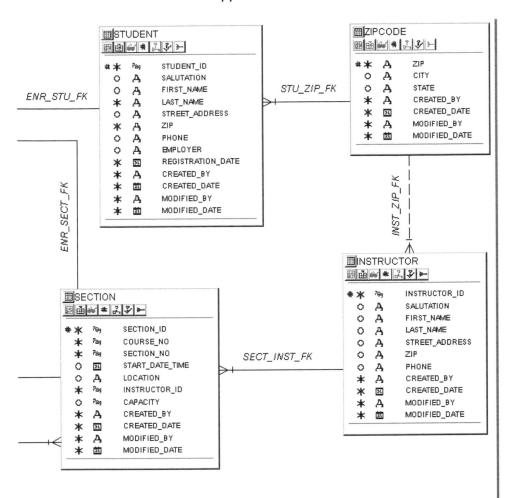

INDEX